Regulation of Cloud Services under US and EU Antitrust, Competition and Privacy Laws

Veröffentlichungen des Instituts für Energie- und Regulierungsrecht Berlin

Herausgegeben von Franz Jürgen Säcker

Band 59

PL ACADEMIC RESEARCH

Sára Gabriella Hoffman

Regulation of Cloud Services under US and EU Antitrust, Competition and Privacy Laws

PL ACADEMIC RESEARCH

Bibliographic Information published by the Deutsche Nationalbibliothek
The Deutsche Nationalbibliothek lists this publication in the Deutsche Nationalbibliografie; detailed bibliographic data is available in the internet at http://dnb.d-nb.de.

Zugl.: Berlin, Humboldt- Univ., Diss., 2016

Library of Congress Cataloging-in-Publication Data
Names: Hoffman, Sára Gabriella, author.
Title: Regulation of cloud services under US and EU antitrust, competition and privacy laws / Sára Gabriella Hoffman.
Description: Frankfurt am Main ; New York : Peter Lang, 2017. | Series: Veröffentlichungen des Instituts für Energie- und Regulierungsrecht Berlin ; vol. 59 | Based on author's thesis (doctoral - Humboldt University of Berlin, 2016).
Identifiers: LCCN 2016050416 | ISBN 9783631677391
Subjects: LCSH: Cloud computing--Law and legislation--European Union countries. | Cloud computing--Law and legislation--United States. | Data processing service centers--Law and legislation--European Union countries. | Data processing service centers--Law and legislation--United States. | Data protection--Law and legislation--United States. | Data protection--Law and legislation--European Union countries. | Antitrust law--United States. | Antitrust law--European Union countries.
Classification: LCC K564.C6 .H644 2017 | DDC 343.2409/944--dc23
LC record available at https://lccn.loc.gov/2016050416

11
ISSN 2363-684X
ISBN 978-3-631-67739-1 (Print)
E-ISBN 978-3-653-07267-9 (E-PDF)
E-ISBN 978-3-631-70348-9 (EPUB)
E-ISBN 978-3-631-70349-6 (MOBI)
DOI 10.3726/b10643

PL Academic Research is an Imprint of Peter Lang GmbH.

Peter Lang – Frankfurt am Main · Bern · Bruxelles · New York · Oxford · Warszawa · Wien

This publication has been peer reviewed.

www.peterlang.com

For
Frida Hoffman
– my very unique companion –

Acknowledgement

This work would not have been possible without Prof. Dr. iur. Dr. rer. pol. Dr. h.c. Christian Kirchner, LL.M. (Harvard). Professor Kirchner had the ability to kindle his students' curiosity with ease and passion for his subject. This curiosity ended up shaping his students' careers for life. His presence in the academic community is greatly missed.

I would like to thank Prof. Dr. Theo Bodewig and Prof. Dr. Heike Schweitzer, LL.M. (Yale) for being the academic advisors and for their very valuable guidance during the last year of my Ph.D. program. With many thanks also to Professor Dr. Harald Koch for chairing my defense committee.

The scholarships and grants of the German Academic Exchange Service (DAAD), Berlin's Elsa-Neumann Scholarship (formerly NaFöG), and the generous contribution from Stanford Law School's Microsoft Grant allowed me to expand this research and spend almost two years in the United States.

I would like to thank Professor George A. Hay at Cornell Law School for his advice and a wonderful time at Cornell. Also, with many thanks to Stanford Law School's Professor A. Mitchell Polinsky for introducing me to a community unlike any other that is a continuous source of inspiration in my professional and personal life.

Friends on both sides of the Atlantic are the special ingredient to this amazing time. Thank you for everything.

This work is dedicated to my family, and in particular to two young scientists who were brave enough to try something new in 1990 – and gave their two daughters a life full of opportunities.

Table of Contents

Table of Illustrations

List of Abbreviations

ABA	American Bar Association
ANSI	American National Standards Institute
API	Application Programming Interfaces
ARM	Advanced Risk Machines
AT&T	American Telephone and Telegraph
AUP	Acceptable Use Policy
B2B	Business-to-Business
B2C	Business-to-Consumer
BDSG	German Federal Data Protection Act (*Bundesdatenschutzgesetz*)
BER	Block Exemption Regulation
BITKOM	Federal Association for Information Technology, Telecommunications and New Media (*Bundesverband Informationswirtschaft, Telekommunikation und neue Medien e. V.*)
CDMA	Code Division Multiple Access
CERT-EU	Computer Emergency Response Teams
CFI	Court of First Instance
CI	Critical Infrastructure
Cir.	Circuit
CIS	Center for Internet and Society at Stanford Law School
CISG	United Nations Convention on Contracts for the International Sale of Goods
CJEU	Court of Justice of the European Union
CMLR	Common Market Law Review
CNIL	French data protection authority (*Commission nationale de l'informatique et des libertés*)
Comp.	Competition
CRM	Customer Relationship Management
DBMS	Database Management System
DCS	Digital Control System
DDSI	Dependability Development Support Initiative
DG	Directorate General of the European Commission
DG Comp	Directorate General of Competition
DG JLS	Directorate General of Justice, Freedom and Security
DIW	German Institute for Economic Research (*Deutsches Institut für Wirtschaftsforschung*)

DoJ	U.S. Department of Justice
DoS	Denial of Service
DPA	Data Protection Authority
DPO	Data Protection Officer
EC	Treaty establishing the European Community
EC3	European Cyber Crime Center
ECI	European Critical Infrastructure
ECJ	European Court of Justice
ECPA	Electronic Communications Privacy Act
ECPR	Efficiency Component Pricing Rule
ECR	European Court Reports
ECS	Electronic Communication Services
EDI	European Dependability Initiative
EF	Essential Facility
EFD	Essential Facilities Doctrine
EIBV	German Ordinance on Railway Infrastructure Utilisation (*Eisenbahninfrastruktur-Benutzungsverordnung*)
ENISA	European Network and Information Security Agency
EnWG	German Energy Industry Act (*Energiewirtschaftsgesetz*)
EPCIP	European Programme for Critical Infrastructure Protection
EU	European Union
FCC	U.S. Federal Communications Commission
FCRA	Federal Credit Reporting Act
FRAND	Fair, Reasonable And Non-Discriminatory
FTC	U.S. -Federal Trade Commission
GATT	General Agreement on Tariffs and Trade
GDPR	General Data Protection Regulation
GFT	Google Flu Trend
GLB	Gramm-Leach-Bliley Act
GPS	Global Positioning System
GSM	Global System for Mobility
GWB	German Act Against Restrains of Competition (*Gesetz gegen Wettbewerbsbeschränkungen*)
HIPAA	Health Insurance Portability and Accountability Act
IaaS	Infrastructure as a Service
IBM	International Business Machines
ICN	International Competition Network

ICN UCWG	International Competition Network Unilateral Conduct Working Group
ICT	Information and Communication Technologies
ID	Identity Document
IDW	Institute of Public Auditors in Germany (*Institut für Wirtschaftsprüfer*)
IEC	International Electrotechnical Commission
IJCSNS	International Journal of Computer Science and Network Security
IJDMS	International Journal of Database Management Systems
IPR	Intellectual Property Right
ISACA	Information Systems Audit and Control Association
ISMS	Information Security Management Systems
ISO	International Organization for Standardization
J.	Journal
JV	Joint Venture
L.	Law
MSA	Master Service Agreement
NBER	National Bureau of Economic Research
NCA	National Competition Authority
NIS	Network and Information Security
NIST	U.S. National Institute of Standards and Technology
NSA	National Security Agency
OECD	Organisation for Economic Co-operation and Development
OJ	Official Journal
PaaS	Platform as a Service
PII	Personally Identifiable Information
QoS	Quality of Service
R&D	Research and Development
RCS	Remote Computing Service
Rev.	Review
RSS	Received Signal Strength
RTD	Refusal to Deal
SaaS	Software as a Service
SAP	Systems, Applications & Products in Data Processing
SCA	Stored Communications Act
SCADA	Supervisory Control and Data Acquisition
SLA	Service Level Agreement
SLC	Significant Lessening of Competition

SME	Small and Medium-Sized Enterprises
SMP	Significant Market Power
SQL	Structured Query Language
SSNIP	Small but Significant Non-Transitory Increase in Price
SSO	Storage Service Provider
STEM	Science, Technology, Engineering, and Mathematics
Tech.	Technology
TEU	Revised Treaty on the European Union
TFEU	Treaty on the Functioning of the European Union
TILEC	Tilburg Institute for Law, Technology, and Society
ToS	Terms of Service
TPA	Third Party Access
TRIPS	Agreement on Trade-Related Aspects of Intellectual Property Rights
UMTS	Universal Mobile Telecommunications System
U.S.	United States
U.S.C.	United States Code
USD	United States Dollar
WPS	Wifi-based Positioning System
WuW	Wirtschaft und Wettbewerb
XML	Extensible Markup Language
ZUM	Zeitschrift für Urheber- und Medienrecht
ZWeR	Zeitschrift für Wettbewerbsrecht

1 Introduction

> *„The mismatch between law time and new-economy real time is troubling in two respects. First, an antitrust case involving a new-economy firm may drag on for so long relative to the changing conditions of the industry as to become irrelevant, ineffectual." – Posner (2000)*[1]

The effective use of (big) data has become a competitive advantage in every sector reaching far beyond just technology companies. Every transaction and activity on the internet creates a data trail. This information is used in many ways to create value. Data analysis is continuously replacing intuition as a basis for business decisions.

The innovations associated with cloud computing affect public and private entities and every person individually. This thesis contributes to the understanding of cloud computing from an antitrust, competition and data privacy law perspective. The analysis is based on comparative research in EU and U.S. law.

Data privacy and competition law are two legal fields that are heavily affected by the innovations and disruptions caused by cloud computing. The innovation cloud computing represents is currently not fully covered by the law. The reason is that current legal provisions do not sufficiently take the technical aspects of cloud computing into account. The link between competition and antitrust laws on the one hand and data privacy on the other is innovation and consumer protection. Competition and antitrust laws look at the welfare of consumers. The competitive behavior of an undertaking is analyzed in relation to how a specific conduct affects the consumer. This can be a pro- or an anti-competitive effect. In data privacy law, the protection of personal data is a core concept. It is a form of consumer protection because the protection granted by law is designed to safeguard the privacy sphere of an individual.

The first link that ties data privacy and competition law together is qualitative consumer welfare under competition law. Increasing consumer welfare is not just a quantitative operation triggered by the price of a product or service. Consumer welfare can also be increased by qualitative criteria. These qualitative pro-competitive effects can be created through an elevated level of data protection in the cloud service providers' offerings.

---

1 *Richard Allen Posner*, Antitrust in the New Economy, Chicago John M. Olin Law & Economics Working Paper No. 106, 2nd Series, 2000, p. 9.

The second link between these two areas of law with regard to cloud computing is innovation. The disruptive force of big data analytics enabled through cloud data processing on the technology sector does not stop there. Much rather, this causes a ripple effect into every other industry sector that relies on data analytics. Because of this large market impact, its perception under innovation policy is important. There, laws distinguish between incremental and radical innovation. This distinction becomes important in competition law for the assessment of i.e. barriers to entry. In data privacy law, innovation that enables a different type of personal data processing triggers consumer protection questions.

1.1 Contribution of this thesis

This thesis shows the exposure of cloud service providers to data privacy, competition and antitrust laws. I will illustrate the legal framework cloud computing has to function in, how service providers must act in order to be compliant with the law and what deficiencies current legal provisions have in accommodating cloud computing. Thereby, I examine how the technical conditions of cloud computing are accounted for in the law. This becomes an important factor when legal requirements must be implemented into an IT-framework through privacy engineering.

The hypothesis of this thesis is that current legal provisions in the field of data privacy and competition law are insufficient to harness the regulatory need that the innovations of cloud computing embody. It is also my subject of analysis that technical and business factors make the recently enacted EU data privacy laws lack enforceability and completeness. Furthermore, there are different understandings of data privacy business needs in the EU and the U.S. that leave regulatory gaps. An example for this is data transfer mechanisms based on a safe harbor approach.

My analysis looks at these questions from the perspective of cloud service providers. It is not practical or technically feasible to look at cloud computing from the sole perspective of consumer protection laws. This is owed to the different deployment models of cloud services. As presented in detail below, cloud services can range from an IT-storage space lease agreement to a service provision relationship where the consumer uses the service provider's software. The nature of the legal relationship is also layered by the specific sector the data processing takes place in. The assessment would suffer fragmentation had I adopted the perspective of the data subject or consumer. However, consumer protection laws are a necessary component of the assessment of data privacy law compliance and of the consumer welfare criterion in competition law.

As the following subchapter will outline, research and literature have previously examined the cloud computing market and the potential of big data from several angles. These include the fields of law, business and policy as well as computer and information science, including statistics. These research contributions have all identified major aspects in the fields. The aspect this thesis contributes is to combine a legal and policy analysis with a technical feasibility of implementation analysis.

Laws are sanctioning mechanisms. They are conditioned programs and rely on an enforcement mechanism because legal provisions are structured as "if-then" functions. If legal enforcement is not possible due to technical limits, the value of the law is factually of symbolic nature. Furthermore, policies must reflect the market they are designed to operate in. The effectiveness of a legal provision therefore depends on its practical implementation and sector specific background. For instance, privacy engineers do the implementation of data privacy law requirements. Their task is to take the legal requirement and translate it into a computer science environment.

1.2 Background factors

1.2.1 The use of data as a competitive advantage

The effective use of data yields a competitive advantage to businesses. Data and big data generate insights into the customers' preferences and can predict future customer behavior by projecting consumer behavior patterns. Additionally, the use of data opens up new ways of creating value for the business.

The hypothesis is: A data-driven business and data-based decision making processes lead to a higher level of productivity and with that, a higher return on investment. This hypothesis has been tested numerous times. One of the largest studies on this has been presented by the *McKinsey Global Institute, Big data: The next frontier for innovation, competition, and productivity.*[2] This thesis is built on the assumption that the hypothesis has not been falsified. Hence, I assume that using data as a foundation for business decisions is a route to comparatively higher profitability and more reliable decisions. Consequently, data-driven decision-making will dominate business decisions. The data subjects' information must be subject to a legal system that can accommodate these business motivations.

2 *McKinsey Global Institute, Manyika/Chui/Brown/Bughin/Dobbs/Roxburgh/Byers*, Big data: The next frontier for innovation, competition and productivity, 2011, available at: http://www.mckinsey.com/insights/business_technology/big_data_the_next_frontier_for_innovation, last accessed 26 December 2014 (henceforth cited as: *McKinsey Global Institute*, 2011).

1.2.2 The consumers' perception of security

The perception of cloud security issues is the largest problem U.S. cloud operators face on the EU internal market. The relationship of European consumers to their data is different from the American understanding. The recent political developments make it more necessary than ever to bridge this transatlantic gap in order to do business. Consumers in the EU want to know what happens to their data, how it is used and reused in much greater detail in comparison to U.S. customers. The EU customer holds cloud service providers accountable to a much higher degree. Lock-in effects, the way the service level agreement (SLA) is drafted and data privacy issues are at the forefront of a conscious consumer's concern. Due to that, market penetration and customer acceptance of cloud-based services is different in the EU compared to the U.S. Not every business model that is successful with U.S. customers can be monetized the same way on the European markets. The ability to negotiate in a business-to-business setting whilst being aware of this cultural disconnect will help bridge the gap. And the law must mirror these consumer needs for accountability.

Solutions to the consumers' concerns can be found by establishing data privacy standards. Cloud service providers can cooperate in multiple ways to safe costs and reach a higher standard of protection of consumer data. For the thesis, I have examined data privacy standards through standardization agreements and strategic alliances.

1.2.3 The business culture disconnect in antitrust and competition law

In addition to competition law problems of the cloud, different policy understandings layer the discussion. These different premises can fog up the key items being discussed. U.S. cloud service providers have trouble getting their points across in the EU and run into obstacles that seem baffling to them. Then, in their perspective suddenly, a large fine for EU law infringement is burdening the company. A recent case illustrating this is Google's alleged anticompetitive behavior with regard to its search engine result placement.

Mirroring this, EU competition law policies are aiming to regulate aggressive competitive behavior that inflicts harm on consumers and competition as an institution from a U.S. perspective. The focal point of EU laws is the consumer, not a total welfare approach. This in turn, is difficult to digest for an American business. In the U.S., the private sector views the role of the government differently. Whilst the American private sector expects a minimal presence of government in competition and business decisions, EU policy makers are an expected key player with numerous guidelines, soft laws and proactive involvement.

1.2.4 Incremental and radical innovation

Incremental innovation is the basis of the vast majority of products and services entering the market. But if a product or service rooted in radical innovation emerges, different issues arise depending on the jurisdiction. EU policies prefer incremental innovation with diminished disruptive forces on the market. Generally, business is more risk averse in the EU than it is in the U.S. Social stability, consumer protection and economic growth on a sustainable scale is valued in the EU. This comes as a trade-off decision against disruptive forces going hand in hand with a higher risk of failure. U.S. market understanding is in favor of radical innovation and embraces the Schumpeterian process of creative destruction to a much higher degree, especially in Silicon Valley. Innovation followed by a follow-up innovation is not valued as highly in business culture as the ability to overhaul the existing relevant market – and taking the corresponding business risk. The different approach to innovation and business culture mirrors this in foreign policy and in the law.

1.3 State of research and literature

Research and literature on cloud computing has been published in several fields. In the following, I present the key pieces for this thesis categorized in the fields of law, business and policy, and computer and information sciences. This is to set the scene for the diverse sources of research preexisting to this thesis. This first overview in Chapters 1.3.1 to 1.3.3 is not meant to be comprehensive. Rather, it shall serve as an introduction of the core pieces of research I rely on testing my research hypothesis. For a full overview, I refer to the bibliography and table of cases.

1.3.1 Law

In 2009, *Sluijs/Larouche/Sauter* published the TILEC discussion paper titled *Cloud Computing in the EU Policy Sphere.*[3] It flags three mayor challenges of cloud computing in the EU: data portability and interoperability, vertical integration, and internal market fragmentation. This publication was crucial in identifying how current legislature does not adequately address the needs and potential problems of the cloud market. Furthermore, it outlined how the EU Commission's digital agenda fits into the existing legal framework.

---

3 *Sluijs/Larouche/Sauter*, Cloud Computing in the EU Policy Sphere, Journal of Intellectual Property, Information Technology and e-Commerce Law Vol. 3 Issue 1, 2012 and also available as TILEC Discussion Paper 2011-036 (henceforth cited as: *Sluijs/Larouche/Sauter*, 2012).

With regard to landmark cases, one of the recent cases with large market impact was *Google Spain SL, Google Inc. v Agencia Española de Protección de Datos (AEPD), Mario Costeja González*[4]. It established a so-called "right to be forgotten" whereby a data subject has the right to be removed from the search engine results in order to maintain privacy. This ruling has substantially expanded the scope of data protection under existing EU legislations. It illustrated the balancing test executed between the interest of the public in having access to information, the individual's private life and the role of the person requesting the information be deleted in public life.[5] Circling back to privacy engineering, implementing this balancing test into an algorithm-based environment that can filter through the consumer notices is a task that falls into their scope of work.

Due to the fast developments in this field, this thesis originally considered General Data Protection Regulation in its proposal version and was updated to the final text after the submission of the thesis.[6] With regard to the European Parliament Vote, the version originally considered was the Draft Report on the proposal for a regulation of the European Parliament and of the Council on the protection of individual with regard to the processing of personal data and on the free movement of such data.[7] The manuscript was updated later to reflect the final legislation.

---

4 *Google Spain SL, Google Inc. v Agencia Española de Protección de Datos (AEPD), Mario Costeja González*, Case C-131/12, OJ C 165, 9 June 2012, Court of Justice, Judgment of the Court (Grand Chamber) of 13 May 2014 (henceforth cited as: *Google/Costeja*, C-131/12).

5 See *EU Commission*, Factsheet on the "Right to be Forgotten" ruling (henceforth cited as: *EU Commission*, Factsheet on the "Right to be Forgotten") and *Council of the European Union*, press release No. 10578/14 of June 2014, p. 2 referencing ruling C-131/12, dated 13 May 2014, Ref. 85 (henceforth cited as: *EU Council*, press release No. 10578/14).

6 *EU Commission*, Proposal for a Regulation of the European Parliament and of the Council on the protection of individuals with regard to the processing of personal data and on the free movement of such data ("*General Data Protection Regulation*"), dated 25 January 2012, available at: http://ec.europa.eu/justice/data-protection/document/review2012/com_2012_11_en.pdf, last accessed 19 January 2015; in its final version Regulation (EU) 2016/679 of the European Parliament and of the Council of 27 April 2016 on the protection of natural persons with regard to the processing of personal data and on the free movement of such data, and repealing Directive 95/46/EC (General Data Protection Regulation), O.J. L 119 of 4 May 2016, p. 1, (henceforth cited as: *EU Commission,* General Data Protection Regulation).

7 *EU Commission, Committee on Civil Liberties, Justice and Home Affairs*, Draft Report on the proposal for a regulation of the European Parliament and of the Council on

With regard to the proposed NIS Directive, the version initially considered was the Directive of the European Parliament and of the Council concerning measures to ensure a high common level of network and information security across the Union.[8] Here, the manuscript was updated as well.

With regard to the EU-U.S. Safe Harbor Framework Agreement, the following communication was the initial basis of the assessment: Communication from the Commission to the European Parliament and the Council on the Functioning of the Safe Harbor from the Perspective of EU Citizens and Companies Established in the EU.[9] Since then, the EU-U.S. Safe Harbor Framework Agreement was invalidated by the Court of Justice of the European Union (CJEU) (see in detail Chapter 9.8). The manuscript was updated in July 2016 to reflect the current laws governing international data transfers.

1.3.2 Business and policy

In 2010, IBM published a Whitepaper[10] discussing the core cloud computing inhibitors in the market. The identified key risk such as security, lack of clear value proposition, lack of standardization, software licensing and loss of internal control still hold true for late 2014. From a company's perspective that is implementing cloud services, these risks were and remain highly relevant. IBM's

---

the protection of individual with regard to the processing of personal data and on the free movement of such data, COM(2012)0011 – C7-0025/2012–2012/0011(COD)); available at: http://www.europarl.europa.eu/meetdocs/2009_2014/documents/libe/pr/922/922387/922387en.pdf, last accessed 19 January 2015.

8 *EU Commission,* Proposal for a Directive of the European Parliament and of the Council concerning measures to ensure a high common level of network and information security across the Union, COM(2013) 48 final, 2013/0027 (COD), 7 February 2013 (henceforth cited as: *EU Commission,* NIS Directive). The final version of the NIS Directive is the Directive (EU) 2016/1148 of the European Parliament and of the Council of 6 July 2016 concerning measures for a high common level of security of network and information systems across the Union, O.J. L 194, p. 1, of 19 July 2016.

9 *EU Commission,* Communication from the Commission to the European Parliament and the Council on the Functioning of the Safe Harbour from the Perspective of EU Citizens and Companies Established in the EU, COM(2013) 847 final dated 27 November 2013, available at: http://ec.europa.eu/justice/data-protection/files/com_2013_847_en.pdf, last accessed 31 August 2014 (henceforth cited as: *EU Commission,* Communication on the Functioning of the Safe Harbour).

10 *IBM,* Cloud computing insights from 110 implementation projects, IBM Academy of Technology Survey, Thought Leadership Whitepaper, dated October 2010 (henceforth cited as: *IBM,* Cloud computing insights from 110 implementation projects).

empirical market assessment is a cornerstone in understanding the cloud service business risks from the implementing companies' perspective.

Equally important is the ENISA report issued in 2009.[11] ENISA also identified key cloud security risks from the consumers' perspective. They include the loss of governance over data, lock-in effects, virtualization failures, compliance with data security standards and lawful handling of data. Since ENISA will receive a prolonged mandate[12], its initial market assessments will remain a strong reference point as a benchmark for market standard improvement.

Gasser/Palfrey with *The Berkman Center for Internet & Society at Harvard Law School* presented an approach to interoperability in 2007. By *Gasser/Palfrey*, the question of interoperability is context specific, a technical issue and also a matter of work flow management and the involved personal and legal framework. Their definition of interoperability has received wide market acceptance:

> *„At the definitional core of the multi-layered and multifaceted concept „ICT (Information & Communications Technology) interoperability" is what we might describe as the ability to transfer and render useful data and other information across systems (which may include organizations), applications, or components. (...) The working definition needs to be concretized for each context and use case separately."*[13]

1.3.3 Computer and information science

In law, personal data is a legally defined term. In the field of information science, the distinction between data, information and knowledge is debated. In 2007, *Zins* published *Conceptual Approaches for Defining Data, Information*, a knowl-

---

11 *European Network and Information Security Agency (ENISA)*, Cloud Computing – Benefits, risks and recommendations for information security, 20 November 2009, available at: www.enisa.europa.eu, last accessed 12 May 2011 (henceforth cited as: *ENISA, 2011)*.

12 See press release of the *EU Commission*: European Commission welcomes European Parliament's vote to extend mandate of ENISA and strengthen EU Cybersecurity, dated 16 April 2013, available at: http://europa.eu/rapid/press-release_MEMO-13-341_en.htm, last accessed 29 December 2014 (henceforth cited as: *EU Commission,* press release 16 April 2013).

13 *Gasser/Palfrey* at: *The Berkman Center for Internet & Society at Harvard Law School and Research Center for Information Law University of St. Gallen*, Breaking Down Digital Barriers – When and How ICT Interoperability Drives Innovation, 14 November 2007, p. 4; also available at: http://cyber.law.harvard.edu/interactive/events/2007/11/Palfrey_Gasser, last accessed 19 January 2014 (henceforth cited as: *Gasser/Palfrey*, 2007).

edge mapping research using the critical Delphi methodology.[14] The scope of this study included 57 scholars from 16 countries and is hence due to its size and scope representative of the discussion. I rely on this study to illustrate how an "easy" legal definition is a heavily debated technical term in another academic field. With that, I aim to show the need to cross-reference findings in order to find a harmonious legal solution to a technical definition.

With regard to the foundation of relational database management, *Codd* established in 1970 the organizational pattern of information in rows and columns.[15] These database management systems are still the foundations we use in structured query language (SQL) that are highly relevant for big data.

In legal publications, the terms "cloud computing" and "big data" are oftentimes used interchangeably. This is incorrect as they are two separate things. Big data refers to the analysis of a particular type of data set whereas cloud computing is a hardware-based concept enabled through remote access. *Boyd/Crawford* presented an analysis-driven definition of big data with three main components, them being technology, analysis and mythology.[16] In 2009, the U.S. National Institute of Standards and Technology (NIST) made a working definition of cloud computing available that has gained industry acceptance:

> „*Cloud computing is a model for enabling ubiquitous, convenient, on-demand network access to a shared pool of configurable computing resources (e.g., networks, servers, storage, applications, and services) that can be rapidly provisioned and released with minimal management effort or service provider interaction. This cloud model promotes availability and is composed of five essential characteristics, three service models, and four deployment models.*"[17]

---

14 *Chaim Zins*, Journal of the American Society for Information Science and Technology, Vol. 58 Issue 4, 2007, pp. 479–493, also available at: http://www.success.co.il/is/zins_definitions_dik.pdf, last accessed 19 January 2014 (henceforth cited as: *Zins*, 2007).

15 *Edgar Frank Codd*, A Relational Model of Data for Large Shared Data Banks, Communication of the ACM, Vol. 13 No. 6, 1970, pp. 377–387 (henceforth cited as: *Codd*, 1970).

16 *Boyd/Crawford*, Critical Questions for Big Data, Provocations for a cultural, technological, and scholarly phenomenon, Information, Communication & Society, Vol. 15, Issue 5, 2012, Special Issue: A decade in Internet time: the dynamics of the Internet and society, also available at: http://www.tandfonline.com/doi/abs/10.1080/1369118X.2012.678878#.VJ2C9UAsFA, last accessed 27 December 2014 (henceforth cited as: *Boyd/Crawford*, 2012).

17 *Mell/Grance* with the *National Institute of Standards and Technology (NIST)*, The NIST Definition of Cloud Computing, 2009, p. 6, also available at: http://csrc.nist.gov/publications/drafts/800-145/Draft-SP-800-145_cloud-definition.pdf, last accessed 9 November 2010 (henceforth cited as: *Mell/Grance* with *NIST*, 2009).

1.4 Structure of the thesis

This thesis is divided into four main parts. In Part 1, encompassing Chapters 2 to 5, I present the technical and legal framework of cloud computing. In Part 2, segmented into Chapters 6 to 8, I examine the competition law exposure of cloud computing. In Part 3, (Chapters 9 to 11), my assessment focuses on the data privacy exposure of cloud service operators with regard to the new EU General Data Protection Regulation (GDPR). Lastly, in Part. 4 (Chapters 12 to 13), I take a broader perspective and examine the existing legal cyber security framework and how the new NIS Directive will fit in. With this broader view, I conclude and provide recommendations to achieve better compliance of cloud service providers with EU laws. Chapter 14 provides the interview questions I used to speak to players in the market.

Part 1 details as follows: Chapter 2 illustrates what 'big data' is and how data can be categorized from a technical perspective. I also illustrate the basic functioning of an algorithm and why correlation is not the same as causality. Then I illustrate why the distinction between correlation and causation is important for the law. Chapter 3 explains the components of the cloud and how those components are relevant for a legal analysis. Chapter 4 identifies the main cloud service security risks that businesses and private individuals associate with cloud services. Furthermore, I present customer risk management strategies from the cloud service providers' perspective. In Chapter 5, I provide an overview of the key law and policy players in the EU and the U.S. This includes a brief overview of the relevant legal provisions in data privacy and competition and antitrust laws in both jurisdictions.

Part 2 is structured as follows: Chapter 6 gives a comprehensive overview of cloud service operators' exposure to EU competition law. I illustrate how competition law can apply to the relatively new type of market player, the cloud service provider. Chapter 6.2 examines the relevant market for cloud outsourcing services from a product, geographic and temporal perspective in light of a potential utility service classification. Chapter 6.3 illustrates the exposure cloud service providers have to a potential Art. 102 TFEU proceeding, with particular focus on tying and bundling and exclusive dealing practices. I illustrate the business practices they must not adopt in order to remain compliant with Art. 102 TFEU because their adoption would be harmful to consumers and deemed anticompetitive. Chapter 6.4 shows the legal boundaries of a strategic alliance of cloud service providers under collective dominance pursuant to Art. 102 TFEU. Chapter 7 ties closely to Chapter 6.4 and illustrates the boundaries of a data privacy cartel under Art. 101 TFEU. In Chapter 8, I conclude the competition and antitrust law assessment of cloud computing exposure by examining the link between interoperability and innovation in light of competition policy choices.

Part 3 commences with Chapter 9. There, the data privacy component of cloud service exposure is illustrated. I examine how the proposal for a new General Data Protection Regulation affects the cloud computing market. I go into detail amongst others about the so-called "right to be forgotten" (Chapter 9.3), consent requirements (Chapter 9.4), notification and reporting requirements and safe harbor regimes (Chapter 9.8) and the fines for a data protection law infringement (Chapter 9.8.4). The point is to illustrate the quality of the law and their implementability. In Chapter 10, I discuss the contractual framework between cloud service providers and their customers. There I also examine possible standardization and certification possibilities to introduce a uniform level of protection for the consumer. In Chapter 11, I aim to balance the strict data privacy requirements against society's interests by showing that there is a great public and society use of cloud services for public benefit. There, I examine the utility of big data for society and show the detrimental effects of lacking trust in this new technology.

Part 4 includes the following: In Chapter 12, I change perspectives and examine the cyber foreign policy implications of the governmental use of cloud services and the transatlantic communications that come with it. Summarizing thoughts and recommendations are provided for in Chapter 13. The questionnaire for interviews is summarized and annexed in German and English in Chapter 14.

Part I:
Technical and legal framework of cloud computing

2 What is (big) data?

2.1 Definition and types of data

Data is Latin for *Things Given*. For this thesis, I will present and work with the definitions provided in legal statute. The EU Commission's General Data Protection Regulation[18] (GDPR) provides a definition of the terms "personal data" and "data subject" in Art. 4 para. 1 GDPR.

> "**Personal data** *means any information relating to a data subject*"[19]

> "**Data subject** *means an identified natural person or a natural person who can be identified, directly or indirectly, in particular by reference to an identifier such as a name, an identification number, location data, an online identifier or to one or more factors specific to the physical, physiological, genetic, mental, economic, cultural or social identity of that person.*"[20]

As a general rule, data can appear in digital or analogue form. An example for analogue data is an LP disk. An example for a comparable content in digital form is an mp3-file with the same soundtrack. Data can for example vary in its source, type, format (i.e. audio, video and image), speed of occurrence (i.e. real-time data), and level of structure.

For the purposes of a legal discussion, this level of precision in the definition of "data" is sufficient to move forward with the analysis. However, for a discussion in the field of information science, this would not suffice. There is no uniform definition of the term "data" in STEM. It is scientifically incorrect to state that data equals information. In the field of information science, the terms "data", "information" and "knowledge" interrelate but are separate concepts. Their relation is heavily debated amongst scholars.

For the definition of these terms in information science, I refer to *Zins'* paper *Conceptual Approaches for Defining Data, Information*[21], a knowledge mapping research using the Critical Delphi methodology. The Critical Delphi method is an anonymous panel discussion of leading scholars in the field. Here, 57 scholars from 16 countries submitted answers to the questionnaire in three rounds to narrow down the answer of defining the three terms and their relation to each other.[22]

18 *EU Commission*, General Data Protection Regulation, loc. cit. Fn. 6.

19 Art. 4 para. 1 General Data Protection Regulation.

20 Art. 4 para. 1 General Data Protection Regulation.

21 *Zins*, 2007, loc. cit. Fn. 14, p. 480.

22 *Zins*, 2007, ibd, pp. 489–493.

There are several conceptual approaches that place a different emphasis on the cognitive abilities of a human to perceive certain items either as information or as knowledge. This may depend on the objective or subjective nature of the data under analysis, i.e. whether religious beliefs allow certain data to be assumed as knowledge. *Zins* identifies the mainstream of the field as non-metaphysical, human-centered, cognitive-based and propositional in its approach.[23]

2.2 Definition of big data

Big data is both a technical term and a media buzzword. The media and non-STEM fields refer to it as an abstract concept of vast amount of information that is hard to collect, store and analyze. Simply put, big data is just a really large amount of data. The quantity of data is one component, but does not comprise a complete definition. Rather, it is a data set that is in continuous flux.

The study by the *McKinsey Global Institute* mentioned above provides a suitable definition of big data accounting for this flexibly of the term:

> *"Big data" refers to datasets whose size is beyond the ability of typical database software tools to capture, store, manage, and analyze. This definition is intentionally subjective and incorporates a moving definition of how big a dataset needs to be in order to be considered big data—i.e., we don't define big data in terms of being larger than a certain number of terabytes (thousands of gigabytes). We assume that, as technology advances over time, the size of datasets that qualify as big data will also increase. Also note that the definition can vary by sector, depending on what kinds of software tools are commonly available and what sizes of datasets are common in a particular industry. With those caveats, big data in many sectors today will range from a few dozen terabytes to multiple petabytes (thousands of terabytes)."*[24]

Boyd/Crawford provide an analysis-driven definition with three main components, them being technology, analysis and mythology:

> *„We define Big Data as a cultural, technological, and scholarly phenomenon that rests on the interplay of:*
>
> *(1) Technology: maximizing computation power and algorithmic accuracy to gather, analyze, link, and compare large data sets.*
>
> *(2) Analysis: drawing on large data sets to identify patterns in order to make economic, social, technical, and legal claims.*

---

23 *Zins*, 2007, ibd, p. 489.

24 *McKinsey Global Institute*, 2011, loc. cit. Fn. 2, p. 1

(3) Mythology: the widespread belief that large data sets offer a higher form of intelligence and knowledge that can generate insights that were previously impossible, with the aura of truth, objectivity, and accuracy."[25]

Technically, database management systems (DBMS) and data warehouses make big data possible. A data warehouse is a copy of transaction data specifically structured for query and analysis.[26]

Companies providing this service are for example Oracle, SAP and MySQL. The database is information collected and stored in an organized pattern. There are several possibilities of organizational patterns. The type of information the database is kept for determines the pattern. For example, the database may organize information to make it easy to find vacant seats on an airplane or train. Another example is the geographic location of rental cars available, or the items in stock at an online warehouse. In all cases, DBMS is software that interacts with its user in order to receive and process information. The task is to allow data points to be defined, created, deleted, updated, searched for, and so on.

A very common standard for DBMS is SQL in a relational database management system. SQL stands for structured query language and is a programming language. With SQL, the programmer can write data definitions, data manipulations and conduct data queries.[27] Relational database management refers to the organizational pattern of information in rows and columns.[28] These systems are equipped with receiving and retrieving data and can complete these tasks largely without computational difficulties. Basically, it is a neat way to organize a very large list. The following visual illustration is taken from *Jacobs*[29]:

---

25 *Boyd/Crawford*, 2012, loc. cit. Fn. 16.

26 *Ralph Kimball*, The Data Warehouse Toolkit: Practical Techniques for Building Dimensional Data Warehouses; John Wiley & Sons, 1996, New York.

27 SQL is an American National Standards Institute (ANSI) standard.

28 *Codd*, 1970, loc. cit. Fn. 15, pp. 377–387.

29 *Adam Jacobs*, The Pathologies of Big Data, Communications of the ACM, Vol. 52, Issue 8, August 2009, pp. 36–44, p. 41, also available at: http://dl.acm.org/citation.cfm?id=J79&picked=prox, last accessed 27 December 2014.

Fig. 1: DBMS data recombination

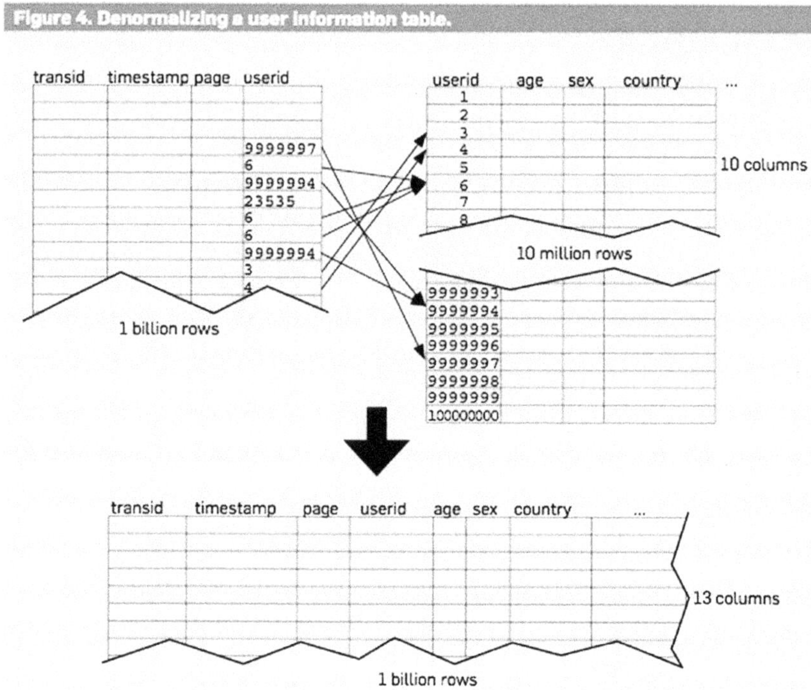

With big data analysis, the data warehouse is now searched for data under a new set of parameters. The purpose of this search is to find out new insights that can only be found out if a very large data pool is available for the search. The algorithm running the recombination is designed to rearrange and analyze the data kept in the rows and columns of the DBMS system. This poses an organizational challenge for the DBMS because the structure the data has been stored for originally may not serve the purpose it is searched for now. An example for this is the collection of Amazon.com purchasing data for each customer and the subsequent analysis requires the search of all customer data for the parameters e.g. female, age 25–34, shipping address in California, USA, amount of purchases for product X over product Y in correlation with an advertisement placement during timeframe Δt.

2.3 Interoperability in database management systems and data integration

Interoperability refers to two systems that are able to exchange and interpret data that the two systems share. It means that two devices, platforms or systems can work together. Interoperability in DBMS is a concern. If the DBMS use proprietary backup formats, the consequence is that access to this data cannot happen with other tools. Whilst originally developed to block interoperability to protect data access, it leads to a heterogeneous DBMS environment with substantial lock in effects.[30] Data integration is not the same as interoperability. Data integration means that data stemming from two separate sources can be combined and processed with the result of having a homogenous perspective on the data.

Pereira Teles/Souto Maior de Barros identified that different sectors such as finance and management protect themselves and their data through increasing the barriers of interoperability by working with and around XML-format. XML stands for extensible markup language and used is to define a set of rules to encode documents. After the encoding process, both machines and humans can read the content of the document.

Interoperability in the field of computer science and cryptography is complemented by the concept of data security. If the DBMS is able to interface with another system, the system becomes more difficult to isolate. And the lower the isolation barriers, the easier it is to trespass on security systems in place. Hence, reaching a low level of interoperability is a valid objective to secure the information stored on the DBMS. This is a point where legal objectives of low lock-in effects, high interoperability and the possibility of data transfers will be opposed by the objectives of data security from a computer science perspective.

2.4 Definition of algorithm

John MacCormick defines an algorithm as a "*precise recipe that specifies the exact sequence of steps required to solve a problem*".[31] There are numerous types of algorithms. One example is the linear search algorithm. There, the task is to find

30 *Pereira Teles/Souto Maior de Barros*, Towards Standardization and Interoperability of Database Backups, International Journal of Computer Science and Network Security (IJCSNS), Vol. 12 No. 8, August 2012, available at: http://paper.ijcsns.org/07_book/201208/20120803.pdf, last accessed 29 December 2014.

31 *John MacCormick*, Nine algorithms that changed the future – The ingenious ideas that drive today's computers, Princeton University Press, 2011, p. 3.

one specific item in an unsorted sequence of items. A linear search algorithm is an automated step-by-step calculation. Consider the following example:

> We have a set of numbers {n}. They are presented in an unsorted list, for example {9; 3; 17; 4}. The goal is to find out which number is the largest one in the list. For that, we must look at each number in the unsorted list, one at a time. The algorithm for this solution is built with the following steps:
> Step one is to figure out if our set of numbers {n} has no number in it. If the set is empty, no element of the set can be the highest number. Secondly, if there is one or more numbers in our set, we first assume that the first number is the largest one. Hence, we assume at the beginning that 9 is the largest number. Now, for each following number in the set, if that number is larger than the current largest one, consider this number the largest one in the set. We go through the questions i) 9 < 3? – no. ii) 9 < 17? – yes. iii) 17 < 4? – no. Once there are no more numbers in our set, consider the last largest number to be the largest one of the set. We have a result showing us that 17 > 9 > 4 > 3 with 17 being the largest element of {n}.

2.5 Causality and correlation

In colloquial language, causality and correlation are often used as terms with identical meaning. From a statistical perspective, this is a wrong statement. Causality and correlation are not the same, nor does correlation imply causality. Correlation is a very important concept for deriving value out of big data. This subchapter serves to introduce these two concepts.

Causation is a term that law students are introduced to in the first semester in criminal law. A prior act is *conditio-sine-qua-non* for the second act. It is a circumstance that cannot be omitted without altering the subsequent chain of events. Counterfactual dependence is necessary to establish causation. For example, the birth of a person is conditio-sine-qua-non for the later act of committing a criminal offence.

Correlation is not causation. Correlation can show that two sets of data have a relationship to each other. This does not mean that a conditional program links them. *Vigen*, a student from Harvard Law, made some entertaining graphs to illustrate these points.[32] As the following example shows, the per capita consumption of cheese in the U.S. correlates with the people who die by getting tangled in their bed sheets at a rate of 94.7 per cent:[33] But that does not mean that eating cheese is conditio-sine-qua-non to the deathly suffocation in bed sheets.

---

32 The illustration below is taken from *Tyler Vigen*, at: http://www.tylervigen.com/, last accessed 27 December 2014.

33 Illustration No. 3 from the top at http://www.tylervigen.com/, last accessed 27 December 2014.

Fig. 2: Correlation

Per capita consumption of cheese (US)

correlates with

Number of people who died by becoming tangled in their bedsheets

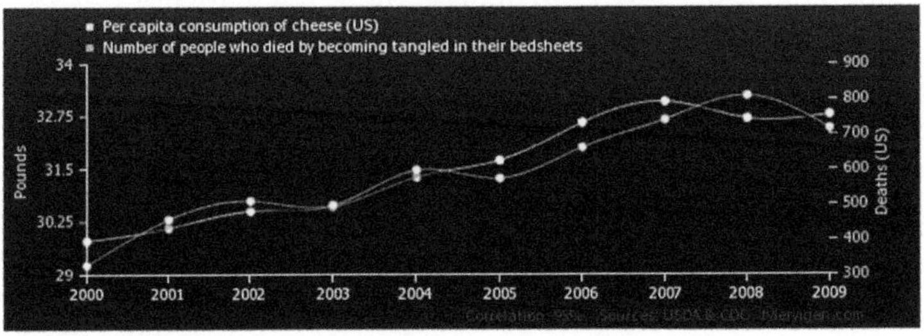

	2000	2001	2002	2003	2004	2005	2006	2007	2008	2009
Per capita consumption of cheese (US) *Pounds (USDA)*	29.8	30.1	30.5	30.6	31.3	31.7	32.6	33.1	32.7	32.8
Number of people who died by becoming tangled in their bedsheets *Deaths (US) (CDC)*	327	456	509	497	596	573	661	741	809	717

Correlation: 0.947091

For big data analysis, this distinction is crucial. The large amount of data that can now be processed can show correlations that remained hidden before. The value of correlation between two or more items is best described in examples (see in detail Chapter 11.5).

Correlation can yield insights into customers' preferences that can provide a competitive edge and a boost in sales through targeted advertisement. And in these instances, correlation is sufficient. A common sense example for correlation is that the higher the temperatures outside, the higher the ice cream sales. Proving causality of summer time and ice cream sales is much more difficult. But here, it is not necessary to do so. Correlation already gave us the relevant commercial insight that we can sell more ice cream in warmer temperatures. An incited that received very large media coverage was a Target customer in Minneapolis. The daughter of the household has been receiving targeted advertisement in the form of coupons for nursery and baby care items. The father called the local Target manager in outrage, asking whether Target is aiming to encourage his daughter to become a teenage mother. Turns out, the daughter was indeed expecting.[34]

34 *Forbes Magazine*: Kashmir Hill, How Target Figured Out A Teen Girl Was Pregnant Before Her Father Did, available at: http://www.forbes.com/sites/kashmirhill/2012/02/16/how-target-figured-out-a-teen-girl-was-pregnant-before-her-father-did/, last accessed 27 December 2014.

The way Target figured this out was by looking at customer shopping data across the U.S. Their data analysis showed that a first trimester pregnancy correlated with intuitively higher purchasing on magnesium and zinc containing products and a quick change of preferences to scent-free moisturizers in the customer bracket of women in a certain age group. The journalist *Charles Duhigg* from the New York Times uncovered Target's coupon practice and the profits it made with it.[35]

For the law, correlation becomes particularly important in criminal prosecution. Innocence must be assumed until the defendant is proven guilty. This fundamental constitutional pillar must be safeguarded against a seemingly persuasive argument of correlation. If in similar situations a crime has occurred in the past, is there room in the criminal justice system to assume a criminal behavior prediction for the future of the person under investigation? Even if the person has not yet committed a criminal act?

Data privacy law and predictive analysis supported by big data and correlation analysis will clash increasingly in the future as more and more companies and government agencies turn into data-driven entities.

2.6 The value of data

Firstly, the value of abundantly available data lies in its ability to reveal the underlying information an action or judgment is based on. This means that access to information results in a higher level of **transparency**.

Because the body of raw information is available, information can be segmented. Segmentation means that data can be reorganized along specific parameters. ***Segmentation*** allows a customized reaction to an observed phenomenon. Legally, data segmentation of personal data is problematic.[36] But at this point, it shall suffice to illustrate that segmentation of data derives a business value. The value of segmentation can be seen in this scenario:

> A clothing store is experiencing a large decline in revenue in the last months. The number of customers buying clothes in the store declined from 10.000/month to only 6.000/month. Based on the rewards cards that have been swiped, we know which customers have returned and which have not visited the store in the time period under examination. Grouping customers into age quintiles, we find out that out of the 4.000

35 *The New York Times*: Charles Duhigg, How companies learn your secrets, available at: http://www.nytimes.com/2012/02/19/magazine/shopping-habits.html?pagewanted=9&_r=1&hp, last accessed 27 December 2014.

36 See in detail Chapter 9.

customers that stayed away, 3.000 of them are female and in the age group of 18 to 25 years old. This segmentation was very valuable for the store. The store now knows the largest driver of declining revenues – namely which customers are no longer coming to purchase. They can act on this information making the store more attractive to this customer segment, target advertisements and market accordingly. Consequently, the invested resources are much more likely to yield the desired effects because they are not data-based and tailor-made for the driver of the problem

The most important value of data is that it is a catalyst for experiments. An experiment is a procedure that one designs to examine the validity of a hypothesis. This means that statements can be falsified based on data analysis. Designing an experiment ideally involves a control group. One parameter at a time is tested. The conditions are to be kept identical for the control group, anything but that one parameter is not to be changed. Assuming a flawless experiment design and repeatable procedures that do not bias the results, the ***relationship of cause and effect*** is demonstrated.

Maybe human intuition already points towards a likely cause or course of action to be taken. In the scenario above, the sales personal may already have a gut feeling that young female customers are not visiting the store as often as before. But looking at the data can support this intuition. Another example where algorithms are used to flag problematic cases is insurance claim audits. Here, the distinction between correlation and causation comes into play again. Maybe the experiment is unable to establish the validity of a hypothesis on the basis of causation. But a very high correlation is certain.

A high correlation alone is enough to build a business model around it. For example, Thanksgiving holidays are not necessarily *condition-sine-qua-non* for many people in the United States to book flights for that weekend and to buy a turkey – people can do that 365 days a year. However, there certainly is a high correlation of "Thanksgiving", "people flying" and "buying a turkey". The correlation is enough to have every airline and grocery store price and stock their services accordingly. Correlating data points drive the business decision.

Data centers processing vast amount of information are the infrastructural underpinning of deriving value from data. The structure of a data center and the functioning of cloud computing is subject of the next chapter.

3 What is the cloud?

„It's called "cloud computing" because the old programs to draw network schematics surrounded the icons for servers with a circle. A cluster of servers in a network diagram had several overlapping circles, which resembled a cloud." – Schmidt/Rosenberg (2014)[37]

This Chapter is dedicated to cloud infrastructure, the innovation it entails and the physical and legal surroundings the cloud requires. Cloud computing has been around since the 1950s. The first cloud architecture was presented by AT&T, a telecommunications company in the U.S., which centralized data storage for this company.[38] Salesforce forecasts that the market for cloud services will exceed USD 241 billion by the year 2020.[39]

A legal assessment of cloud services must start with an understanding of the market and its components. This chapter looks at what cloud computing and data centers are. It will shed light on the type of innovations cloud computing brings and what benefit can be derived from implementing a cloud solution. Furthermore, it looks at the cloud architecture, its cost structure and pricing models.

3.1 Definitions and variations of cloud computing

Cloud computing is the use of centralized information and infrastructure facilities that can be accessed locally on demand via an internet connection.[40] The "cloud" may also be seen as an acronym: Common, Location-independent, Online, Utility and available on Demand.[41] The U.S. National Institute of Standards and Tech-

37 *Schmidt/Rosenberg*, How Google Works, John Murray, 2014, p. 11 footnote No. 10.

38 *Salesforce*, A Complete History of Cloud Computing, available at: http://www.salesforce.com/uk/socialsuccess/cloud-computing/the-complete-history-of-cloud-computing.jsp, last accessed 29 December 2014.

39 *Salesforce*, A Complete History of Cloud Computing, ibd.

40 *Jaeger/Jin/Grimes/Simmons*, Where is the cloud? Geography, economics, environment, and jurisdiction in cloud computing, First Monday, Vol. 14 No. 5, May 2009, p. 1 (henceforth cited as: *Jaeger/Jin/Grimes/Simmons*, 2009).

41 *David C Wyld*, The Utility of Cloud Computing as a New Pricing and Consumption Model for Information Technology, International Journal of Database Management Systems (IJDMS), Vol. 1 No. 1, November 2009, p. 1 (henceforth cited as: *David C Wyld*, 2009).

nology (NIST) provided a working definition of cloud computing that has gained industry acceptance:[42]

> *„Cloud computing is a model for enabling ubiquitous, convenient, on-demand network access to a shared pool of configurable computing resources (e.g., networks, servers, storage, applications, and services) that can be rapidly provisioned and released with minimal management effort or service provider interaction. This cloud model promotes availability and is composed of five essential characteristics, three service models, and four deployment models.*"[43]

The NIST lists the following ***five essential characteristics***:[44] On-demand self-service, broad network access, resource pooling, rapid elasticity and measured service. Self-service means that the customer is able to upload, build, deploy, schedule, manage and report the services himself on demand.[45] Broad network access refers to the capabilities of the system that are available over the network and accessed through a standard mechanism.[46] Resource pooling means that one standardized, scalable, physical and stable resource is used to serve more than one customer at the same time.[47] Rapid elasticity refers to the ability to quickly scale the pooled resource on demand.[48] Lastly, measured service refers to the ability to use a metering capability that enables the customers and the service provider to control and optimize the use of the resource.[49] In addition to the five key characteristics proposed by NIST, the *Cloud Security Alliance* suggests a sixth key characteristic called ***multi-tenacity***. It is the defined as the "*need for policy-driven*

---

42 On industry acceptance: *Khajeh-Hosseini/Sommerville/Sriram*, Research Challenges for Enterprise Cloud Computing, available through the Cornell University Library under http://arxiv.org/abs/1001.3257, last accessed 29 December 2014, p. 1 (henceforth cited as: *Khajeh-Hosseini/Sommerville/Sriram*, 2010).

43 *Mell/Grance* with *NIST*, 2009, loc. cit. Fn. 17, p. 6.

44 *Mell/Grance* with *NIST*, 2009, ibd, p. 6.

45 *Dave Malcom Surgient*, The Five Defining Characteristics of Cloud Computing, ZDNet, Virtualization, dated 9 September 2009, also available at: http://www.zdnet.com/article/the-five-defining-characteristics-of-cloud-computing/, last accessed 29 December 2014 (henceforth cited as: *Dave Malcom Surgient*, 2009).

46 *Mell/Grance* with *NIST*, 2009, loc. cit. Fn. 17, p. 6.

47 *Dave Malcom Surgient*, 2009, loc. cit. Fn. 45.

48 *Dave Malcom Surgient*, 2009, ibd.

49 *Information Systems Audit and Control Association (ISACA)*, Essential Characteristics of Cloud Computing, also available at: http://www.isaca.org/Groups/Professional-English/cloud-computing/GroupDocuments/Essential%20characteristics%20of%20 Cloud %20Computing.pdf, last accessed 29 December 2014 (henceforth cited as: *ISACA*).

enforcement, segmentation, isolation, governance, service levels, and chargeback/ billing models for different consumer constituencies".[50]

Furthermore, according to the NIST[51], cloud computing consists of ***three service models***, Saas, PaaS, IaaS and ***four deployment models***; private, community, public and hybrid cloud.

Software as a Service (SaaS) allows users to access software that provides an application through the internet. The service offered by the cloud is in this case an end-user application. The program is not installed on the user's hardware but merely accessed from it. The SaaS provider installs the software on its servers and the customer accesses it remotely.[52] The customers addressed are those requiring end-user applications. Examples are GoogleDocs and Microsoft Online Services.

Platform as a Service (PaaS) offers a platform for collaboration for experiments, communication and joint development of new programs. These applications are run on the cloud provider's infrastructure and are also made available from there to end users. The cloud service provider makes an entire platform available that is hosted on the provider's server including operating systems and development tools.[53] PaaS customers are programmers that develop a service for end users. Examples are Amazon Web Service and Google App Engine.

Infrastructure as a Service (IaaS) provides services for system administrators in need of general data processing, data storage, database management and large server capacities. Customers receive virtual server storage space where they can install, run and maintain their own software.[54] These customers use the cloud infrastructure and pay for the amount of capacities used. The targeted customers are providers of IT services with large hardware capacity demand. Examples are EC2-Service – Amazon's Elastic Compute Cloud and HP Cloud Enabling Computing.

Also, clouds may be divided into clusters based on the degree of exclusivity into ***deployment models***. Only members of one organization or company can access private clouds.[55] It is an internal data center for the administration of the work flow within one organizational structure, e.g. a company. A community cloud can be

50 *ISACA*, ibd.
51 *Mell/Grance* with *NIST*, 2009, loc. cit. Fn. 17, p. 7.
52 *Mell/Grance* with *NIST*, 2009, ibd, p. 7.
53 *Mell/Grance* with *NIST*, 2009, ibd, p. 7.
54 *Mell/Grance* with *NIST*, 2009, ibd, p. 7.
55 *Mell/Grance* with *NIST*, 2009, ibd, p. 7.

accessed by all members of the user groups. It is less exclusive than a private cloud, but more exclusive than a public cloud. The infrastructure is shared in use and cost between several user groups that have a common issue, e.g. administration of specific data or governmental issues. The public cloud can be accessed by the general public to whom the service is provided.[56] The technological advantage lies in the shift of the private cloud technology to the application of the same principles in a public cloud.[57] A hybrid cloud's access structure depends on the independent community. Two or more independent cloud entities, e.g. a private and a public cloud, are linked together.[58]

The storage of data and data processing takes place in cloud units operated by the respective hard- and software, called ***data centers***.[59] Cloud computing can be used to different degrees depending on the amount of software or hardware to be outsourced. The cloud itself divides the tasks of running applications and data storage into small packages. These then are distributed among the servers for processing.[60] The possibility of distributing the information to be processed into small data packages opens up the possibility of ***scale earnings***. The following diagram illustrates the effect of economies of scale in cloud computing in comparison to a mainframe and a client server solution:[61]

56 *Mell/Grance* with *NIST*, 2009, ibd, p. 7.

57 *Kerr/Teng*, Cloud Computing: Legal and Privacy Issues, Prepared for the Academy of Business Disciplines' Conference, taking place 10 to 13 November 2010 in Ft. Myers, Florida, dated 15 September 2010, p. 5, also available at: http://www.g-casa.com/conferences/vietnam/paper/JDK_CLOUDING_9_21_10_Paper-1[11].pdf, last accessed 29 December 2014 (henceforth cited as: *Kerr/Teng*, 2010).

58 *Mell/Grance* with *NIST*, 2009, loc. cit. Fn. 17, p. 7.

59 *Armbrust/Fox/Griffith/Joseph/Katz/Konwinski/Lee/Patterson/Rabkin/Stoica/Zaharia*, Clearing the clouds away from the true potential and obstacles posed by this computing capability, Communications of the ACM, Vol. 53 No. 4, April 2010, p. 52 (henceforth cited as: *Armbrust/Fox/Griffith/Joseph/Katz/Konwinski/Lee/Patterson/Rabkin/Stoica/Zaharia*, 2010).

60 *William Jeremy Robinson*, Free at What Cost? Cloud Computing Privacy Under the Stored Communications Act, The Georgetown Law Journal, Vol. 98 No. 4, 2010, pp. 1195 et seqq. at p. 1199 (henceforth cited as: *William Jeremy Robinson*, 2010).

61 *Pavel/Mattes*, Cloud Computing: Großes Wachstumspotential, Wochenbericht des DIW Berlin Nr. 48/2010, p. 11, available at: http://www.diw.de/documents/publikationen/73/diw_01.c.364145.de/10-48-3.pdf, accessed 14 March 2011.

Fig. 3: Economies of scale of cloud computing

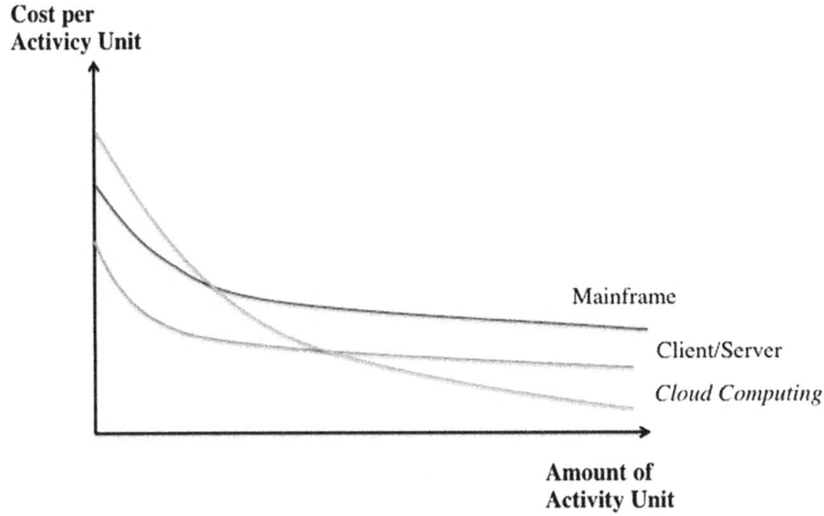

The data processing costs decrease with every unit of production. Scale earnings result from fixed costs irrespective of the amount of data units processed, competitive advantages due to specialization and know-how.[62]

3.2 The benefit of could computing

Without having to manage complex hardware and software, cloud computing is an option for sophisticated IT service providers and developers as well as end users. The benefit of outsourcing to cloud computing is illustrated by the following example: On every Friday evening between 8 and 10 p.m. local time, "*Fictional News TV Weekly*" is broadcast discussing current political issues. After the broadcast, viewers visit *"FictionalNewsTVWeekly.com"* eagerly for further information on this week's topics. During the week, this website is not frequented to this degree. To meet the demand during peak times, the capacity corresponding to peak demand would need to be maintained constantly. Through cloud computing, resources booked correspond directly to the resources demanded. In result, this innovation saves the amount 'Resources constantly maintained' minus 'Resources required'. The duty of payment is only for the amount of resources used.

62 *Helmut Bester*, Theorie der Industrieökonomik, 4th Edition, 2007, Springer, p. 150 et seqq. (henceforth cited as: *Helmut Bester*, 2007).

Fig. 4: The benefit of cloud computing

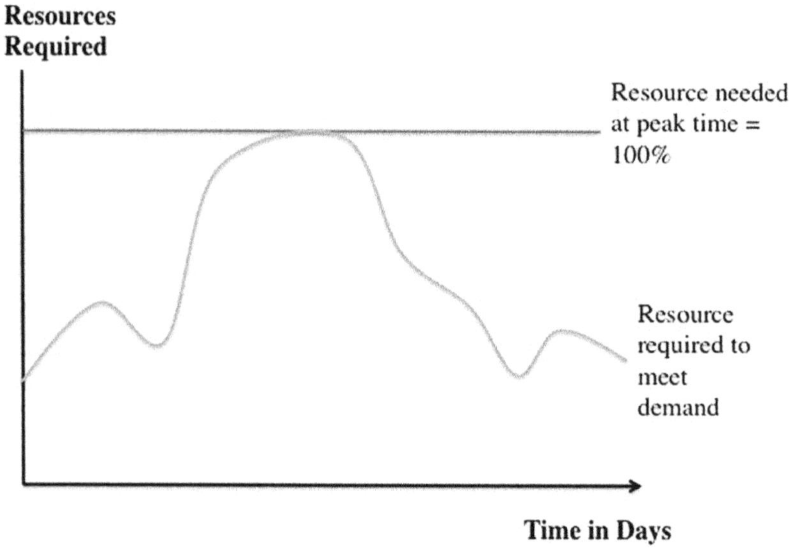

If the website operator can outsource the web traffic computing needs, he will save the difference between outsourcing costs and the in-house IT maintenance costs plus the costs for idle in-house capacity going unused. The benefit of cloud computing is the ***elimination of decentralized overcapacity***. *Benkler* captured the personal computer as a 'lumpy good'. Lumpy is defined as the "*provision of functionality in discrete packages rather than in a smooth flow*".[63] The minimum unit of purchase is 1 PC – whether you need all the computing capacity of this unit is irrelevant after the time of purchase. Private ownership is wide-spread of this resource and overflow capacity in relation to the owner's demand present.

3.3 The innovations of cloud computing

Cloud computing is a new business model on the IT market. It provides the market with a new standard of information technology. It poses new challenges in several legal fields such as competition law, intellectual property law, business and

63 *Yochai Benkler*, Sharing Nicely: On Shareable Goods and the Emergence of Sharing as a Modality of Economic Production, The Yale Law Journal Vol. 114, 2004, pp. 273–358, at pp. 276–277 (henceforth cited as: *Yochai Benkler*, 2004).

corporate law. Cloud computing causes an organizational shift in the IT market and is intertwined with new security, legal and privacy issues. This is rooted in its inherent innovations. Cloud computing is an innovation in two ways:

Firstly, it is a ***product innovation:*** An existing product is made available in a new way forming a new product for data storage, data processing and server capacities. The degree of elasticity of resources is unprecedented in the IT market and the necessity of long-term planning of the IT resources is diminished significantly.[64] Secondly, it also is an ***institutional innovation:*** The contractual relationship of the market players is required to regulate a new set of problems on the level of private ordering. On the level of public ordering, existing and planned regulations of the cloud computing sector need to be analyzed from the angle of positive theory and with regard to intended and non-intended effects of regulation.[65]

Looking at the cost structure of IT solutions, cloud computing shifts IT expenses from sunk costs to variable costs. The elasticity and scalability of the server resources and the transfer of risks from the in-house IT department to the cloud service provider open up new possibilities for risk management.[66] The main burden of an in-house IT structure is the ***risk of over- and underprovisioning.***[67] In the case of overprovisioning, resources remain not utilized and are a deadweight. In the case of underprovisioning, the facilities are at complete saturation but beyond complete saturation, the demand of user n + 1 after saturation cannot be met anymore and is therefore a lost potential. In this case, the company must also account for the reputation mechanism initiated by a rejected user. It is therefore more likely that a company risks deadweight server capacities than risking a lost customer or negative reputation. It is estimated that the average server utilization of a conventional data center that is not member of a public cloud is at 5 to 20 per cent.[68] This mirrors deadweight due to overprovisioning at minimum at 80 per cent.

---

64 *Kirchner/Käseberg*, Cloud Computing im Lichte des europäischen Wettbewerbsrechts, in: *Bechtold/Jickeli/Rohe* (eds.), Recht, Ordnung und Wettbewerb: Festschrift zum 70. Geburtstag von Wernhard Möschel, Nomos, 5 July 2011 (henceforth cited as: *Kirchner/Käseberg*, 2011).

65 *Kirchner/Käseberg*, 2011, ibd.

66 On risk management see in detail Chapter 3.6.

67 *Armbrust/Fox/Griffith/Joseph/Katz/Konwinski/Lee/Patterson/Rabkin/Stoica/Zaharia*, 2010, loc. cit. Fn. 59, p. 53.

68 With further references see *Armbrust/Fox/Griffith/Joseph/Katz/Konwinski/Lee/Patterson/Rabkin/Stoica/Zaharia*, ibd, p. 53.

With regard to the economics of cloud computing, there are three possible scenarios where cloud computing is favorable in comparison to owning the infrastructure itself.[69] Firstly, the ***demand*** for computing service is ***not constant*** and time-dependent with large peak loads. This means that resources are not constantly needed at the same capacity all the time. Secondly, the demand for computing service is ***not always predictable*** beforehand. This means that unforeseeable events may lead to a surge in capacity on short notice. Thirdly, the recipient of the computing service performs ***batch analytic services***. This means that either one server working for 100 hours or 100 servers working for one hour in order to process the required data can perform the computational output.

3.4 Key legal issues of the cloud

An IT revolution like cloud computing triggered several legal problem areas. To get a first sense of the affected legal fields, this subchapter serves as an introduction to the initially identified problematic issues. The European Network and Information Security Agency (ENISA) identified the following ***five key legal issues*** of cloud computing:[70]

- Data protection including data availability and integrity and minimum protection standards
- Confidentiality
- Intellectual property rights
- Professional negligence
- Outsourcing services and changes in control.

It is surprising that the ENISA report does not mention competition law within the five legal key issues. With exception to lock-in effects[71], no question of competition law is tackled in detail.

Within the Commission, the Directorate-General Information Society and Media initiated calls for papers on cloud computing and thoroughly researches the aspect of data security within cloud computing. Until 2012, the Directorate-General did not issue a call for papers with regard to the competition law im-

69 *Armbrust/Fox/Griffith/Joseph/Katz/Konwinski/Lee/Patterson/Rabkin/Stoica/Zaharia*, ibd, p. 52.

70 *ENISA*, 2011, loc. cit. Fn. 11, p. 97.

71 *ENISA*, 2011, ibd, p. 25.

plications of cloud computing.[72] In the field of cloud computing in particular, the questions of data security standards and competition law concerns are strongly intertwined.[73] *Ms Neelie Kroes,* the former DG Information Society and Media Commissioner, participated in the opening of the new Microsoft Cloud and Interoperability Centre in Brussels on 23 March 2011.[74] With regard to the high speed of adaptation in the IT sector, competition law questions should be assessed as much in advance as possible to assist the market with the predictability of the EU Commission's expectations in this field. Cooperation between DG Competition and DG Information Society and Media should have been initiated much earlier to give an exchange of thought accessible for market participants.

From a competition law perspective, cloud computing poses several questions that have never been asked before for a product market comparable to the cloud. New up and coming technological milestones (or components of it) may also be regarded as essential facilities (EF) with all the consequences attached to it. Aside from the "classic examples" of an EF – such as regional electricity distribution networks[75], rail networks[76], airport terminals[77], gas storage

72 See for the call for papers and research work program for the years 2011 and 2012: http://cordis.europa.eu/fp7/ict/home_en.html and ftp://ftp.cordis.europa.eu/pub/fp7/ict/docs/ict-wp-2011-12_en.pdf, last accessed 6 June 2012.

73 See in detail Chapter 7 on data privacy standardization cartels.

74 See the press release at: http://lucvdv.wordpress.com/2011/03/23/ microsoft-opens-european-cloud-and-interoperability-center-second-microsoft-innovation-center-in-brussels/, last accessed 29 December 2014.

75 In the United States of America see: *Otter Tail Power Co. v. United States*, 410 U.S. 366 (1973); In the European Union see for Germany Sec. 20 German Energy Industry Act (*Energiewirtschaftsgesetz – EnWG*).

76 In the United States of America see: *Delaware & Hudson Ry. Co. v. Consolidated Rail Corp.*, 902 F. 2d 174 (2d Cir. 1990); In the EU see for Germany the German Ordinance on Railway Infrastructure Utilisation (*Eisenbahninfrastruktur-Benutzungsverordnung – EIBV*).

77 In the United States of America see: *Interface Group, Inc. v. Massachusetts Port Auth.*, 816 F.2d 9 (1st Cir. 1987); in the EU see the case concerning Frankfurt am Main International Airport and the liberalization of the ground services: Commission Decision dated 14 January 1998 – IV/34.801 FAG, O.J. No. L 072, pp. 30–50 – *Flughafen Frankfurt/Main AG.*

facilities[78], bridges[79], harbors[80], television guide listings[81] up to information on interoperability[82] – the Commission has extended its interpretation of „facility" to immaterial property rights such as patents and trade secrets. Interoperability is enabled through source code and – if considered as an EF – would be the most "technical" facility to date. The closest in case law history to this degree of technicality applied in a refusal to deal or supply case was the API information concerning work group servers.[83]

Furthermore, interoperability information is also protected by IPRs and trade secrets. Also, the cloud facility may pose an issue for foreign direct investment and a corporate governance risk.[84] The privacy and security issues may be addressed through an agreement or common standard of practice developed by the cloud operators on the market. This agreement must also be subject of competition law assessment.[85] For market players facing API or interoperability information of cloud services being a potential Art. 102 TFEU target for disclosure, their exposure to lawsuits should be examined by the market player beforehand.

The ***market value of interoperability information*** is the first indicator towards competition law-relevant behavior in the future. If the information is able to inhibit dynamic competition through i.e. lock-in effects and network effects, competition law scrutiny may occur in the near future. Using past IT-sector cases as an indicator, competition law proceedings on interoperability will be a long (judicial

---

78 *EU Commission*, Commission Staff Working Paper, Interpretative Note on Directive 2998/73/EC concerning Common Rules for the Internal Market in Natural Gas – Third-Party Access to Storage Facilities, dated 22 January 2010.

79 In the United States of America see: The leading decision *United States v. Terminal Railroad Association*, 224 U.S. 383 (1912).

80 In The European Union: *Sea Containers v. Stena Sealink*; Commission Decision dated 21 December 1993 - IV/34.689 – O.J. No. L 015, pp. 8–19.

81 In the European Union: *Radio Telefis Eireann (RTE) and Independent Television Publications Ltd. (ITP) v. Commission*; Joined Cases C-241/91 P and C-242/91 P, [1995] E.C.R. I-743 [1995] 4 C.M.L.R. 718 (henceforth cited as: *Magill*). This case caused great controversy as it was unclear whether merely any competitive advantage could be considered an essential facility. Also, the scope of intellectual property rights captured by the EFD may be extended to technical know-how or trade secrets.

82 *EU Commission*, Decision dated 24 March 2004, Case COMP/C-3/37.792 – *Microsoft* (henceforth: *Microsoft*, COMP/C-3/37.792).

83 *Microsoft*, COMP/C-3/37.792, ibd.

84 See also: *Kerr/Teng*, 2010, loc. cit. Fn. 57, p. 2.

85 See below Chapter 6.4 on strategic alliances.

and enforcement) process with the market moving faster than the litigation itself. For example, the Microsoft[86] cases lasted over a decade.

An additional layer of problem will be added by ***defining the applicable law*** – especially if the servers of the cloud facility are located outside the jurisdiction of the relevant market under examination. The more precisely the SLA is drafted, the more this may be used as an indicator in favor of the defendant, in particular for non-discriminatory licensing and other factors that may "drive up" the fines the Commission is able to sentence.

As a further area of necessary legal analysis, cloud operators are affected by a potential change in policy regarding ***network neutrality***.[87] Net neutrality may heavily impact the market for cloud services. Network neutrality stipulates the equal treatment of all data packages. A ‚smart grid' is able to distinguish between different kinds of data packages and prioritize them e.g. according to time critical content or the application responsible for the data packages sent/received.[88] Internet services connect the front end and the back end devices with each other. In the case of an internet flat rate, the ***common pool problem*** emerges and the marginal costs for a data unit transmitted is zero. A change in policy of network neutrality is subject to a heated discussion[89] in the US, where currently also many cloud data centers reside. This question is also necessarily intertwined with the question of the contractual clauses stipulating regulations for internet data transfer.

3.5 Market impact

To illustrate the scale of resources concerned with cloud computing, a few figures as of 2010. The amount of data stored by Amazon Web Services in the last months of 2007 comprises 14 billion units, the units varying in size from a few bytes to

86 *Microsoft*, COMP/C-3/37.792, loc. cit. Fn. 82.

87 The Quality of Service (QoS) is a concern with regard to network neutrality and therefor for cloud service providers, see e.g.: *Sluijs/Larouche/Sauter*, 2012, loc. cit. Fn. 3. In the scope of this work, it is not possible to analyze the full legal and economic impact of network neutrality on cloud computing. This must be subject of a subsequent paper.

88 For example, data packages for video online streaming or video chat are more time sensitive than emails during the transmission process.

89 See the two landmark cases in the U.S., *Comcast Corp. v. FCC*,[1] 600 F.3d 642 and *Verizon v. FCC*, 740 F.3d 623 (D.C. Cir. 2014). On the forefront of contributions see i.e. Stanford Law School, Center for Internet and Society (CIS), *Barbara van Schewick*, Network Neutrality and Quality of Service, What a Non-Discrimination Rule Should Look Like, Center for Internet and Society Whitepaper, 11 July 2012.

5 gigabytes.[90] Amazon's s3 storage services handles approximately 30.000 requests per second. Amazon charges 0.15 $ for one gigabyte of data storage and 0.10 $ per hour for a server rented (equals 876 $ per year for non-stop usage).[91] Google is able to sort one petabyte[92] of data via the cloud architecture in approximately six hours using 4.000 computers. The market for cloud computing services had a volume of $16 billion in the year 2008 and was estimated to grow up to $42 billion by the year 2012.[93] The market has long exceeded these expectations. Google alone was operating more than 450.000 servers per conservative estimate back in 2007.[94] The figure by the *IBM Whitepaper* illustrates the workloads anticipated for cloud computing in the following years to 2010:[95]

The workload anticipation shows that in every examined segment, the workload was projected to increase. Particularly high projections were expected for transaction processing, decision support and analytics and high performance computing. Specifically with decision support, this backs up the premise stated in the outline that intuitive decision-making has become more and more supported by data-driven assessments to verify business decisions.

---

90 *Grzegorz Czajkowski*, Sorting 1 PB with MapReduce, The Official Google Blog, 21 November 2008, available at: http://googleblog.blogspot.com/2008/11/sorting-1pb-with-mapreduce.html, last accessed 20 February 2011; *Hardy*, The Death of Hardware, Forbes Magazine, 11 February 2008, available at: http://www.forbes.com/forbes/2008/0211/036.html, last accessed 20 February 2011.

91 See: http://aws.amazon.com/de/ec2/pricing/, last accessed 20 February 2011.

92 A petabyte is a unit of information that equals 1000 terabytes. On the dimension of data processed, see *Gilder*, The Information Factories. Wired, Vol. 14 No. 10, 2007 (henceforth cited as: *Gilder*, 2007).

93 *Khajeh-Hosseini/Sommerville/Sriram*, 2010, loc. cit. Fn. 42, p. 1; *Gleeson*, Computing industry set for a shocking change, Moneyweek dated 24 April 2009, available at: http://www.moneyweek.com/investment-advice/computing-industry-set-for-a-shocking-change-43226, last accessed 10 May 2011; *Kerr/Teng*, 2010, loc. cit. Fn. 57, p. 6.

94 This references physical servers, not virtual servers. 450.000 physical servers is the lowest estimation according to *Gilder*, 2007, loc. cit. Fn. 92.

95 *IBM*, Cloud computing insights from 110 implementation projects, loc. cit. Fn. 10, p. 4, Fig. 3.

Fig. 5: Anticipated cloud computing workload

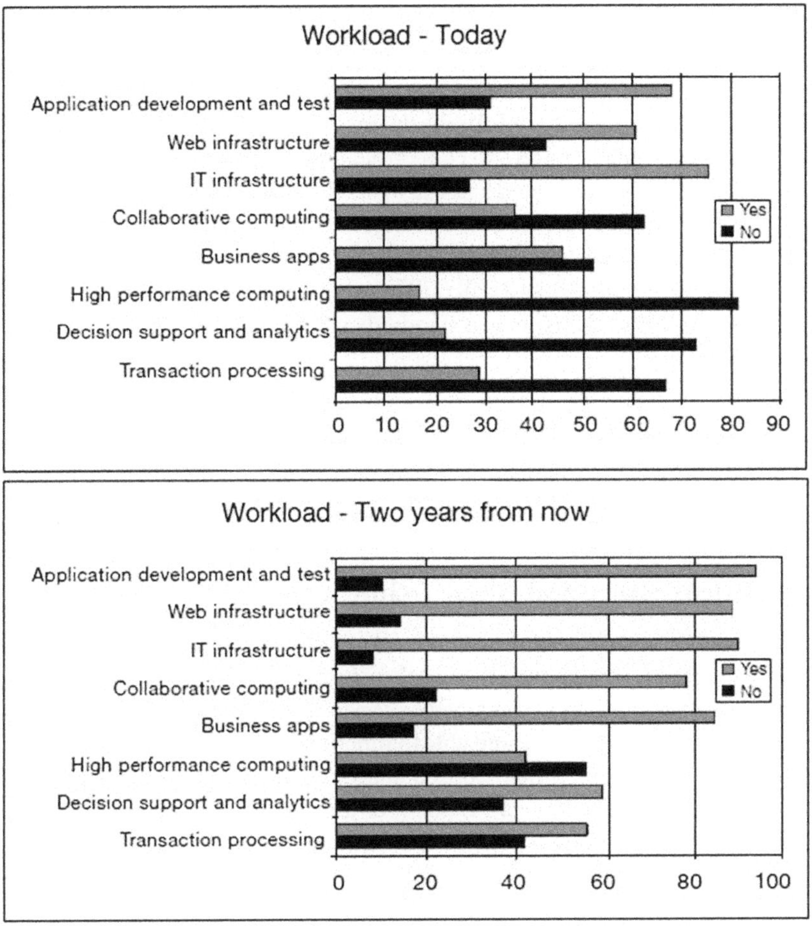

3.6 Risk management

Cloud operators that want to enter, expand or remain in the EU internal market need to work with and abide by the legal institutions and laws of the EU. These institutions and provisions are a mirror of the economic, political, social and historical background the cloud services have to operate in for serving their customers. Their understanding is a component of risk management due diligence. The policy makers are introduced in detail in Chapter 5.

Risk management can be divided into five categories.[96] Firstly, there is risk ***identification***. The risky factor must be identified and isolated from non-risk factors. This allows us to know the driving factor or issue of the uncertainty. Secondly, the risk can be ***avoided*** if it can be eliminated completely. Thirdly, the risk can be ***reduced***. This occurs if the risk is still present, but to a smaller degree. Fourthly, the risk can be ***shared***. This is the case if more than one individual must burden the risk if the risk were to come true. Lastly, there is risk ***retention***. This implies that the risk is accepted and calculated in its initial form.

Pricing the regulatory risk needs to account for the decision-making costs-related to the cultural surroundings of the site of the business activity. The perception of justice, fairness and trust in enforcement with a subjective lens is as equally important as the objective standards written as laws. On this matter by *Douglass North*:

> *"Ideology is the subjective perception that people have about what the world is like and what it ought to be; ideology therefore affects people's perception about the fairness or justice of the institutions of a political economics system. Institutions (...) are the humanly devised constraints on repeated human interaction, that is, the rules of the fame – both formal rules and informal rules of behaviour and the way they are enforced."*[97]

3.7 Cost structure and cloud architecture

A data center and the cloud facility is a construction of numerous components with each component relying on the other. Prima facie, data centers need real estate, electricity, cooling and maintenance services. But there is much more to it. The cloud is only profitable and able to function at all if these components can communicate with each other. Consequently, the cloud components and their degree of interoperability are an element of the cost structure. This subchapter presents those components and what it costs to set them up.

3.7.1 Cloud architecture

For the data exchange between customer and the cloud to work, both parties need to be equipped with certain facilities. The customer must be able to utilize the performance provided by the cloud operator and the cloud facility must be equipped to perform the offered services. The ***front end*** is the part of the cloud

---

96 ISO 31000:2009.

97 *Douglass C North*, Ideology and Political/Economic Institutions, Cato Journal, Vol. 8 No. 1, Spring/Summer 1988.

architecture visible to the client of the cloud facility. Components of the front end may be the client's network, computer, smart phone or any other hardware device and the application with which the client is accessing the cloud performance. The ***back end*** is the cloud itself providing the performance. In the back end, the servers, data storage facilities and resources are located to operate the computations in the cloud. The back end of the cloud architecture is examined in detail as follows.

3.7.2 Data center equipment and setup

The operation of these large data centers (the back end) requires constant technology development, a physical infrastructure, process management, electricity, cooling, software and hardware engineers and many more. The construction of a data center without any pre-established conditions has been analyzed in Iceland.[98] Several surrounding parameters are necessary for the basic functioning of a data center:[99] Firstly, data racks must be places low and with high density. The data racks must be equipped with switching, routing and telephony equipment to reach the individual components remotely and quickly for trouble-shooting. Secondly, there needs to be fiber optic cabling and horizontal copper cabling in place. This ensures that the wires are in place to connect the racks and also enables data transmission at high speed. Thirdly, a heavy security detail must be in place. This entails safety and security measures on the site such as access registration, intrusion detection, fire detection and emergency fire extinguishing gas that does not harm the equipment. Since equipment is fragile and relies on optics, there must be fully installed raised floor and dust limiting wall painting. Fifthly, the data centers would heat up substantially without a sophisticated temperature control and air conditioning system in place. The optimal temperature is a crucial factor to operate the center efficiently. Lastly, electrical power installation including transformers, low and high-tension cabinets, additional batteries and generators, grounding and lighting are necessary.[100] The total costs for establishing these data center surrounding parameters have been estimated at 27.049.000 Euros in the

---

98 *PriceWaterhouseCoopers*, Invest in Iceland Agency, Benchmarking Study on Iceland as a Location for Data Centre Activity, 2007, available at: http://www.invest.is/resources/files/invest.is/BDC%20Report.pdf, accessed 15 May 2010 (henceforth cited as: *PriceWaterhouseCoopers*, 2007).

99 *PriceWaterhouseCoopers*, 2007, ibd, p. 43 et seqq.

100 These components #1 through #7 are in line with my on-site observations and the criteria presented by: *PriceWaterhouseCoopers*, 2007, ibd, p. 43 et seqq.

year 2007 for a facility of 800m².[101] Here, the real estate and electricity costs were not included yet.

A dynamic infrastructure service such as a data center is organized in a multi-layer facility. Each layer has its own function and can be customized and monitored independently. Particularly important is the component of ***virtualization***. Virtualization is what enables the economies of scale due to systematic over-capacity of computing goods that enable a form of sharing practice.[102] As *Benkler* analyzed from the perspective of the economic analysis of sharing, he pointed out about distributed computing, already in 2005:

> *„Parallel computing will achieve similar results to a single processor at lower cost if the total amount of overhead lost to parallelization is less than the cost differential for building the added computation capacity into one computer. This simplified explanation describes more or less why, by the end of the twentieth century, most supercomputers were made of thousands of simple processors lashed together and why parallelization became an important field in computer science".*[103]

In order to support a ***dynamic infrastructure***[104], certain physical infrastructure components are needed within a data center. There are physical components such as power systems, blade center, system X, mainframe, storage and networking. These are the hardware components of the data center. These parts need to be connected to each other, set up in an appropriate location and shall provide the service that is sold through the cloud. The key element layered on top of the physical components is the virtualization of servers, storage and networks. Virtualization is defined by IBM as

> *"the abstraction of logical resources away from their underlying physical resources in order to improve agility and flexibility, reduce costs and thus enhance business value."*[105]

Virtualization can be considered as the core piece of the data center. It allows a number of underutilized (larger) units to be consolidated into smaller units. These units are then used to their full capacity. Hence, the resources are shared, managed and isolated from one another allowing users to share the resource

101 *PriceWaterhouseCoopers*, 2007, ibd, p. 50.

102 *Yochai Benkler*, 2004, loc. cit. Fn. 63, p. 357.

103 *Yochai Benkler*, 2004, loc. cit. Fn. 63, p. 290.

104 *IBM*, Seeding the Clouds: Key Infrastructure Elements for Cloud Computing, February 2009, available at www.ibm.com with document reference No. OIW03022-USEN-00, p. 9 (henceforth cited as: *IBM*, Seeding the Clouds). The definitions and product descriptions in this chart are those of IBM, see p. 10 et seqq.; the elements of monitoring are described in p. 14.

105 *IBM*, Seeding the Clouds, ibd, p. 10.

without affecting one another. In essence, virtualization achieves the isolation of the user from the underlying infrastructure. The following image is taken from *Majd F Sakr's* presentation at Carnegie Mellon Qatar dated 14 January 2010:[106]

Fig. 6: Correct virtualization.

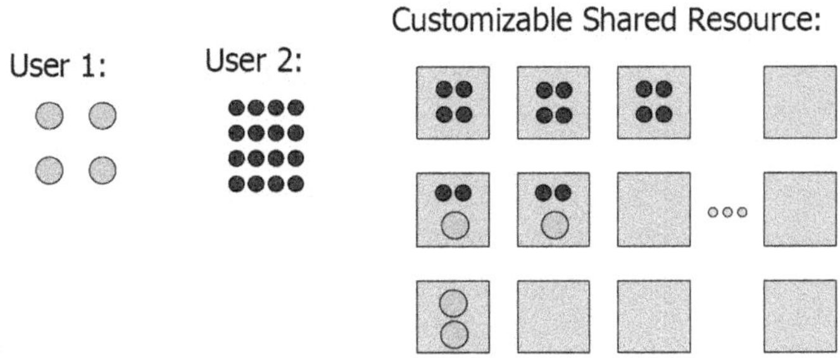

This image illustrates that two users are able to share a resource without knowing from each other's joint use of the same physical platform. In essence, a software layer virtually isolates them from each other, making a physical resource appear exactly as large as the individual user's needs.

Next, data centers need to be managed through dynamic provisioning, dynamic scheduling, self-service portals for users, monitoring and service level agreement capacity planning. Infrastructure management is the component ***organizing the potential enabled through virtualization***. The element of monitoring illustrates the components that need to be observed in order to allow virtualization to function to its full potential. Firstly, the system must collect data in order to plan for medium and long-term future data center resources and resource placement. Secondly, real-time data streams for capacity requirements on short notice must be captured. A method for this is to measure the service level agreement performances. Next, one must continuously observe whether there are application problems within the system. Lastly, the system must report data on the currently used resources for efficient cost allocation, e.g. by shutting down servers. Users may contribute to the management of the data center through performing the more ‚simple' tasks of e.g. starting and stopping servers if the project demands more resources.

106 *Majd F Sakr*, Introduction to cloud computing, lecture at Carnegie Mellon Qatar dated 14 January 2010, also available at: http://www.qatar.cmu.edu/~msakr/15319-s10/lectures/lecture02.pdf, last accessed 29 December 2014 (henceforth cited as: *Majd F Sakr*, 2010).

3.7.3 Location

For the customer, who may access his e-mails from any place at any time, the question of the cloud's location is not at the forefront. But for the cloud service provider, the question of location is of vital importance.[107]

In general, the infrastructure back end, with the elements as described above[108], is centralized in a few locations in data centers. The demand of space, cooling, electricity and other available resources are enormous and intrinsically tied to very high costs. When deciding where to build a data center, it is of paramount importance to the investor to examine the physical location and the surrounding parameters of the real estate in question. This includes the available resources and the governing jurisdiction.[109] For the construction of a data center numerous real estate parameters are decisive.[110] Firstly, there needs to be enough space to build warehouse-sized buildings. Secondly, the ground needs to be a flat surface or suitable for an underground location.[111] Thirdly, the real estate should be located in stable climate and weather where there is low likelihood of natural disasters such as earthquakes. Preferably, there are natural features allowing energy saving such as water for cooling through a nearby river. Fourthly, the chosen area must be in a safe area where the security of the facility can be easily ensured against criminality and corporate espionage. Fifthly, a high capacity internet connection should be available nearby. Next, affordable[112] electricity and cooling should be obtainable. Second to last, the data center should be sufficiently distant to facilities posing a danger to the data center, such as chemical plants through evacuation requirements.[113] Lastly and most importantly, data center investors will consider

107 *Jaeger/Jin/Grimes/Simmons*, 2009, loc. cit. Fn. 40.

108 *Mell/Grance* with *NIST*, 2009, loc. cit. Fn. 17, p. 7. The definition as presented in Chapter 3.1.

109 *Jaeger/Jin/Grimes/Simmons*, 2009, loc. cit. Fn. 40.

110 *Jaeger/Jin/Grimes/Simmons*, 2009, ibd.

111 Examples of such favorable locations are underground facilities, empty malls, abandoned mines and bunkers; see also *Gilder*, 2007, loc. cit. Fn. 92.

112 Electricity is one of the major cost factors with one data center consuming approximately as much electricity as an aluminum smelter (200 MW); see *Ahmed*, Google search finds seafaring solution, The Sunday Times, 15 September 2008 available at: http://technology.timesonline.co.uk/tol/news/tech_and_web/the_web/article4753389.ece, last accessed 20 February 2011 (henceforth cited as: *Ahmed*, 2008).

113 *The Boyd Company*, Location Factors for Data Centers, Area Development, Site and Facility Planning, August 2009, available at: http://www.theboydcompany.com/pdf/

the laws, policies and regulations of the jurisdiction that shall be data center friendly.

The "Data Center Map"[114] illustrates where data centers and cloud servers are located worldwide. The locations of preference are e.g. Iowa, Oregon and Washington State in the U.S., Iceland and Siberia.[115] Mainly so, Siberia and Iceland have low electricity costs and U.S. States Iowa, Oregon and Washington have wind power and hydroelectric power facilities available. These geographic locations were chosen for a reason. The two main concerns of a facility operator in cloud computing are the ***electricity costs*** and the ***characteristics of the jurisdiction*** governing the location.

3.7.4 Electricity costs

Electricity costs are the overriding recurring cost factor of a data center. The price per kWh[116] depends largely on the region electricity is consumed and also on the governing energy law for production facilities with especially high electricity consumption.[117] In addition to the geographically fortunate conditions of wind and hydro power, Iowa also encourages the construction of data centers through tax reliefs for large manufacturing companies in the form of no sales tax on the equipment and electricity used for the construction and operation of the facilities.[118] According to the survey conducted by *Boyd* in 2009[119], the operation of a new data center with 125.000 square feet (11.612,88 square meters) and 125 employees can cost $12 million in Iowa, $23 million in San Francisco and $28 million in New York.[120]

Area_Development_Data_Centers.pdf, last accessed 15 May 2011 (henceforth cited as: *The Boyd Company*, 2009).

114 See: http://www.datacentermap.com (accessed 21 February 2011).

115 *Jaeger/Jin/Grimes/Simmons*, 2009, loc. cit. Fn. 40, p. 7; *Gilder*, 2007, loc. cit. Fn. 92.

116 "kWh" stands for Kilowatt-hour measuring one unit of electricity delivered to a consumer.

117 For example, under the German Sec. 60 et seqq. Renewable Energies Act (*Erneuerbare-Energien-Gesetz* – "EEG"), facilities with especially high electricity consumption such as railway transportation companies or manufacturing companies are granted certain reliefs of EEG-surcharge payments for electricity consumption linked to the business performance of the company.

118 *Foley*, Why Google And Microsoft Are Building Data Centers In Iowa, Information Week dated 4 August 2008, available at: http://www.informationweek.com/blog/229210089, accessed 10 May 2011 (henceforth cited as: *Foley*, 2008).

119 *The Boyd Company*, 2009, loc. cit. Fn. 113.

120 *Foley*, 2008, loc. cit. Fn. 118.

The five globally leading search companies operate approximately 2 million physical servers producing approximately 600 MW of heat per year. An additional amount is needed for the cooling of the servers. Also, one must account for electricity inefficiencies due to transformers, converters and other electro-technical difficulties. Already in 2006, 5 GW were needed to power the servers on their basic load.[121]

The significance of ***cooling*** with stable and cost efficient electricity procurement is probably best illustrated by how creatively data center operators try to save on these costs. There are developments of hosting a data center in international waters using the ocean for power and cooling to safe electricity. Google filed a patent registration, in the media cited as *The Google Navy*.[122] However, this project suffers from large security concerns and was to public knowledge not realized until this day.

3.8 Forum shopping

The Google Navy raised one additional point very clearly that should alert policy makers[123]: The issues of forum shopping and high quality public ordering are tackled to a dissatisfying degree to the players on the market. The degree of dissatisfaction is high enough to set sail to go beyond territorial governmental reach. This is detrimental for consumer protection and the accountability of cloud service providers. Hence, we must ask ourselves how to organize the legal environment of a cloud facility to find balanced regulations that meet the service providers' business needs as well as society's demands for consumer and data protection laws.

The law is governed by the principle of territoriality. As a general rule, the location of the facility determines the applicable law. It is possible for the (*private*) parties to agree on a certain applicable law on the level of private ordering. Nevertheless, this is not possible to override elements of compulsory public ordering through private ordering. An example would be the regulations for electricity grid access that are considered elements of compulsory public order under German law. Furthermore, the density of regulations is substantially increased once the cloud facility operates for governmental purposes. The quality of the law is a cost factor. Unclear or unfavorable legal regimes translate into risks. Hence, forum shopping is a cost-benefit calculation. There is a trade-off between more sophis-

121 *Gilder*, 2007, loc. cit. Fn. 92. This estimation is based on the year 2006. The demand was significantly increasing since then.

122 *Ahmed*, 2008, loc. cit. Fn. 112.

123 *Jaeger/Jin/Grimes/Simmons*, 2009, loc. cit. Fn. 40.

ticated consumer protection and data privacy laws and lower transaction costs through higher enforceability and security of legal titles.

An investor or service provider compares different jurisdictions and choses the most convenient for the investment or business purpose. During this assessment, the investor considers numerous factors. One mayor factor is the overall costs of business activities in that particular jurisdiction such as taxes, regulatory requirements, availability of skilled employees on the market. Secondly, a data center causes a very large carbon footprint due to its high electricity consumption. Environmental requirements and in particular the cost of the carbon foot print of a data center are a major concern.[124] Thirdly, the technology and the data stored and processed involved are oftentimes subject to IPR.

The concerns of data privacy, confidentiality, accessibility through third parties and data property hit the core of the cloud service providers' business. From the customers' perspective, the aspect of data portability and the hinged standard of consumer welfare under the jurisdiction in question are important. Lastly, the governing legal system may be set for possible short-term governmental interference. This could be disruptive for a long-term investment. With that, the enforceability of legal titles is essential. The vast majority of interview partners raised jurisdictional concerns as a key concern for their operations in Europe. A considerable effort is linked to avoiding jurisdiction (*Gerichtsbarkeit*) in legal regimes associated with expensive data privacy standards and intransparent governmental interference through foreseeable changes in the law.

3.9 Conclusion

Cloud computing introduced two major innovations to the market. Firstly, the ***product innovation*** made a new type of IT resources available to private individuals, companies and the public sector. The processing capacities have become available to an unprecedentedly diverse group of customers with large elasticity of procurement on the customers' side. Secondly, the ***institutional innovation*** led to a need to regulate a new type of legal relationship. Cloud service providers on SaaS, IaaS and PaaS level have emerged as new contractual partners. The handling of the data in remote physical locations raises new problems of data portability, data protection and enforceability. Investors are actively forum shopping and compare jurisdictions in a risk mapping exercise. They identified numerous legal parameters that are important for their decision-making process. These are in

124 *Jaeger/Jin/Grimes/Simmons*, 2009, ibd.

particular the governing IP and data protection laws and the likelihood of quick changes in the legal structure.

A lot of upfront planning is necessary to build a data center. Once the physical infrastructure is built, the investment becomes a sunk cost. Specific real estate parameters must be given in order to accommodate technically difficult setups and sufficient security and connectivity. Beyond the real estate parameters, remote access via sufficient peripheral infrastructure is necessary to enable global remote access to the facility.

When policy makers choose to redraft data privacy, IP and cyber security laws, the IT sector is closely watching whether the factual requirements of building a data center are sufficiently accounted for. Equally, this is true for the level of consumer protection for IT-based services.

4 Cloud security risks

The demand for cloud computing services has significantly increased. A survey by Mimecast.com[125] stipulates that the sectors with the highest cloud adaptation are the technology sector with 53 %, financial services with 41 % and legal services with 37 %. The data transferred to the cloud in these sectors is confidential. The relevant information may affect IPRs, influence the reaction on stock markets and information falling under the attorney-client-privilege.

European and U.S. customers have a different understanding of their relationship with personal data. European customers are very data-conscious, aware and keen to know what happens with their personal data. The "click and agree" policies are being challenged by critical questions and the data processor and data controller are held accountable by consumer pressure as well as the law. This concept of privacy and fragmented data handling must be mirrored when dealing with the EU internal market. Looking at the German Data Protection Act *(Bundesdatenschutzgesetz)*, there is a specific legal basis for data storage, processing, deleting, third party inquiries, transfers, damages in case of unlawful use, and so on.

4.1 Identified security concerns (B2B)

Therefore, ***security concerns*** are the largest group of perceived cloud computing risks. The *IBM Whitepaper*[126] describing the core cloud computing inhibitors also illustrates this in the following chart:

125 For the survey see: www.mimecast.com also partially referenced in *Kerr/Teng*, 2010, loc. cit. Fn. 57, p. 17 et seqq.

126 *IBM*, Cloud computing insights from 110 implementation projects, loc. cit. Fn. 10, p. 6, Fig. 5.

Fig. 7: Inhibiting factors to cloud computing

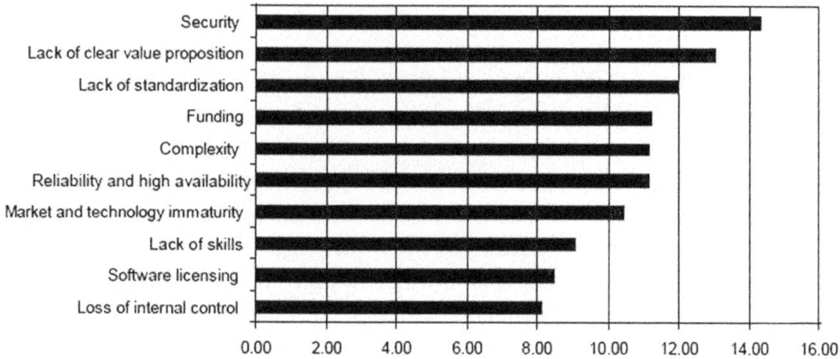

The *IBM Whitepaper* identified security, the lack of a clear value proposition and the lack of standardization as the three main inhibitors to cloud service implementation. The ten listed inhibitors show that the focus point lies on the business implementation possibilities of cloud services.

The *ENISA report* also identified eight key risks strongly related to data security issues:[127] Firstly, ***governance over data*** could be lost completely. This means that the cloud service provider ceases to have control over the data stored on its platforms. Secondly, a concern is ***lock-in effects***. These refer to the inability to remove data from the DBMS and integrate the data on a different management system.[128] The consequence is that the customer is effectively bound to stay with that cloud service provider because only that data processor can render the services associated with the legible data on the platform. Proprietary interfaces of cloud service providers hinder the consumer from switching between cloud service providers through ***high switching costs***.[129] A possible solution to data lock-in effects is setting up a trading platform for resource allocation of cloud capacities lowering switching costs. Concepts for the realization of such plat-

127 *ENISA*, 2011, loc. cit. Fn. 11, p. 9 et seqq.

128 See in detail Chapter 2.3.

129 *Buyya/Yeo/Venugopal/Broberg/Brandic*, Cloud Computing and Emerging IT Platforms: Vision, Hype and Reality for Delivering Computing as the 5th Utility, Grid Computing and Distributed Systems Laboratory, Department of Computer Science and Software Engineering, University of Melbourne, Australia; Manjrasoft Pty Ltd, Melbourne, Australia; Institute of Information Systems, Vienna University of Technology, Vienna, Austria, 2009, p. 10 (henceforth cited as: *Buyya/Yeo/Venugopal/Broberg/Brandic*, 2009).

forms are circulating for nearly a decade[130] but have not been executed to their full potential yet. A prerequisite for its functionality were to be the standardization of interfaces. Creating a global trading platform for data processing is an option for cost reduction but is prohibitively inhibited by data security concerns and the question of the enforceability of contractual rights under the SLA. Linked to lock-in effects is the issue of ***compliance with data privacy standards***.[131] In the EU, data privacy provisions are stipulated by both national authorities and the EU. Compliance is specific to Member States and cloud service providers must adapt to national regulatory needs.[132] Next, ENISA has raised concern that the ***security of customer management interfaces*** through web browser access may be insecure. This refers to the connection and data transmission process between the front and back end. The cloud service provider can only partially control this process because the customer using the front end device must ensure on his end that his device is not compromised, i.e. affected by malware. During the transfer process, data must be ***transferred and retained*** lawfully within the cloud. This is governed by national data privacy laws and by the GDPR, once it has come into effect on 25 May 2018. In conjunction with this, ENISA's next key concern is ***insecure or incomplete deleting*** of the data. This means that data that was supposed to be deleted was either not deleted or deleted in such fashion that a reconstruction of the data remains possible. Second to last, a malicious insider such as a system administrator of the cloud service provider could pose an inside security risk by abusing his position in the company.[133] Lastly, the problem of ***virtualization failure*** is a large technical concern. This technical problem leads to a failure of isolation within a data center. The following two images were adopted from *Majd F Sakr's* presentation at Carnegie Mellon Qatar dated 14 January 2010:[134]

130 *Fu/Chase/Chun/Schwab/Vahdat*, SHARP: An Architecture for Secure Resource Peering, Department of Computer Science, Duke University, Intel Research Berkeley and Network Associates Laboratories, 2003, available under: http://issg.cs.duke.edu/publications/sharp-sosp03.pdf, last accessed 31 May 2011.

131 *ENISA*, 2011, loc. cit. Fn. 11, p. 9 et seqq.

132 See in detail for the relevant product market definition and on product segmentation Chapter 6.2.3.1.

133 *ENISA*, 2011, loc. cit. Fn. 11, p. 9 et seqq.

134 *Majd F Sakr*, 2010, loc. cit. Fn. 106.

Fig. 8: Correct virtualization

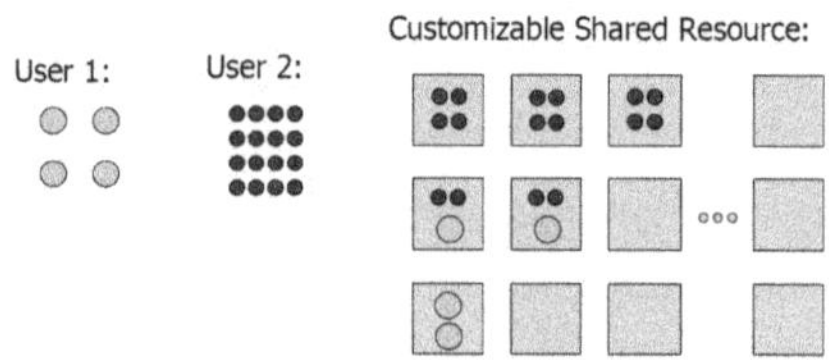

Fig. 9: Virtualization failure

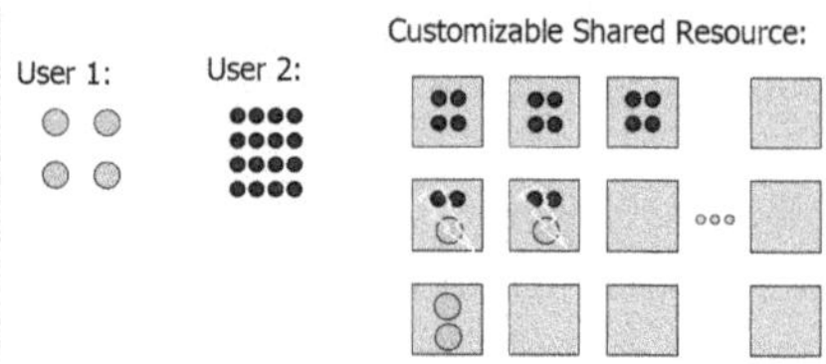

They illustrate the technical status with and without a virtualization failure. In the left image, visualization is functioning. User 1 and User 2 can share the same physical resource represented by the grey boxes. They remain unaware of each other's existence. On the right hand side, User 1 and User 2 become aware of each other because the virtualization layer that is supposed to isolate the two users from each other has broken down. This can lead to numerous subsequent technical failures, such as the breakdown of the computing resource or the access or transmission of malware.

4.2 Customers' concerns of privacy risks with big data (B2C)

The European and particularly the German understanding of data privacy issues are much more about personal space. Data is not primarily perceived as a business or as a remuneration for receiving services. These sensibilities must be accounted for. A tremendous amount of effort on both sides of the Atlantic goes into drafting policies and agreements around these issues. But their worth is hinged to an understanding that goes beyond the legal question at hand. In Germany, the right to privacy and the right to the integrity of information technology systems are rooted in Art. 1 in conjunction with Art. 2 of the German *Grundgesetz*. This is a historically developed cornerstone of German law and a key to the protection of citizens. No personal information of a person shall serve as a target against this citizen through abusive governmental or third party conduct.

To illustrate the point of customer concerns associated with big data, I will first present the Eurobarometer study results on *Attitudes on Data Protection and Electronic Identity in the European Union*[135]. Secondly, I reference a personal experience from a work discussion whilst I was a law clerk at a German Federal Ministry.

4.2.1 Eurobarometer on attitudes on data protection and electronic identity in the EU

In Winter 2010, *Eurobarometer* published a survey conducted by TNS Opinion & Social at the request of Directorate-General Justice, Information & Society & Media and Joint Research Centre.[136] The findings were published in June 2011. It is a comprehensive survey that maps the EU citizens' attitude towards identity management, data protection and privacy.[137] One of the core takeaways of the study was the relative lack of trust in commercial companies collecting data.

> *"Less than one-third trust phone companies, mobile phone companies and Internet service providers (32 %); and just over one-fifth trust Internet companies such as search engines, social networking sites and e-mail services (22 %)."*[138]

In EU-average and based on the whole sample, 74 % of Europeans consider it an increasing part of their lives to disclose personal data such as financial and medical information, credit card numbers and ID numbers.[139] The full bandwidth of information and data that survey participants considered personal are:[140]

---

135 *Eurobarometer*, Attitudes on Data Protection and Electronic Identity in the European Union, 2010, available at: http://ec.europa.eu/public_opinion/archives/ebs/ebs_359_en.pdf, last accessed 29 December 2014 (henceforth cited as: *Eurobarometer*, 2010).

136 *Eurobarometer*, 2010, ibd.

137 *Eurobarometer*, 2010, ibd, p. 1.

138 *Eurobarometer*, 2010, ibd, p. 2, bullet point No. 6.

139 *Eurobarometer*, 2010, ibd, p. 1, bullet points No. 1 and 2.

140 *Eurobarometer*, 2010, ibd, p. 12.

Fig. 10: Eurobarometer 2010; Question on personal information.

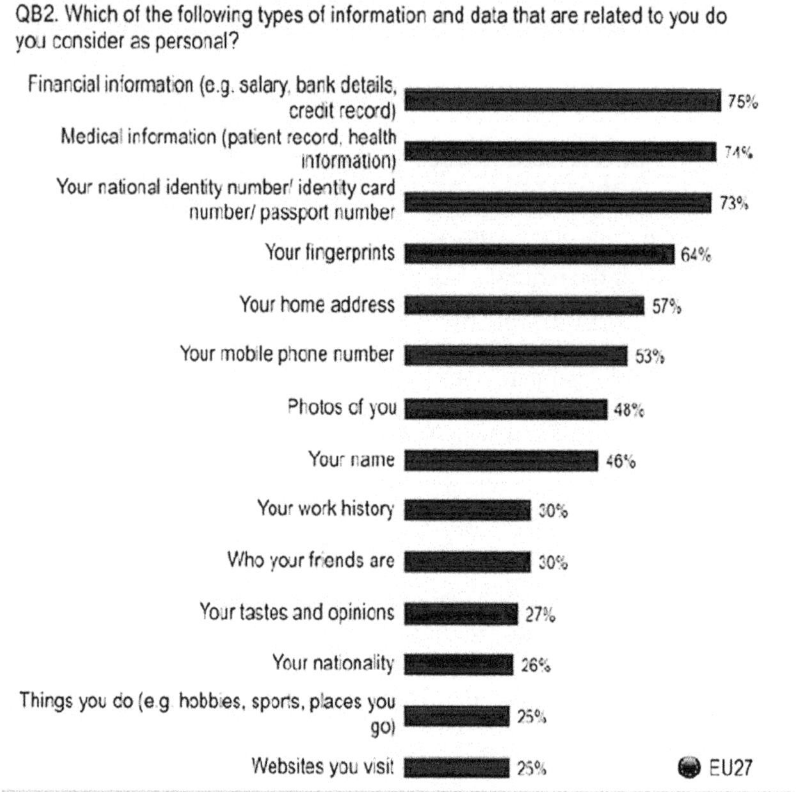

Base: Whole sample

This illustrates that the survey participants do not differentiate between the different spheres of their lives as a distinguishing factor with regards to data handling. The responders consider information from their professional sphere, their social activities and their post unique identifiers such as ID numbers and home addresses personal. However, not every EU Member State shows the same level of concern. For example with regard to medical information, there is a clear image that different countries show on in average different concern levels:

Fig. 11: Eurobarometer 2010; Question on medical information.

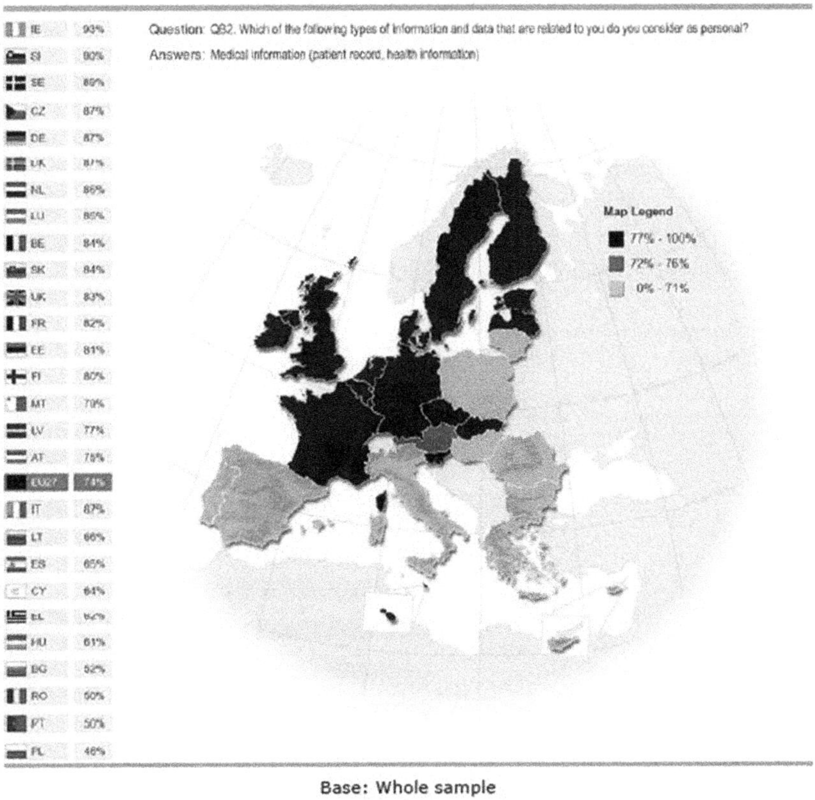

These results can be tied back to the definition of the relevant product and geographic market from a demand-side perspective.[141] If certain Member States show the same level of privacy concern in a defined sector, the supplier may use this information to customize its product or service in accordance to the required level of privacy standard beyond legal requirements. In that case, the service provider does not only comply with national laws, but rather he brackets his products and services in line with similar customer demand standards in those regions.

For another sector, the survey shows that on EU-average, 61 % of the survey participants consider disclosing personal data necessary to access social network-

141 See in detail Chapter 6.2.3.1 and 6.2.3.2.

ing sites and 79 % find it unavoidable for online shopping.[142] This shows that the choice of disclosing personal information is factually not a choice for those respondents having answered in the affirmative. The choice is made prior to that, whether or not to participate in and rely on those services.

With regard to potential remedies, 51 % of the survey participants believe that companies using personal data without informing the data subject should be fined, 40 % would ban the company from future data use and 39 % would compel the company to compensate the victims of unlawful use of personal data.[143] The range of responses were much broader, including better technical solutions, warning systems and class action lawsuit organisation:[144]

Fig. 12: Eurobarometer 2010: Question on possible remedies against unlawful personal data use.

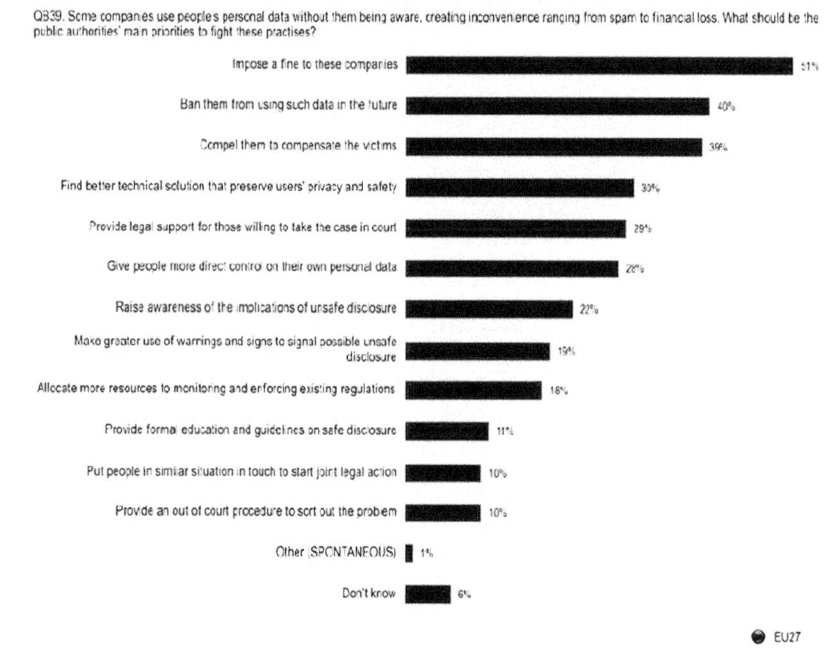

Base: Whole sample

142 *Eurobarometer*, 2010, loc. cit. Fn. 135, p. 1, bullet points No. 4.

143 *Eurobarometer*, 2010, ibd, p. 3, bullet point No. 1.

144 *Eurobarometer*, 2010, ibd, p. 190.

The responses range from cooperative measures, legal assistance and punitive remedies such as fines and help with legal proceedings. The diverse remedy suggestions imply the multiple levels a data subject may seek remedies or compensation to amend the unlawful data use. Preventive methods such as better warning systems and more control options as well as punitive recourses such as class action suits and victim compensation schemes, i.e. damages, may come into play.

4.2.2 Discussion on big data and cyber foreign policy

As part of my training in Germany, law clerks are mandated to do several rotations in governmental service. I did one rotation at a German Federal Minstry. Once a week, the department I was assigned to had lunch talks to discuss current political affairs. This was shortly after news coverage began on Edward Snowden. In this context, I gave a presentation on the introduction to cloud computing. I spoke about big data, introduced the book by *Viktor Mayer-Schönberger and Kenneth Cukier*[145] and illustrated the example of the Target customer referenced above[146] to show the market value of information derived from correlation versus causality for targeted advertising.

The audience was a highly skilled group of professionals with substantial international experience and education, dealing with complex economic issues every day. They were women and men, between 30 and 60 years of age, many of them trained in law and all in possession of rewards cards, smart phones and leading a "connected life". Their reactions to the targeted advertising were disbelief, outrage, disgust and general great personal interest. Their questions were pinpointed to one core issue: Big data infringed personal space. After this example, the discussion was no longer about how these calculations work, the cloud, policy options or the industry. It was a matter of personal privacy for everyone individually. A few months later, I gave the same presentation in San Francisco. The audience was mostly German legal professionals who moved to Silicon Valley. The same presentation to this audience left the point of privacy barely touched upon. This goes to show that our consumer behavior and relationship to data is much more deeply rooted than the governing law of the jurisdiction we are a part of. It is a question of societal conduct and expectation that shapes our relationship to our personal information.

---

145 *Mayer-Schönberger/Cukier*, Big Data: A Revolution That Will Transform How We Live, Work, and Think, Eamon Dolan/Houghton Mifflin Harcourt; 1st Ed., 2013.

146 See Chapter 2.5 on causality and correlation.

4.3 Customer risk management strategies

Depending on the most favorable risk-benefit-ratio, the cloud service consumer sorts the danger of data privacy infringement into one of the four possible risk management categories.[147] Depending on the type and preference structure of customer, the conduct of the customer can be accommodated in one of four strategies:

Firstly, the risk of data privacy infringement can be ***avoided*** in total if the company does not engage in cloud computing services. This means that the risk leads to a complete rejection of the potential benefits of cloud-enabled services because the risks are perceived as not worth it. Secondly, the risk of data privacy infringement is a question of the negotiated contractual terms between the cloud service provider and the customer. Consequently, the risk can be ***reduced*** through designing the appropriate individual contractual clauses. Using a private instead of a public cloud and through further safety measures the infringement risk is mitigated. These risk reduction mechanisms are factored into the pricing model of the cloud service. Thirdly, the risk can be shared. ***Risk sharing*** by buying an insurance against data privacy infringement is a rather unlikely model due to its expense factor and predictability. An insurance provider will assess the risk by calculating the probability of the event occurring in ratio to the impact of the risk event. Another option is to willingly pay a higher price for a certified service provider.[148] This is to assume that an ISO certification such as ISO/IEC 27018 in combination with ISO/IEC 27001 and ISO/IEC 27002 serves as a de facto insurance for the cloud service provider's compliance when acting as a data processor. Lastly, the customer ***retains*** the risk without any avoidance strategy and factors the risks into his calculation to its full extend.

Data security concerns of customers can be mirrored as a performance risk of cloud operators. The cloud service provider must account for the reputation mechanism with regard to the availability of service even though demand may fluctuate or be unknown in advance. Data lock-in, data confidentiality and data transfer bottlenecks must be managed in light of the customer's concerns.[149] Within risk management, the precise identification of the risk is

---

147 See Chapter 3.6 on risk management.

148 See in detail chapter 10.2 on certification possibilities.

149 In detail on cloud computing obstacles also mirroring *ENISA*, 2011, loc. cit. Fn. 11, see: *Armbrust/Fox/Griffith/Joseph/Katz/Konwinski/Lee/Patterson/Rabkin/Stoica/Zaharia*, 2010, loc. cit. Fn. 59.

essential. Risks can be categorized into simple and complex and certain and uncertain issues. The complexity and uncertainty of a risk is in direct connection to the likelihood of the investment or service provision decision to be positive or negative. From an investor's perspective, the more the risk can be moved into the category of 'certain' or 'simple', the investment project becomes more manageable.

Certain and simple risks are those that are easy to handle with existing standards and mechanisms already present on the relevant market for these investment structures. If the risk is certain but more complex, the risk management options must address all of the risk components that render it complex. The risk assessment should therefore be conducted through an analysis of possibly more than one person. Only if the components are fully identified can subsequent decisions be made about risk tolerability. If the risk is uncertain, the degree of complexity is also uncertain *ex ante*. Therefore, the risk assessment of an investor may take the following two steps to further identify the nature of the risk: Firstly, if the assessment leads to risk components that are ambiguous, actors within the investment structure may interpret the factor differently. Conflicting interests and evaluation outcomes between shareholders and management must be resolved. The reputation mechanism is to be considered when the public forms an opinion about risk assessment factors. Secondly, mechanisms must be introduced to analyze an uncertain risk in small components and sequentially in order to avoid irreversible decisions.

I do not advocate drafting legal provisions that eliminate entrepreneurial risk. However, the law should make the risk calculable and compliance with the law implementable. The market shall reward risk taking, but it must be clear which risk is taken. In result, this would meet the market's desire for certainty and lower transaction costs.

Risks can be visualized in a ***risk tolerability matrix*** that may look as follows. The concrete risk tolerability depends on the individual parameters of the concrete investment decision to be analyzed.

The category of risk and the level of risk tolerance accepted by the investor will determine many parameters of the investment making process. In particular, the type of project financing will depend on the risk structure of the investment deal. Pricing the rate of return of such investment projects is one of the major challenges in risk calculation.

Fig. 13: Risk tolerance matrix

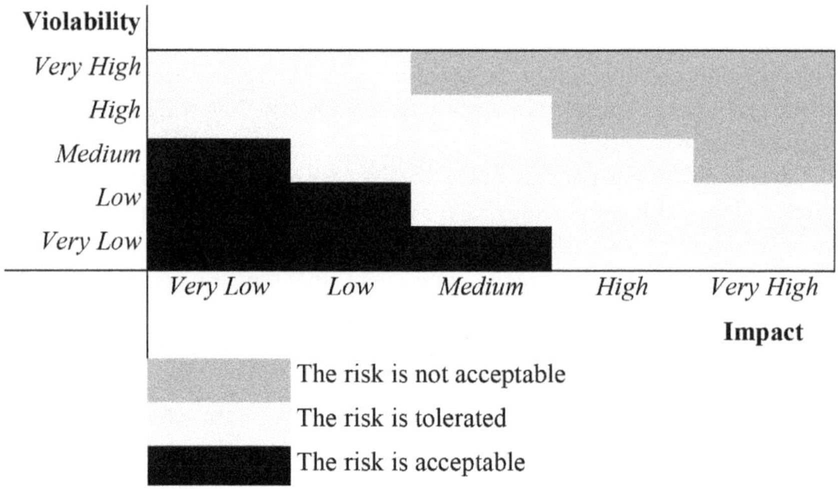

4.4 Summary

Customers and policy makers associate several security concerns with cloud services. But the most severe one is that upon which the consumer loses faith in the service and rejects it in the end. Not understanding the European "data mentality" stands in a direct causal link to losing business opportunities for U.S. cloud service providers in the EU because service providers fail to cater to the customers' needs around privacy accountability.

The Eurobarometer survey showed that customers see numerous creative and diverse possible remedy courses. Increased technical abilities to ensure the privacy of the data subject, better warning systems and other preventive measures as well as punitive proceedings and civil suits for damages are possible recourses.

Risk management strategies should differentiate between B2B relationships of cloud service providers and B2C service provision to individual data subjects. Cloud service providers must employ two separate remedy sets to accommodate security concerns and data privacy concerns. Whilst security and privacy concerns are not mutually exclusive, B2B and B2C have different priorities. In B2B relationships, the identified security concerns are rooted in the security of the data and compliance with data privacy standards. If a company chooses to outsource its IT business and migrate to the cloud, the service buyer must still ensure to its own customers that the compliance standards are upheld and that the business remains running smoothly. Hence, a technically flawless day-to-day operation is an absolute necessity for the business customer. In B2C relationships the most common constellation is where the customer uses a cloud-based software as a service. Here, the cloud service provider's customer is either a corporation or an individual private person. Privacy concerns revolve around ID-information such as date of birth, financial data such as credit card information and medical data. The perceived individual threat to privacy is much higher.

5 Overview of laws and policy makers in the EU and the U.S.

Cloud computing has come to the attention of policymakers on both sides of the Atlantic. Identifying the key players and their stakes in shaping the legal environment of the cloud is necessary in order to see what considerations drive legal reforms in the field. This chapter serves as an overview of the applicable legal provisions and the responsible policy makers in the EU and the U.S. The legal environment for data privacy is very fragmented in the U.S. in comparison to the EU and its Member States (with special emphasis on Germany). In contrast, competition and antitrust laws are systematically more homogenous.

5.1 Policy makers in the U.S.

In the U.S. the leading government body dealing with cloud computing is the *Congressional Subcommittee on Courts, Intellectual Property and the Internet*[150]. It is a subcommittee of the *Judiciary Committee at the United States House of Representatives*. It was established in 2011.[151] It has jurisdiction over amongst others information technology, trademark, copyright and patent law.[152] Secondly, the *Federal Communication Commission* (FCC) plays a major role in developing laws for the cloud sector. The FCC is the regulatory authority for international communication by radio, television, wire, satellite and cable.[153] It is in charge of communications law, technical innovation and promoting a legal framework that accommodates the "*unfolding of the communications revolution*".[154] Thirdly, the *Federal Trade Commission* (FTC) is the agency in charge of protecting con-

---

150 Internet presence of the *Congressional Subcommittee on Courts, Intellectual Property and the Internet* at: http://judiciary.house.gov/index.cfm/subcommittee-on-courts-intellectual-property-and-the-internet, last accessed 29 December 2014.

151 Press release of *Chairman Smith* dated 7 January 2011 available at: http://judiciary.house.gov/news/2011/jan/110107_subcommittee_chairmen.html, last accessed 29 December 2014.

152 Competency statement at: http://judiciary.house.gov/index.cfm/subcommittee-on-courts-intellectual-property-and-the-internet, last accessed 29 December 2014.

153 See *FCC's* mission statement at: http://www.fcc.gov/what-we-do, last accessed 29 December 2014 (henceforth cited as: *FCC's* mission statement).

154 See *FCC's* mission statement, ibd.

sumers and promoting competition.[155] It develops policies to enhance competition through keeping prices at a competitively low level whilst encouraging a selection and high quality of goods and services.[156] Furthermore, the FTC collects and evaluates complaints "*about hundreds of issues from data security and deceptive advertising to identity theft and Do Not Call violations, and make[s] them available to law enforcement agencies worldwide for follow-up*".[157]

5.1.1 Data privacy laws

The data privacy laws of the U.S. are fragmented by sector. However, the Uniting and Strengthening America by Providing Appropriate Tools Required to Intercept and Obstruct Terrorism, the U.S. Patriot Act, uniformly applies across all sectors.[158] The Patriot Act has established numerous subsequent acts that entitle agencies to surveillance procedures stipulated in Title II, Sections 201 to 225 Patriot Act. Under these provisions, authorities are entitled to intercept wire, oral and electronic communication. The interception target may be data stored outside of the jurisdiction of the U.S. If the servers are owned by a U.S. company, the Patriot Act still applies and interception must be made possible by the company.

There are numerous sector specific data privacy laws in the U.S. In the following, I will provide a brief overview of the most important ones. The Fair Credit Reporting Act[159] (FCRA) regulates the collection of personal data around credit card information. This includes collecting customer data, purchasing and credit score information and the dissemination of this information. The Health Insurance Portability and Accountability Act[160] (HIPAA) stipulates rules for the use and disclosure of protected health information in Title II HIPAA. The Electronic Communications Privacy Act[161] (ECPA) is hinged to the Stored Communications Act. It stipulates the criteria to obtain a search warrant for the interception of electronic communication. Pursuant to 18 U.S.C. § 2510, "*electronic communication entails any transfer of signs, signals, writing, images, sounds, data, or intelligence of any nature transmitted in whole or in part by a wire, radio, electromagnetic, photo*

155 See *FCC's* mission statement, ibd.
156 See *FCC's* mission statement, ibd.
157 See *FCC's* mission statement, ibd.
158 Public Law 107–56-Oct. 26, 2001; 115 Stat. 272, also available at: http://www.gpo.gov/fdsys/pkg/PLAW-107publ56/pdf/PLAW-107publ56.pdf, last accessed 29 December 2014.
159 Public Law 91–508, October 26, 1970; 84 Stat. 1127.
160 Public Law 104–191, August 21, 1996; 110 Stat. 1936.
161 18 U.S.C. § 2510 (2012) et. seqq.

electronic or photo optical system that affects interstate or foreign commerce". The Stored Communications Act[162] (SCA) is Title II of the ECPA. It stipulates how third party internet service providers can be compelled to provide information on stored wire and electronic communications and transactional records. Sec. 2703 SCA differentiates between two types of information, electronic communication services (ECS) and remote computing services (RCS). This distinction matters because there are different criteria applicable to compel internet service providers to disclose information. ECS is defined in 18 U.S.C. § 2510(15) as "*any service which provides to users thereof the ability to send or receive wire or electronic communications*". RCS is defined in 18 U.S.C. § 2711(2) as "*the provision to the public of computer storage or processing services by means of an electronic communications system*". Stored data (RCS) is given less protection under the law than ECS because RCS refers to stored or "idle" data, whereby ECS refers to data that is currently in transmission. From a procedural law perspective, this matters because access to the information can be obtained by either a search warrant, a subpoena or a court order pursuant to Sec. 2703(d) SCA on "*specific and articulable facts*". Technically speaking, this law from 1986 is outdated. It is no longer possible to distinguish between transmission and storage competencies within a company. Circling back to the definition of RCS, it entails two main criteria: the provision of computer storage and of processing services. The storage component is easy to define and can be compared to a physical storage space of i.e. furniture. In exchange for money, data can be stored. But the criterion of "processing services" cannot be clearly defined nor has it clear boundaries in today's information technology age. Every website that receives data must automatically process them in order to interact with its users.[163]

5.1.2 Antitrust laws

For this thesis, the relevant antitrust act is the Sherman Act.[164] Sec. 1 Sherman Act stipulates that "*every contract, combination in the form of trust or otherwise, or conspiracy, in restraint of trade or commerce among the several States, or with foreign nations, is declared to be illegal*". In essence, Sec. 1 Sherman Act prohibits

162 18 U.S.C. §§ 2701 to 2712.

163 *Orin S. Kerr*, A User's Guide to the Stored Communications Act – and a Legislator's Guide to amending it, George Washington Law Review, Vol. 72, p. 1700 et seqq., also available at: http://courses.ischool.berkeley.edu/i205/s10/readings/week10/kerr-storedcomm.pdf, last accessed 29 December 2014.

164 15 U.S.C. §§ 1 to 7, 26 Stat. 209.

cartels. Sec. 2 Sherman Act declares that the intent to monopolize is criminalized: "*Every person who shall monopolize, or attempt to monopolize, or combine or conspire with any other person or persons, to monopolize any part of the trade or commerce among the several States, or with foreign nations, shall be deemed guilty of a felony*".The antitrust approach to monopolizing firm behaviour is very cautious of causing false positive / Type I errors running the risk of penalising legitimate but not courteous competitive behaviour.[165] The two most recent precedents for this tendency are *Trinko*[166] and *linkLine*[167]. In *Trinko*, the Court held:

> „*Compelling such firms to share the source of their advantage is in some tension with the underlying purpose of antitrust law, since it may lessen the incentive for the monopolist, the rival, or both to invest in those economically beneficial facilities.*"[168]

The *Antitrust Modernization Commission*[169] has given the incentive structure and enforcement policy of monopolisation claims under Sec. 2 Sherman Act thought in great detail. The report acknowledges the conduct of the antitrust courts to protect vigorous competition, the aggressive pursuit of business objectives and the recognition of efficiency as a proper aim even if at the loss of competitors.[170] The report furthermore asks for more clarity and better standards of the law with regard to the assessment of bundled discount rates and rebates, the unilateral refusals to deal with competitors present in the same relevant market and sees this to be the duty of the judiciary to provide more specific standards.[171] Antitrust enforcement shall focus on the core issues of fostering innovation, protecting and promoting competition and welfare and the thorough prosecution of cartels with a more alert perspective on "*other conduct that may offer substantial benefits*".[172]

---

165 In agreement with *Hay/McMahon*, The Diverging Approach to Price Squeezes in the United States and Europe, Journal of Competition Law & Economics, Vol. 8 No. 2, April 2012, pp. 259–296, p. 261

166 *Verizon Communications Inc. v. Law Office of Curtis v. Trinko*, 540 U.S. 398 (2004).

167 *Pacific Bell Telephone Co., dba AT&T California, et al. v linkLine Communications Inc., et al.*, 129 S. Ct. 1109, 555 U.S. 438 Supreme Court of the United States, 25 February 2009.

168 *Verizon Communications Inc. v. Law Office of Curtis v. Trinko*, 540 U.S. 398 (2004), Ref. 411.

169 *Antitrust Modernization Commission*, Chair *Deborah A. Garza*, Report and Recommendations, April 2007, available at http://govinfo.library.unt.edu/amc/, last accessed 24 August 2012 (henceforth cited as: *Deborah A. Garza*, 2007).

170 *Deborah A. Garza*, 2007, ibd, p. 3.

171 *Deborah A. Garza*, 2007, ibd, p. 3.

172 *Deborah A. Garza*, 2007, ibd, p. 2.

The policy recommendations of the *Antitrust Modernization Commission* suggest that in general, firms do not have a duty to deal with competitors in the same market and that market power should not be assumed form a patent, copyright or trademark in a tying case.[173]

5.2 Policy makers in the EU

Within the European Commission, the *Directorate-Generale for Communications Networks, Content and Technology* has a designated *Software & Services, Cloud Unit*, Unit E.2.[174] The Unit's main mandate is to fully implement the *Cloud Computing Communication* from 2012.[175] In 2015, the Unit desires to develop a fully updated agenda of specific policy actions for the new cloud policy agenda. Its aim is to strengthen the EU-based cloud service market.[176] A lot of these efforts are targeted together with the EU Commission's Directorate-Generale for Justice and Consumers. The *Cloud Computing Communication*[177] has initiated a major push for reforms in enabling and adopting cloud computing solutions faster within the EU internal market. In this communication, the Commission identified steps to be implemented in order to help market penetration of cloud computing services in the EU internal market. Firstly, the Commission identified that the fragmentation of the EU internal market due to different Member State data privacy laws is the single largest hurdle in adopting cloud services.[178] Secondly, contract design must meet the customers' concerns around compensation for server downtime, data loss and data ownership. The Commission views it as unclear how these disputes will be resolved and what legal liabilities the customers in the EU will be com-

173 *Deborah A. Garza*, 2007, ibd, p. 83 recommendation No. 18 and 19.

174 See their online presence at: http://ec.europa.eu/dgs/connect/en/content/software-services-cloud-european-cloud-computing-strategy, last accessed 29 December 2014.

175 *EU Commission*, Unleashing the Potential of Cloud Computing in Europe, Communication from the Commission to the European Parliament, the Council, the European Economic and Social Committee and the Committee of the Regions, COM(2012) 529 final, dated 27 September 2012 (henceforth cited as: *EU Commission*, Unleashing the Potential of Cloud Computing in Europe).

176 *EU Commission*, Communication of Unit 5.2 of the EU Commission, DG Communications Networks, Content and Technology, available at: http://ec.europa.eu/dgs/connect/en/content/software-services-cloud-european-cloud-computing-strategy, last accessed 29 December 2014.

177 *EU Commission*, Unleashing the Potential of Cloud Computing in Europe, loc. cit. Fn. 175, p. 2.

178 *EU Commission*, Unleashing the Potential of Cloud Computing in Europe, ibd, p. 5.

pensated for.[179] Thirdly, with regard to technical standards, it is unclear which technical standard shall prevail that also provides an adequate level of interoperability of data formats to permit data portability.[180]

5.2.1 Competition laws

The two main provisions in competition law relevant for the scope of this thesis are Art. 101 and 102 of the Treaty on the Functioning of the European Union (TFEU)[181]. Art. 101 TFEU (formerly Art. 81 TEU) stipulates that any agreement "*shall be prohibited as incompatible with the internal market (...) which have as their objective or effect the prevention, restriction or distortion of competition within the internal market (...)*". Art. 102 TFEU (formerly Art. 82 TEU) prohibits the abuse of a dominant position on the relevant market and reads: "*Any abuse by one or more undertakings of a dominant position within the internal market or in a substantial part of it shall be prohibited as incompatible with the internal market in so far as it may affect trade between Member States.*" I will examine the exposure of cloud computing to EU competition law in detail below.

5.2.2 Data privacy laws

In the EU, data privacy rules are stipulated in one main piece of legislature, namely Directive 95/46/EC of the European Parliament and of the Council of 24 October 1995 on the protection of individuals with regard to the processing of personal data and on the free movement of such data[182]. The new GDPR will enter into force on 25 May 2016 and will replace Directive 95/46/EC. Until that time, national laws in combination with Directive 95/46/EC will continue to govern EU privacy and data protection laws. Additionally, there is the Directive 2002/58/EC of the European Parliament and of the Council of 12 July 2002 concerning the processing of personal data and the protection of privacy in the electronic

179 *EU Commission*, Unleashing the Potential of Cloud Computing in Europe, ibd, p. 5.

180 *EU Commission*, Unleashing the Potential of Cloud Computing in Europe, ibd, p. 5.

181 Treaty on the Functioning of the European Union ("*TFEU*"), O. J. C 326/88, 26 October 2012, also available at: http://eur-lex.europa.eu/legal-content/EN/TXT/PDF/?uri=CELEX:12012E/TXT&from=EN, last accessed 29 December 2014.

182 Directive 95/46/EC of the European Parliament and of the Council of 24 October 1995 on the protection of individuals with regard to the processing of personal data and on the free movement of such data, O.J. L 281, 23 November 1995 (henceforth cited as: Directive 95/46/EC).

communications sector.[183] Its regulatory aim is to improve the legal framework of the telecommunications sector. Furthermore, there is the Art. 29 Working Party Group, which holds advisory status within the EU Commission.[184] Their position was created under Directive 95/46/EC and aims to protect individuals with regard to processing and the free movement of such personal data. Their legal basis is established in Art. 30 Directive 95/46/EC and Art. 15 Directive 2002/58/EC.

Since Directives are not directly applicable in EU Member States, the Member States are obligated to implement the EU Directives within a given time frame. In Germany, this implementation took place in the form of the *Bundesdatenschutzgesetz* (Federal Data Protection Law)[185]. It stipulates a uniformly applicable law across all sectors when it comes to the processing of personal data by information technology systems or human manual processing. It can be assumed that the Federal Data Protection Act applies to cloud service operators across the board because the collection of personal data is touched upon as a general rule. Furthermore, cloud service operators must examine whether the *Telemediengesetz* (German Telemedia Act) applies as well. The Telemedia Act applies if electronic communication and broadcasting services are involved. This includes for example music download platforms, VoIP and online shopping platforms. I will examine the exposure of cloud computing to EU data privacy laws and the newly proposed General Data Protection Regulation in detail below.

183 Directive 2002/58/EC of the European Parliament and of the Council of 12 July 2002 concerning the processing of personal data and the protection of privacy in the electronic communications sector , O.J. L 201, 31 July 2002 (henceforth cited as: Directive 2002/58/EC).

184 See their online presence at: http://ec.europa.eu/justice/data-protection/article-29/index_en.htm, last accessed 29 December 2014.

185 An English version of the German Federal Data Protection Act is available here: http://www.gesetze-im-internet.de/englisch_bdsg/index.html, last accessed 29 December 2014.

Part II: Cloud computing and competition law

6 Cloud computing and EU competition law

6.1 Introduction

In the following chapter, I examine the competition law exposure of cloud services. First, I determine the relevant market for cloud services. Next, I will look into specific types of conduct under Art. 101 and 102 TFEU that could exposure cloud service operators to competition law liability. The assessment of a competition law proceeding always begins with the definition of the relevant market. The relevant market assessment is needed for both Art. 101 and Art. 102 TFEU proceedings. For Art. 102 TFEU, the definition of the relevant market is immediately triggered by the question of dominance on the relevant market. But also for Art. 101 TFEU proceedings, the relevant market must be defined. Numerous competition law instruments rely on defining the relevant market and the undertakings' market share. For example, claiming the privilege of the De Minimis Notification and block exemption regulations is only possible if the relevant conduct under competition law remains under a certain market threshold.

The De Minimis Notification has the legal effect that Art. 101 para. 1 TFEU cannot be applied where the anti-competitive effects of a cartel agreement on the EU internal market is not noticeable due to its small impact.[186][187] Using market share thresholds, the De Minimis Notification creates a safe harbor and reduces compliance costs for mostly small enterprises. If SMEs conclude agreements with competitors, block exemptions very often fail to cover these under Art. 101 para. 3 TFEU.[188] The De Minimis Notification catches these cases. To stipulate to the De Minimis safe harbor, the aggregate market share of the parties to the horizontal agreement must not exceed 10 % on the relevant market; in the case of vertical agreements the threshold is at 15 %; in the case of cumulative network effects, the

186 *EU Commission*, Commission Notice on agreements of minor importance which do not appreciably restrict competition under Article 81(1) of the Treaty establishing the European Community (de minimis), O.J. C 368 dated 2 December 2001 (henceforth cited as: *EU Commission*, de minimis notice). Note that the competition law safe harbor under De Minimis is not equal to the Safe Harbor framework in data privacy law. This is unfortunately the same terminology in two distinct fields of law.

187 The de minimis Notification does not exempt hard-core cartels from being nill and void under Art. 101 para. 1 TFEU.

188 *EU Commission*, de minimis notice, loc. cit. Fn. 186.

threshold lies at 5 %.[189] In order to establish whether a De Minimis Notification is an option, the relevant market must always be defined in order to benchmark the market share thresholds.

The definition of the relevant market under Art. 101 TFEU is also relevant for the assessment of block exemption regulations (BER). For example, in the case of vertical restraints, if the market share of the supplier and buyer in a vertical chain each does not exceed 30 %, the safe harbor of the BER applies.[190] Both BER and the De Minimis Notification show that for companies to enjoy a safe harbor privilege, the market shares on the relevant market are the linchpin of the exemption regulation. If an undertaking is too present on a relevant market, it can no longer stipulate that the EU internal market is not affected by its anticompetitive conduct.

6.2 The relevant market for cloud computing

The definition of the relevant market is the first step of any competition law assessment. Here, I preface the definition of the relevant geographic, product and timely market with two aspects that are influencing definition factors for the relevant product and geographic market for cloud services. Firstly, cloud computing can be defined as a utility service. Secondly, the consequence of a utility service is that it also has a specific utility pricing scheme. This would strongly impact the demand-side substitution assessment of the relevant product market.

6.2.1 Cloud computing as a utility service

Several papers[191] discuss the possibility of categorizing cloud computing as the next utility service after gas, electricity, water and telecommunication. With technological improvement, utility services are provided by a few suppliers specialized on this service, i.e. through an oligopolistic market structure. The benefit in common of utility services is that the user of the services rendered does not

---

189 *EU Commission*, de minimis notice, ibd.

190 *EU Commission*, Guidelines on Vertical Restraints, SEC(2010) 411, p. 9, also available at: http://ec.europa.eu/competition/antitrust/legislation/guidelines_vertical_en.pdf, last accessed 29 December 2014.

191 *Buyya/Yeo/Venugopal/Broberg/Brandic*, 2009, loc. cit. Fn. 129; *Picker*, Competition and Privacy in Web 2.0 and the Cloud, Chicago John M. Olin Law & Economics Working Paper No. 414 (2D Series), June 2008, p. 6 (henceforth cited as: *Picker*, 2009); *Sluijs/Larouche/Sauter*, 2012, loc. cit. Fn. 3, p. 6; *David C Wyld*, 2009, loc. cit. Fn. 41, p. 3.

need to manage the network in order to benefit from it. Especially for small and medium-sized enterprises (SME), cloud computing lowers the barriers of entry significantly by lessening the investment costs in an IT infrastructure indispensable for market entrance.

Utility computing refers to a market where the cloud computing service provider offers the computing resource and infrastructure management on demand. The goal is to maximize the efficiency of the resources and to reduce the input costs as much as possible. In essence, the computation resource becomes subject to a rent agreement. Utility computing is linked to the concept of grid computing. Grid computing refers to a situation where there is a sudden spike of computation demand. Numerous computers that can distribute the information to be processed to numerous computation units buffer this spike. Distributed computing plays a large role in grid computing. It means that one operation can be run on more than one device. To illustrate this, consider the mathematical operation

$$2+2+2+2=8.$$

We can distribute this operation into three component pieces:

$$2+2=4$$
$$2+2=4$$
$$4+4=8$$

Technically, this includes that there is no single point of failure in the IT system for a more complex calculation. An example for a business use is the aircraft control system for real-time process controlling. Furthermore, it allows the separate component calculations to run in a distributed way. This makes the operation run faster in total. However, to avoid a single point of failure disrupting the system, redundancy layers have to be built into the system.

6.2.2 Pricing models of cloud utility and consequences for defining the relevant market

There are similarities between the structure of utility services and cloud computing. Before installing the electricity grid, every household was stocked with candles, generators or wood. Before installing gas pipelines, firewood or gas cylinders were stocked for the preparation of food and heating. With cloud computing, the procurement of the IT facilities is no longer necessary. Three possible pricing models are applied:[192] ***tiered pricing, price per unit*** and ***subscription-based pricing.***

---

192 *Khajeh-Hosseini/Sommerville/Sriram*, 2010, loc. cit. Fn. 42, p. 3 et seqq; *Sluijs/Larouche/Sauter*, 2012, loc. cit. Fn. 3, p. 6 et seqq.

Tiered pricing means that different pricing rates are offered to different consumer brackets. An example is the different rate of electricity pricing depending on domestic or industrial use. The price per unit method refers to a linear pricing mechanism where each unit of output is priced at the same rate. Subscription-based pricing refers to a base rate fee that is payable disregarding the concrete amount of units consumed. Utility pricing models for cloud computing services have been in discussion on several bases. Most market players work with a subscription based pricing mechanism. However, some companies pushed forward with new metric called service units per seconds (SU/sec).[193] The problem with this metric is that it is unclear what constitutes a service unit. Parallels to the electricity sector cannot be assumed that easily because a service unit is not a unit defined by the law of physics such as a kilowatt-hour or Joule. It is possible that different service providers charge a different SU-price for running a computation on a different platform, i.e. Linux versus HP-UX. For cloud computing to become a utility service, there must be a pricing mechanism in place that allows a comparison of the different service providers.

6.2.3 The relevant market

Interpreting cloud computing as a utility service poses large difficulties for the definition of the relevant market in competition law. Competition law assessments commence with the definition of the relevant market and define the level playing field of the subsequent legal analysis. The definition of the relevant market shapes the investigation process and the potential enforcement recommendations of the competition authorities.[194] For instance, the broader the market is defined, the more unlikely a dominant position on that market occurs.[195] The definition of the relevant market is the point in competition and antitrust law, where regardless of the jurisdiction, legal criteria are specified through an economic analysis. According to *Carlton/Perloff*:

> *A market definition specifies the competing products and geographic area in which competition occurs that determines the price for a given product.*[196]

---

193 As seen by *Microsoft*: Best Practices for the Design of Large-Scale Services on Azure Cloud Services dated 14 October 2014, available at: http://msdn.microsoft.com/en-us/library/azure/jj717232.aspx, last accessed 29 December 2014.

194 *Harbour/Koslov*, Section 2 in a Web 2.0 World: An Expanded Vision of Relevant Product Markets, Antitrust Law Journal, Vol. 76, 2010 p. 769 et seqq. at p. 775 (henceforth cited as: *Harbour/Koslov*, 2010).

195 *Helmut Bester*, 2007, loc. cit. Fn. 62, p. 20 et seqq.

196 *Carlton/Perloff*, Modern Industrial Organisation, 4th Ed., 2005, Pearson, p. 644 (henceforth cited as: *Carlton/Perloff*, 2005).

6.2.3.1 The relevant product market

The relevant product market is separated from neighboring markets by analyzing the interchangeability and substitutability of the products. The *Commission Notice on the definition of the relevant market for the purposes of Community competition law* defines the product market as follows:

> *„A relevant product market comprises all those products and/or services which are regarded as interchangeable or substitutable by the consumer, by reason of the products' characteristics, their prices and their intended use.“*[197]

The relevant product market must be segmented into the relevant demand-side and supply-side product market. Demand-side substitution identifies those products that are effective substitutes by consumers. The SSNIP-Test[198] analyses the possibilities of the consumer to switch to a comparable product satisfying a comparable need. The analysis is conducted through the calculation of the cross-price-elasticity putting a relative increase in price of product A into relation to the relative demand increase of product B.[199]

Cloud computing services can be categorized into Saas, IaaS and PaaS. A service that SaaS can be benchmarked against for determining cross price elasticity is UMTS coverage[200]. UMTS and cloud service users need to be differentiated between private and business related use. The UMTS network aims at high interoperability and portability and is consequently preferred for business related use. If the purpose of services used is within the same category, cloud service providers on the level of SaaS may likely compete for customers with software providers.

Supply-side substitution describes the possibility of a supplier to switch its production to the relevant market without significant costs or risks if a SSNIP

---

197 *EU Commission*, Commission Notice on the definition of the relevant market for the purposes of Community competition law, O. J. C 372 dated 9 December 1997, Ref. 7 (henceforth cited as: *EU Commission*, Notice on the definition of the relevant market).

198 SSNIP stands for „Small but Significant Non-Transitory Increase in Price“; see *EU Commission*, Notice on the definition of the relevant market, loc. cit. Fn. 197, Ref. 17.

199 $\epsilon = \frac{\%\ change\ in\ quantity\ of\ demand\ in\ A}{\%\ change\ in\ price\ of\ B}$. The point of economic concern of ε remains the Cellophane Fallacy (*United States v. E. K. du Pont de Nemours & Co.*, 351 U.S. 377 (1956). The pricing strategy of the suppliers determines the factor ε and is therefore determined endogenously through the market players' own competitive behavior.

200 UMTS stands for „Universal Mobile Telecommunications System“.

occurs.[201] Here again, cloud computing services must not be regarded as one entity but as numerous kinds of services with different product dimensions. As illustrated by the U.S.-case *Broadcom v. Qualcomm*[202], it is important to distinguish between the different product types within the same market:

> *"In the context of a claim of monopoly power in violation of the Sherman Act, competing products are in the same market if they are readily substitutable for one another; a market's outer boundaries are determined by the reasonable interchangeability of use between a product and its substitute, or by their cross-elasticity of demand."*[203]

The same market segmentation pattern along product lines was argued in the *IBM Italia v. UBIS*[204]. There, the Commission segmented into a total of seven categories: hardware maintenance, software maintenance and support, consulting, development and integration, IT outsourcing, business process outsourcing, management services and education and training.[205]

Considering the very fast innovation cycles of the IT-industry, the U.S. authors *Harbour/Koslov* propose a different dynamic approach to the product market definition in Web 2.0 markets.[206] They suggest that the definition of markets for data be separated from markets utilizing data for service provisions.[207] In the authors' opinion, this would lead to the definition of the relevant product markets based on privacy issues.[208] The market definition shall be used as an incentive mechanism to foster innovation in technologies that are enhancing data privacy standards.[209] With regard to the product market, the segmentation by IT service functionality only partially depicts the business reality. From the supply-side perspective, these functionalities service different customer needs. Also from the demand-side, the segmentation can occur with respect to the functionality of the service and the different sector in question.[210] However, the inherent innovation of

201 *EU Commission*, Notice on the definition of the relevant market, loc. cit. Fn. 197, Ref. 20.

202 *Broadcom Corp. v. Qualcomm Inc.*, 501 F.3d 297, United States Court of Appeals 3rd Cir., No. 06–4292, 4 September 2007.

203 *Broadcom Corp. v. Qualcomm Inc.*, ibd, Ref. 307.

204 *IBM Italia v UBIS*, Case COMP/M.6921, O.J. C 163 dated 8 June 2013 (henceforth cited as: *IBM Italia v UBIS).*

205 *IBM Italia v UBIS*, ibd, Ref. 12.

206 *Harbour/Koslov*, 2010, loc. cit. Fn. 194, p. 773 and 784.

207 *Harbour/Koslov*, 2010, ibd, p. 773.

208 *Harbour/Koslov*, 2010, ibd, p. 784.

209 *Harbour/Koslov*, 2010, ibd, p. 795.

210 In line with *IBM Italia v UBIS*, loc. cit. Fn. 204, Ref. 10.

cloud computing is that the risk of overcapacity and idle resources is outsourced to the cloud service provider. This entails that hardware and software IT support, hardware and software provisioning as well as the recurring IT maintenance costs are outsourced to the cloud service provider.

6.2.3.2 The relevant geographic market

The relevant geographic market is characterized by supply-side and demand-side geographic market definition. The *Commission Notice on the definition of the relevant market for the purposes of Community competition law* defines the geographic market as follows:

> *"The relevant geographic market comprises the area in which the undertakings concerned are involved in the supply and demand of products or services, in which the conditions of competition are sufficiently homogeneous and which can be distinguished from neighbouring areas because the conditions of competition are appreciably different in those area.*"[211]

From the supply-side, the market is represented by IT companies that operate globally and issue worldwide or EEA-wide tenders.[212] These parameters are unlikely to chance in favor of a more local supplier structure. The market players are mostly of comparable size and equipped for global operation. On the demand-side, customers frequently demand a more customized user experience and service which entails linguistic adaptation of the service and compliance with national laws and requirements. However, the core customer service requests do not differ. In *IBM Italia v. UBIS*, it was not necessary to decide what the geographic relevant market was in the IT outsourcing business.[213] Defining the relevant geographic market for cloud computing is not possible within the scope of the provided public ordering definition. The Commission is focusing on the market integration within the EU. The customer of cloud computing services is acting globally or having data stored on a global scale and has consequently a broader scope of action not bound to geographic boarders. Switching a cloud computing service supplier is possible without relevance of the geographic position of customer or supplier.[214] In terms of the IT sector, the relevance of the geographic factor for competition law assessments must be redefined in its scope and legal impact on a competition law assess-

---

211 *EU Commission*, Notice on the definition of the relevant market, loc. cit. Fn. 197, Ref. 8.

212 *IBM Italia v UBIS*, loc. cit. Fn. 204, Ref. 28.

213 *IBM Italia v UBIS*, ibd, Ref. 30.

214 This statement disregards the burden of switching costs. Those are case-by-case calculations that must be accounted for individually.

ment. The business of IT outsourcing and cloud computing is designed around the notion that location and the nature of the front-end device plays a marginal role. Whether in Norway or the Netherlands, the UK or the U.S., the access to web-based email service via an iPhone will be an identical service experience. This is a major selling point for suppliers and a big factor in why the services are attractive for consumers. Therefore, the factors of both demand and supply-side speak strongly for an emphasis on a broader geographic market definition.

6.2.3.3 *The relevant temporal market*

The market for cloud computing must be analyzed with a temporal dimension as well. The Commission has identified that markets with high technological progress are subject to significant changes of market conditions. Therefore, markets shall be defined narrower.[215] The TILEC Discussion paper by *Sluijs/Larouche/Sauter* has identified 3 major issues of cloud computing:[216] Data portability and interoperability, vertical integration and internal market fragmentation. The IT sector is strongly characterized by a high level of innovation and strongly present elements of Schumpeterian competition. For the definition of the relevant temporal market, the time frame of the market must be identified correctly by identifying those leap-frog or incremental innovations that elevate the standard on the market away from the product or service under competition law scrutiny.

6.2.4 Conclusion on defining the relevant market

Defining the relevant market is the first step of every competition law investigation. The alleged anticompetitive conduct – be it under Art. 101, 102 TFEU or under merger control Regulation EC 139/2004 – must always be tied to the precisely defined field of investigation. This includes a product, geographic and timely component from a demand and a supply perspective as seen in this chapter.

The definition of these criteria is rendered particularly challenging for the cloud computing market. The nature of the cloud infrastructure and the services provided through the cloud are designed to make geography a non-issue with a service available world-wide. The Commission was able to make a finding in *IBM Italia v. UBIS* without having to decide whether the product and geographic

215 *Tetra Pak International SA v. Commission*, 1996, Case C-333/94, E.C.R. I-5951, 4 C.M.L.R. 662, para. 94, also discussed in *Sluijs/Larouche/Sauter*, 2012, loc. cit. Fn. 3, p. 15.

216 *Sluijs/Larouche/Sauter*, 2012, ibd, p. 15.

market for IT outsourcing services is of national or EEA scope.[217] This however, will not always be the case. Proceedings will appear before the Commission where the agency will need to take a position. Very strong indicators speak in favor of an EEA-wide geographic market. The expansion of the relevant geographical market is favorable for a defendant. If the basis of the market is considered larger, the proportional market share is lower. As an indicator for market dominance and market power, the definition of the relevant market gives leverage. Also with regard to the relevant product market, a segmentation of services does not mirror the business reality. Cloud services are attractive because the hard- and software as well as its maintenance and support services can be outsourced into one external hand. Economies of scale and scope are responsible for the cloud service providers' margin. A fragmentation of the product market would artificially dissect this business from the supply-side product market. Therefore, maintenance services rendered in connection with IT outsourcing services should be considered in the same relevant product market.

6.3 Abuse of a dominant position, Art. 102 TFEU

For the infringement of Art. 102 TFEU, the following five criteria must be given: (i) one undertaking[218], (ii) must be holding a dominant position, (iii) within the relevant internal market, (iv) and unilaterally abuse its position[219], (v) in a way that has an effect on the internal market. *Hoffmann-La Roche* defined the key term of a dominant position in the market. A dominant position

> *"relates to a position of economic strength enjoyed by an undertaking which enables it to prevent effective competition being maintained on the relevant market by affording it the power to behave to an appreciable extent independently of its competitors, its customers and ultimately of the consumers. Such a position does not preclude some competition, which it does where there is a monopoly or quasi-monopoly, but enables the undertaking, which profits by it, if not to determine, at least to have an appreciable influence on the conditions under which that competition will develop, and in any case to act largely in disregard of it so long as such conduct does not operate to its detriment."*[220]

217 *IBM Italia v UBIS*, loc. cit. Fn. 204, Ref. 25 and 30.

218 Or several undertakings in the form or collective dominance.

219 In comparison to Art. 101 para. 3 TFEU, the defendant(s) do not have the possibility of an individual or block exemption regulation in their favor. The defendant merely may illustrate an objective justification for the unilateral conduct under examination.

220 *Hoffmann-La Roche & Co. v. Commission*, Case 85/76, 13 February 1979, ECJ [1979] ECR 461, [1979] 3 C.M.L.R. 211.

The basis of what constitutes an abusive conduct in terms of Art. 102 TFEU has also been defined by the ECJ in this leading case, *Hoffmann-La Roche:*

> *"(...) The concept of abuse is an objective concept relating to the behaviour of an undertaking in a dominant position which is* **such as to influence the structure of a market** *where, as a result of the very presence of the undertaking in question, the degree of competition is weakened and which, through recourse to methods different from those which condition normal competition in products or services on the basis of the transactions of commercial operators, has the* **effect of hindering the maintenance of the degree of competition still existing in the market or the growth of that competition.**".[221] *[emphasis added]*

Currently, there is no cloud service provider that can claim sufficient market power. The number of market players is very high and the number of factual and potential market entries is not predictable to establish market power under Art. 102 TFEU. However, there are two issues that are already at this stage relevant for cloud service providers regarding anticompetitive conduct under Art. 102 TFEU. Given numerous cloud service providers on the market, one must firstly ask what happens to those customers after they have made the choice for a particular supplier in terms of lock-in effects. Secondly, cloud service providers could tie their service to products on the aftermarket and leverage their market power by combining a necessary maintenance product with the cloud service. Equally, there could be an exclusionary practice by refusing to let any other supplier of a necessary maintenance product offer their services. In the following, I examine these two conduct scenarios under Art. 102 TFEU.

6.3.1 Conduct: Tying and bundling

Tying occurs when two components that face insufficient individual demand are supplied together. Tying and bundling occurs when a supplier offers two products, whereby the tying product can only be purchased with the tied product.[222] Tying and bundling in combination with aftermarkets occurs when the customer must purchase a follow-on product on the aftermarket in order to be able to use the product from the foremarket.[223] A classic example of this is the printer and the color cartridge.

---

221 *Hoffmann-La Roche & Co. v. Commission*, Case 85/76, 13 February 1979, ECJ [1979] ECR 461, [1979] 3 C.M.L.R. 211, also quoted in *Nederlandsche Banden Industrie Michelin v. Commission*, Case 322/81, 9 November 1983, ECJ [1983] ECR 3461, [1985] 1 C.M.L.R. 282.

222 *O'Donoghue/Padilla*, The Law and Economics of Article 82 EC, Oxford and Portland 2006, Ref. 3.5.2 (henceforth cited as: *O'Donoghue/Padilla*, 2006).

223 *O'Donoghue/Padilla*, 2006, ibd, Ref. 3.5.3.

In this scenario, a cloud service provider is active on two markets, (i) the market of cloud services, e.g. storage capacities for data (IaaS), and (ii) the market for virus detection software, data packaging software, data presenting software or any other type of data processing related software. The cloud service provider is one of numerous participants with no large market share on market (i) (polypoly) and a player with high market shares and substantial market power on market (ii). Depending on the circumstances, the plaintiff's claim has a potentially high chance of success. This significantly depends upon the ***contract***. If the cloud service provider *a priori* discloses the 'full package', a claim based on Art. 102 lit. (d) TFEU is not likely to succeed. If however the cloud service provider is utilizing the changes in the equilibrium of forces between the contractual parties and *ex post* imposes limitations to consumer choice, a liability is given. This liability is rooted in the fact that the customer is effectively locked in to using the product the cloud service provider has chosen for the aftermarket. There are several technical and legal indicators that a competition authority would consider in assessing whether the cloud service provider engaged in anticompetitive conduct when linking his services to another service within the cloud service he provides.[224] A very good indicator is quantifying the switching costs. If the switching costs reach the threshold of constituting a lock-in effect, Art. 102 TFEU is infringed. The quantification of this cost is a complex economic problem that exceeds the scope of this thesis. Firstly, we must establish whether there is an available substitute for the after-market service. If the customer can effectively exercise a choice, it is a strong indicator against lock in effects.[225] Secondly, we must price how much it would cost the customer to migrate its data from his current cloud service provider to a competitor's service platform.[226] Thirdly, we must assess whether the security of the data would be compromised due to interoperability issues if customer data were migrated to another service provider's platform.[227]

6.3.2 Conduct: Exclusive dealing

Exclusive dealings constitute a barrier to entry. It entails an agreement along the vertical supply chain that the supplier on the foremarket will contract exclusively with one business partner on the aftermarket. In this scenario, the

224 In line with *Feinstein*, Transcending the Cloud, A Legal Guide to the Risks and Rewards of Cloud Computing, Chapter 7: Tying Up the cloud: A Study in Antitrust Issues in Cloud Computing, ReedSmith 2011 (henceforth cited as: *Feinstein*, 2011).

225 *Feinstein*, 2011, ibd, p. 34.

226 *Feinstein*, 2011, ibd, p. 34.

227 *Feinstein*, 2011, ibd, p. 34.

cloud service provider informs the customer that there is an exclusive contractual partner of the cloud service provider performing IT-maintenance and customer support help. For any software updates, service pack actualization and other comparable services the only contact person for customers of this cloud service provider is the exclusive partner X. Again, this may be subject of Art. 102 TFEU liability. However, the chances of a successful lawsuit are significantly lower than in the tying scenario. If the contracting parties are clear about the technical requirements of the cloud service operation, the provisions will also stipulate that technical maintenance services need to be customized to the cloud service provider's platform. A customer will have a very heavy burden of proof to show that other service providers for the aftermarket were subject of a refusal to deal and that this refusal also impacted the EU internal market negatively. In comparison, this scenario is far less likely than the previously presented one on tying and bundling. Mostly so, because the customer as a plaintiff can more easily quantify his damage resulting from tying and bundling in comparison to exclusive dealings.

6.3.3 Conclusion on Art. 102 TFEU

The cloud market does not have a large exposure to Art. 102 TFEU proceedings at this stage. There are a large amount of market players and numerous potential entrants that exert a sufficient amount of competitive pressure on the market. Consequently, establishing a dominant position for one player is very unlikely at this point. The competitive pressures present in this polipoly structure are enough to maintain a sufficiently high level of competition that does not reach the threshold of consumer harm through anticompetitive behavior. This is enhanced by the fact that the definition of the relevant product and geographic market is at least national if not EEA-wide. With that, the pool of players is even larger in relation to one undertaking exerting dominance. However, the constellation of tying and bundling as a form of abusive conduct can under specific circumstances seen above establish a liability under Art. 102 TFEU. This liability will depend on quantifying the switching costs customers have in order to establish a lock-in effect.

6.4 Strategic alliance of cloud service providers

Forming a strategic alliance is the most common form of cooperation in the IT sector. The ***speed of innovation*** in the market is so high that collaborations are utilized to remain part of the market for innovation.[228] From a business perspective, a competitive advantage and benefit should be obtained also at the expense of fellow competitors. With regard to cooperation, the parties may develop complementary resources through joint effort.[229] From a legal point of view, the possibilities and limits to this form of cooperation between competitors need to be analyzed. From an economic point of view, it must be asked why strategic alliances are popular amongst the market participants in the IT sector. These strategic motivators will play a key role in an Art. 102 TFEU proceeding. This chapter examines the options for a strategic alliance from a competition law perspective. That is to give an illustration of the boundaries of practice cloud operators on the EU internal market.

6.4.1 Definition of the strategic alliance

A strategic alliance is a type of corporate partnering for the purpose of using the complementary assets of another firm.[230] A strategic alliance can be concluded for various purposes such as technology licensing concepts, manufacturing relationships, research and development agreements and may also result in the founding of a joint venture.[231] The economic functions of a strategic alliance are widespread. They can encompass setting new industry standards, market access, risk spreading and capital obtainment or technology transfer.[232] A joint venture is a strategic alliance where the collaborative effort presents itself in the form of a new

---

228 An example for an outpaced competitor on the market for computer chips is Intel in comparison to Advanced Risk Machines (ARM) for processors used in portable devices such as smart phones, see: *Rohwetter*, Intel – Gefräßige Chips, Die Zeit, 26 May 2011, available at: http://www.zeit.de/2011/22/Chip-War-Intel-vs-ARM, last accessed 30 May 2011.

229 *Abdallah/Wadhwa*, Collaborating with your rivals: Identifying sources of coopetitive performance, Paper to be presented at the Summer Conferences 2009, Copenhagen Business School, 17–19 June 2009, p. 2.

230 *Barrett*, The European Commission's Antitrust Analysis of High-Technology Joint Ventures and Strategic Alliances: A Diverging Analysis?, The Transnational Lawyer Vol. 12, 1999, p. 512 (henceforth cited as: *Barrett*, 1999).

231 *Barrett*, 1999, ibd, p. 513; *Kolasky*, Antitrust Enforcement Guidelines For Strategic Alliances, presented at the Federal Trade Commissions's Hearings on Joint Ventures, 1 July 1997, p. 1 (henceforth cited as: *Kolasky*, 1997); *Flohr/Pohl*, in: *Martinek/Semler/Habermeier/Flohr*, Vertriebsrecht, 3rd Ed., C. H. Beck, 2010, § 40 Ref. 62.

232 *Chang/Tsai*, How Do Strategic Alliances Affect Suppliers, Customers and Rivals?, National Cheng Kung University, 1 February 2008, p. 2.

legal entity on the relevant market.[233] For the purpose of this analysis, a strategic alliance is understood as collaboration on a contractual basis without forming a joint venture. The alliance partners remain separate and independent companies without a corporate law overlap.

6.4.2 Strategic alliance and Art. 102 TFEU exposure

Strategic alliances are *prima facie* a problem of Art. 101 para. 1 TFEU. But at second glance, the assessment of a strategic alliance turns out to be relevant under Art. 102 TFEU in the form of ***collective dominance*** of the alliance members held on the relevant market. Developing and launching infrastructures and services are so intensive on R&D and sunk costs that the innovation may only occur in the form of a collectively guided investment process as one company alone is unable to sustain the upfront costs. The alliance members may exclude non-members of the strategic alliance from the resource since they have not contributed to the investment costs of the facility *ex ante* and burdened the shared risk.

6.4.2.1 Collective dominance in European competition law

Collective dominance is a legal problem under both European merger control and Art. 102 TFEU proceedings. The difference in analysis is the timely component of the legal analysis. Merger control conducts the ex ante observation of the creation or strengthening of a collective dominance position. Art. 102 TFEU analysis is focused on the examination of the ex post abuse of the collective dominance position by the member undertakings. Whilst different in their approach, Art. 102 TFEU analyses strongly depend on the findings in European merger control cases on collective dominance.[234] The criteria for collective dominance have been established in *Airtours*: (i) an incentive to arrive at tacit collusion, (ii) the ability to sustain tacit collusion and (iii) the inability of a non-participating rival to destabilize the tacit agreement in place.[235] Tacit collusion – distinguished from explicit collusion targeted under Art. 101 TFEU as a cartel – may arise when firms interact in a series of occasions. Tacit collusion is the economic basis of collective dominance cases under Art. 102 TFEU. The long-term scope of interaction allows

233 *Barrett*, 1999, loc. cit. Fn. 230, p. 514.

234 See commentary by *Ezrachi*, EC Competition Law – An Analytical Guide to the Leading Cases, Hart Publishing, 2008, p. 200.

235 *Airtours/First Choice* – Case No. IV/M.1524 dated 22 September 1999. The decision is subject to judicial amendment after *Sony/BMG* – Case No COMP/M.3333, limiting the scope of application of the three criteria test.

the participants to tacitly agree on the fact that *any form of deviation from the collusive path triggers retaliation.*[236]

From a game theory perspective, the dominant strategy is to deviate from the cartel. Hence, the members must take countermeasures to balance the benefit of deviation through punitive measures to incentivize further cooperation. But retaliation or punishment of the remaining members comes at a price as well. The short-term costs generated through the resources required to punish the deviating participant must be balanced by long-term gains obtained through punishment.[237]

Examining the factors that facilitate tacit collusion, *Ivaldi/Jullien/Rey/Seabright/Tirole* identified the following criteria: Firstly, the number of market players in the relevant market is important.[238] An oligopolistic market facilitates decisions based on strategic interdependence. Hence, the smaller the number of players, the higher the game theory based strategic interdependence of the players. Linking to this, the market shares of the market players in the relevant market further facilitates this strategic interdependence.[239] Thirdly, entry barriers have a correlating relationship to collusion possibilities.[240] Barriers to entry facilitate a resistance against competitive pressure from potential entrants. Next, the density and frequency of interaction opportunities between the market players is relevant.[241] Tacit collusion can only occur if there is an opportunity for it. Frequent interaction enhances the opportunities to interact. Furthermore, an innovative market renders collusion more difficult.[242] Recurring changes in the market make it necessary to frequently adapt to the new conditions. Lastly, market transparency, demand curve examinations of the relevant market, business and demand fluctuation and product differentiation[243] represent access to information.

---

236 *Ivaldi/Jullien/Rey/Seabright/Tirole*, The Economics of Tacit Collusion, Final Report for DG Competition, European Commission, IDEI, Toulouse, March 2003, p. 5, also available at http://ec.europa.eu/competition/mergers/studies_reports/the_economics_of_tacit_collusion_en.pdf, last accessed 24 October 2012 (henceforth cited as: *Ivaldi/Jullien/Rey/Seabright/Tirole*, 2003).

237 *Ivaldi/Jullien/Rey/Seabright/Tirole*, 2003, ibd, p. 7.

238 *Ivaldi/Jullien/Rey/Seabright/Tirole*, 2003, ibd, p. 12.

239 *Ivaldi/Jullien/Rey/Seabright/Tirole*, 2003, ibd, p. 14.

240 *Ivaldi/Jullien/Rey/Seabright/Tirole*, 2003, ibd, p. 16.

241 *Ivaldi/Jullien/Rey/Seabright/Tirole*, 2003, ibd, p. 19.

242 *Ivaldi/Jullien/Rey/Seabright/Tirole*, 2003, ibd, p. 29.

243 *Ivaldi/Jullien/Rey/Seabright/Tirole*, 2003, ibd, p. 32 et seqq.

6.4.2.2 The concept of collective dominance in U.S. antitrust law

The concept of collective dominance under competition law does not have a parallel provision in antitrust law. The reason for a lack of this construction in antitrust law is the scope of the Clayton Act and the Sherman Act. In antitrust law, EU collective dominance cases fall under Clayton Act's significant lessening of competition (SLC-Test). Consequently, under antitrust law there is no need to go through Sec. 2 Sherman Act to handle these case characteristics with collective dominance. Similarly, Sec. 1 Sherman Act is also not able to cover collective unilateral price discrimination cases because Sec. 1 Sherman Act[244] demands monopoly power. With that, Sec. 1 Sherman Act has a higher threshold than the dominance criterion under competition law. For a tacit agreement case, the relevant factor under antitrust law is the facilitating practices-test[245] and whether there has been an actual agreement between the parties to exclude a competitor. This would fall under Sec. 1 Sherman Act. This boycott case requires evidentiary support of an agreement illustrating a market conduct phenomenon parallel to collective dominance. Another alternative of handling these cases would be under the category of coordinated effects.[246]

6.4.3 The necessity of strategic alliances

The need for a strategic alliance amongst cloud service providers may be rooted in different reasons, for example the high R&D costs, understanding and entering foreign markets, up- and downstream market integration and penetration amongst many. A paper presented by *Armbrust/Fox/Griffith/Joseph/Katz/Konwinski/Lee/Patterson/Rabkin/Stoica/ Zaharia* in 2010 already suggests the possibility of an agreement between cloud service providers with regard to a business-continuity strategy for the case a cloud provider goes out of business or has a complete failure of supply:

> *„We believe the best chance for independent software stacks is for them to be* **provided by different companies**, *as it has been difficult for one company to justify creating and maintain two stacks in the name of software dependability.“*[247] *[emphasis added]*

244 Sec. 1 Sherman Act covers cartel proceedings.

245 See i.e. *Kaplow*, On the Meaning of Horizontal Agreements in Competition Law, California Law Review Vol. 99 No. 3, June 2011, pp. 683–818 at p. 715.

246 *Ivaldi/Jullien/Rey/Seabright/Tirole*, 2003, loc. cit. Fn. 236, p. 4.

247 *Armbrust/Fox/Griffith/Joseph/Katz/Konwinski/Lee/Patterson/Rabkin/Stoica/Zaharia*, 2010, loc. cit. Fn. 59, p. 54; The Acknowledgements (p. 58) inform about the companies supporting the quoted research paper.

Also, the code of practice presented by *BITKOM* suggests that cloud service providers are working on the standardization of IaaS and PaaS application interfaces. The paper also references the *Open Cloud Manifesto*[248], supporting the open source format for cloud computing. The German original reads as follows:

> „*Cloud Computing erfordert eine weitgehende Interoperabilität von spezifischen Produkten und Lösungen. Hierzu ist insbesondere eine Standardisierung der Anwenderschnittstellen zur Kontrolle von Clouds notwendig.* **Die Frage der Standardisierung wird für IaaS- und PaaS-Angebote industrieweit bei Anbietern und Nutzern von Clouds diskutiert**". *[emphasis added]*

The English translation reads:

> „*Cloud computing requires an extensive interoperability of specific products and solutions. For this, the standardization of application interfaces is necessary for the control of clouds.* **The question of standardisation for IaaS- and PaaS products is discussed amongst the industry by both users and provides of cloud services.**"[249] *[emphasis added]*

The availability of the cloud service is a quality characteristic directly linked to the reputation mechanism. Internet services are very reliant on a positive reputation amongst users.[250] Users remember a website failure, i.e. they immediately notice that Facebook is not reachable for 5 minutes and this information hits the 6pm news cycle. One of the IT sector's core principles is "no single point of failure".[251] Yet, this principle is nearly impossible to realize in a cloud architecture with regard to virtualization, the common software infrastructure required for the data centers and the aspect of interoperability. Furthermore, a Denial of Service (DoS) attack launched would make the service provided by

248 www.opencloudmanifesto.org, last accessed 4 April 2010. The site has been taken down at last attempt of access dated 29 December 2014. Substantial opposition was made public to the Open Cloud Manifesto by Microsoft and Amazon.

249 *Bundesverband Informationswirtschaft, Telekommunikation und neue Medien e. V. (BITKOM)*, Cloud Computing – Evolution in der Technik, Revolution im Business; BITKOM-Leitfaden, October 2009, p. 43, also available at: http://www.bitkom.org/de/themen/36129_61111.aspx, last accessed 30 August 2011 (henceforth cited as: *BITKOM*-Leitfaden, 2009).

250 *Buyya/Yeo/Venugopal/Broberg/Brandic*, 2009, loc. cit. Fn. 129, p. 9 et seqq.

251 *Armbrust/Fox/Griffith/Joseph/Katz/Konwinski/Lee/Patterson/Rabkin/Stoica/Zaharia*, Above the Clouds: A Berkeley View of Cloud Computing, Electrical Engineering and Computer Sciences University of California at Berkeley, Technical Report No. UCB/EECS-2009–28, 10 February 2009, p. 14 (henceforth cited as: *Armbrust/Fox/Griffith/Joseph/Katz/Konwinski/Lee/Patterson/Rabkin/Stoica/Zaharia*, 2009).

the cloud unavailable to its users and possibly frustrate potential users.[252] This may pose a severe availability obstacle for the cloud provider. Also, the EU Commission's Work Program 2011–2012 for Information and Communication Technologies (ICT) listed the following target outcome for cloud computing coordination and support actions:

> "– *Support for standardisation and collaboration in software and services technologies.*
>
> – *Support for the uptake of open source development models in Europe and beyond.*
>
> – **Collaboration with Japanese entities** *on: cloud computing, particularly on* **common standards for data portability and on interoperability**; *services having more efficient energy usage."*[253] *[emphasis added]*

As the papers cited above documents, companies active in the market for cloud services realized that strategic alliances may come with certain benefits and competitive advantages that cannot be achieved alone at lower costs. Market learning for low risk and low costs is expected to emerge from collaboration. But cooperation also goes hand in hand with certain risks. The costs and benefits of strategic alliances between cloud operators are subject henceforth.

6.4.4 Strategic alliance cost and benefits for cloud operators

As expressed by *Hamel/Doz/Prahalad*, collaboration is competition in a different form. It is a shift in competitive tactics while still striving for the same competitive goals.[254] The cloud operators are players on the market for the most procreative strategic alliance that best complements one's own core competencies. Strategic alliances can only function profitably for both partners if the contractual partners are willing to exchange certain know-how (within the scope of the agreement) and learn from the obtained knowledge. The underlying assumption is that the players act alongside the characteristics of bounded rationality, incomplete information

---

252 This example is also mentioned in *Armbrust/Fox/Griffith/Joseph/Katz/Konwinski/Lee/Patterson/Rabkin/Stoica/Zaharia*, 2009, ibd, p. 14.

253 *International Competition Network (ICN)*, Unilateral Conduct Workbook Chapter 3: Assessment of Dominance, prepared by The Unilateral Conduct Working Group, Presented at the 10th Annual ICN Conference, The Hague, May 2011, p. 16, also available at: http://www.internationalcompetitionnetwork.org/working-groups/current/unilateral.aspx, last accessed 9 February 2012.

254 *Hamel/Doz/Prahalad*, Collaborate with Your Competitors – and Win, Harvard Business Review, January-February 1989 (henceforth cited as: *Hamel/Doz/Prahalad*, 1989); *Kolasky*, 1997, loc. cit. Fn. 231, p. 2.

and opportunism.[255] The goal of each alliance partner is to exit from the strategic alliance with more competitive ability in comparison to before and without the alliance. The following subchapters illustrate the core elements of possible costs and benefits of a strategic alliance and presents best practice points for cloud operators entering a strategic alliance.

6.4.4.1 Barriers to entry in a foreign market

Entering a foreign market is intertwined with very high information costs. The entrant does not have sufficient knowledge to estimate the risks and challenges associated with the desired entry. Information on the market structure, the consumer preferences and the density of the market need to be obtained to have data for a risk assessment. Accessing a foreign market through an alliance with a competitor already present on this market transfers the home field advantage of one alliance partner to the other lowering the costs of market entry.[256] The risk factor here is the information gatekeeper checking what information is made available to the competitor. Gatekeepers of information flows are of paramount importance. The person performing the information exchange and the information exchanged must be under strong supervision because the system is perceptive to abusive information over-gathering. The information made available to the alliance partner must not allow the competitor a larger regain of time than the speed of innovation of the incumbent company. A protection mechanism against this risk is to work with the aspect of information portability. Information on source codes, virtualization and other elements of programming are easily portable on small items or transferrable via an internet connection. The alliance partners must clearly identify restricted information and must impose a tight controlling system on information transfer. Additionally, privacy regulations must be accounted for. Regulations on data privacy vary strongly between jurisdictions. As a cloud operator, an alliance between a U.S. and a European provider has great potential of knowledge gain because data privacy and data security requirements differ.

---

255 *Oliver E Williamson*, The Economic Institutions of Capitalism – Firms, Markets, Relational Contracting, The Free Press, 1985, p. 29.

256 *Barrett*, 1999, loc. cit. Fn. 230, p. 515 et seqq.; *Hamel/Doz/Prahalad*, 1989, loc. cit. Fn. 254; *Kolasky*, 1997, loc. cit. Fn. 231, p. 3; *Prahalad/Hamel*, The Core Competence of the Corporation, Harvard Business Review, May-June 1990 (henceforth cited as: *Prahalad/Hamel*, 1990); *Sidak/Teece*, Dynamic Competition in Antitrust Law, Journal of Competition Law & Economics, 2009, p. 592 (henceforth cited as: *Sidak/Teece*, 2009).

6.4.4.2 *Flexibility*

The IT-sector is characteristically a fast product cycle industry. A strategic alliance is in essence a long-term contractual relationship that ex ante provides a framework for future actions that may be flexibly agreed upon at a later moment in time.[257] The danger of a strategic alliance based on a contractual relationship is the possibility of ex post opportunism, where the contractual partner diverges from the original agreement. Mechanisms of supervision and (contractual) penalties and its enforcement must be identified as a transaction cost factor in a strategic alliance. This means that the contractual parties can be in a position to abuse their established relationship from the past to yield a future self-serving profit. To work around this danger, the contractual relationship stipulating the framework for the alliance should be drafted with regard to a few essential points. The area of collaboration and the department in charge in each alliance company must be clearly defined. There should be designated soft- and hardware facilities in place for technology exchange. This includes an email monitoring or tracking server software for the identification of breach of contract or competition law infringements. This includes a content screen for trigger words such as "agree on price" or "level of output in service region X". Furthermore, the contract must ensure that the alliance partners are compliant with data privacy regulations of both jurisdictions if a deviation is given. From a corporate organization point of view, the alliance partners ought to appoint a compliancy officer overlooking the alliance from a competition law point of view. Looking into the future, the contractual partners should ex ante stipulate how the results of their collaboration be used in the future. Lastly, the contract should stipulate a clear exit option from the alliance.

6.4.4.3 *Skills acquisition*

Choosing an alliance partner, the choice should be made depending on the market penetration and the core competences of the company. The knowledge transferring company should complement the characteristics of the knowledge acquiring alliance partner. Acquiring new skills by learning from the alliance partner is less expensive than developing the skill in-house without external input.[258] However, learning skills from an alliance partner means that there is an imbalance of knowl-

---

257 *Barrett*, 1999, ibd, p. 515 et seqq.; *Hamel/Doz/Prahalad*, 1989, ibd; *Kolasky*, 1997, ibd, p. 3; *Prahalad/Hamel*, 1990, ibd; *Sidak/Teece*, 2009, ibd, p. 592.

258 *Barrett*, 1999, ibd, p. 515 et seqq.; *Hamel/Doz/Prahalad*, 1989, ibd; *Kolasky*, 1997, ibd, p. 3; *Prahalad/Hamel*, 1990, ibd; *Sidak/Teece*, 2009, ibd, p. 592.

edge between the two parties. The cost of this imbalanced contribution must be accounted for. If the collaboration is utilized to close a specific lack of knowledge compensating a prior failure, the costs of keeping the alliance partner interested in the alliance will rise exponentially with time. With growing dependency, the asymmetry in the revealed information increases. The more information is exchanged, the more it will become possible to exert leverage.

6.4.4.4 *Speed of adaptation*

Implementing a new industry standard is simplified if the standard can be allocated on up- and downstream markets quickly through alliance partners. The large inherent danger is the transfer of core skills from one partner to the other. The new technology standard to be implemented through a manufacturer should ideally not enable him entering the downstream market with the same or more sophisticated products. The control over core technology elements is essential. Information packages concerning technology and the related competence must be disconnected from each other. The core skill of a company is intertwined with the brand. Hence, the costs of protecting skills mirrored in the value of the brand.[259] Entering the strategic alliance should be made in confidence if the alliance partner's conduct may diminish brand value.

6.4.4.5 *Interpersonal relationships*

In addition to the issues mentioned above, strategic alliance partners must also account for costs and risks related to the newly formed interpersonal relationships between the collaborating partners. Globally active cloud service providers ought to consider the different cultural background, language barriers and differences in management philosophy.[260] It will take additional resources to build trust amongst the collaborating entities. Additionally, the collaborating teams including operating procedures and attitude towards problem solving must be coordinated prior to any joint engagement. It is necessary to do recurring loops of feedback with regard to relational risk. This allows the parties to evaluate the probability of lack of commitment and identify opportunistic behavior of the alliance partner. Lastly, it is reasonable to monitor the parameters surrounding the field of action of the

---

259 *Barrett*, 1999, ibd, p. 515 et seqq.; *Hamel/Doz/Prahalad*, 1989, ibd; *Kolasky*, 1997, ibd, p. 3; *Prahalad/Hamel*, 1990, ibd; *Sidak/Teece*, 2009, ibd, p. 592.

260 *Barrett*, 1999, ibd, p. 515 et seqq.; *Hamel/Doz/Prahalad*, 1989, ibd; *Kolasky*, 1997, ibd, p. 3; *Prahalad/Hamel*, 1990, ibd; *Sidak/Teece*, 2009, ibd, p. 592.

alliance partner such as governmental policies, strong shifts in market structure, economic recession or other similar developments.

6.4.5 Legal evaluation of admissible strategic alliance conduct

Not admissible conduct under Art. 101 para. 1 TFEU is the formation of a hard-core cartel.[261] The OECD presented the following widely accepted definition of a hard core cartel:

> *„For purposes of this Recommendation, a "hard core cartel" is an anticompetitive agreement, anticompetitive concerted practice, or anticompetitive arrangement by competitors to fix prices, make rigged bids (collusive tenders), establish output restrictions or quotas, or share or divide markets by allocating customers, suppliers, territories, or lines of commerce".*[262]

Under the antitrust regime, Sec. 1 Sherman Act stipulates:

> *„Every contract, combination in the form of trust or otherwise, or conspiracy, in restraint of trade or commerce among the several States, or with foreign nations, is declared to be illegal. (...)"*

Antitrust law differentiates between per se assessment and the rule of reason. Under the per se analysis, agreements are challenged that under EU law fall under the comparable category of the hard-core cartel. Is the strategic alliance between competitors concluded for the purpose of overcoming a market failure with a defined and specific objective, the collaboration may be admissible under competition law. The agreement must be analyzed in more detail for pro-competitive and anti-competitive effects and their treatment under the jurisdiction in question. Pro-competitive effects may include the gain of enhanced economic efficiencies on the market and a decreased rate of wasteful duplication. Anti-competitive effects of a strategic alliance may be summarized in the categories of collusion effects and exclusion effects. Relevant for the admissibility of the agreement under Art. 101 para. 1 TFEU is whether the alliance partners remain with a competitive freedom of action. Collusion effects can include reducing rivalry amongst competitors and a decrease in the level of competition. Strategic alliances are numerously formed in the IT sector with the main goal of innovation enhancement. Exclusionary practices are necessary to protect the investment made into the

---

261 *Kling/Thomas*, Kartellrecht, Verlag Franz Vahlen München 2007, p. 150 et seqq.

262 *OECD*, Report: Fighting Hard Core Cartels: Harm, Effective Sanctions and Leniency Programmes, p. 106, also available at: http://www.oecd.org/dataoecd/49/16/2474442.pdf, last accessed 14 May 2011.

cooperation and the innovation achieved. More importantly, exclusionary practices are a protection mechanism against free-riding. Exclusionary practices may present itself as market power leveraging, increased barriers to entry and raising rivals‘ costs, tying agreements, cross licensing, vertical integration and exclusive dealings. A concerted practice can generally be excluded if the unilateral announcement is of a genuinely public nature, i.e. in a newspaper. However, even in this case the specific circumstances of the situation may give grounds for a finding of concerted practice.[263] The horizontal guidelines for Art. 101 para. 1 TFEU for information exchange may be applied *mutatis mutandis* for cases of unilateral information disclosure.[264]

6.4.6 Conclusion on strategic alliances

Engaging in a strategic alliance as a cloud service provider is a balancing act of admissible conduct and competition law infringement. The competitive process is shifted from an external to an internal relationship. Competition and antitrust authorities have a broad scope of discretion when evaluating these cases. From the market players' internal perspective, tactic behavior is necessary. The alliance partner must be monitored to track the likelihood and danger of eased opportunistic behavior. A strategic alliance only makes sense if the scope of alliance is clearly defined and appropriate company-internal measures are in place to understand the interests of the alliance partner to protect oneself against potential opportunistic behavior.

As the next chapters will show, the EU and the U.S. have a very different understanding of handling data privacy and data security issues. Strategic alliances may become an integral part of easing U.S.-based companies into EU data privacy law compliance. However, this is a two-edged sword. As shown, the potential benefits of a strategic alliance come hand in hand with risks to the company's proprietary information, business strategy and branding.

263 *OECD*, Working Party No. 3 on Co-operation and Enforcement, Unilateral Disclosure of Information with Anticompetitive Effects (e.g. Through Press Announcements), OECD Directorate for Financial and Enterprise Affairs, Competition Committee, European Union, DAF/COMP/WP3/WD(2012)21, dated 14 February 2012, p. 6 (henceforth cited as: *OECD*, Working Party No. 3, 2012).

264 *OECD*, Working Party No. 3, 2012, ibd, p. 6.

6.5 Conclusion

Cloud service providers face three main questions with regard to core competition law exposure. Firstly, the definition of the relevant market is the first criterion that must be examined for Art. 101 and 102 TFEU proceedings. The definition poses challenges for the cloud service market, both from a product and a geographic perspective. Cloud services are designed to make geographic boundaries be less relevant for the consumer. From the product market perspective, it is highly questionable whether a legal segmentation of the relevant supply-side product market reflects business realities and the customers' demand for a one-stop-shop for outsourced IT services. From a defendant's perspective, a broader definition of the relevant market is beneficial because it makes the relative position of the defendant on the market appear proportionally smaller. This bears consequences for Art. 101 para. 1 TFEU in light of safe harbors for De Minimis Notifications and BER as well as for Art. 102 TFEU in establishing dominance.

Currently, cloud service providers do not face a likely exposure to Art. 102 TFEU liability given the polypolistic structure of the market for cloud services. Competitive pressures are still sufficient in the market to suppress market dominance by one player. However, the one constellation to be aware of is the conduct of tying and bundling under Art. 102 lit. d TFEU. The best way to preempt this exposure is to draft contractual provisions that explicitly inform the customer of the service packages. That way, the potential plaintiff's claim of no prior knowledge can be countered through the contract document, shifting the burden of proof back to plaintiff. Customers on the other hand should be made aware to notice any explicit information directed at them. It must not be that explicit information policies become a blank check to escape competition law liability for anticompetitive unilateral conduct. Legally, a balancing test is necessary to mitigate customer information and service provider notices with their respective interests.

Strategic alliances are necessary to keep up with the rapid speed of innovations on the market. Aside from the necessary business mindset of knowing your alliance partners and their strategic objectives, the strategic alliance must also comply with the legal boundaries of Art. 102 TFEU from a collective dominance perspective. From an internal perspective, alliance partners must take precaution measures to protect themselves against opportunistic behaviors from within. Externally, the collectively dominant alliance must remain aware of a legal liability under Art. 102 TFEU for a refusal to deal with non-alliance members.

7 Data privacy standardization cartel

Since the services of the cloud are globally accessible via the World Wide Web, the cloud operates globally. This poses the problem of ***uniform data protection levels***. The scope of data protection is stipulated in the privacy and data protection laws. The legal provisions are governed by the principle of territoriality.[265] This poses a problem for the regulation for cloud service operators. The cloud user demands data protection regardless to the country they access their data from or to the place the data is processed and stored. Also, virtualization is responsible for an additional layer of data privacy concern in the case of an attack user vs. user trespassing on the virtual server boundaries within the data center. It would ease compliance costs if service providers could use a joint forum to analyze technical failures. This would elevate data privacy standards and mitigate IT forensics expenses because resources and knowledge would be shared.

7.1 International data privacy standards

On the level of international public ordering, setting up international data privacy standards is theoretically possible. Reaching an understanding between the U.S. and the EU Member States was not possible so far due to different understandings of data privacy standards.[266] The two systems of law have two different bottom lines regarding the commitment and the balance of interest of open information flows versus privacy.[267] A very detailed legal framework in the Member States of the EU and the EU itself protects personally identifiable information.[268] Mitigating differences in data privacy standards is under constant controversy, as is the safe harbor regulation for international data flows[269] between the EU and the U.S. Control over personal data and the efficiency of information flows are two interests in a conflict of objectives that is to date far from being resolved

265 *Nägele/Jacobs*, Rechtsfragen des Cloud Computing, Zeitschrift für Urheber- und Medienrecht (ZUM), 2010, p. 281.

266 As an attempt see for instance the *World Summit for the Information Society*, http://www.itu.int/wsis/index.html, last access 24 November 2014.

267 *Andreșan-Grigorio*, European Union/United States Data Protection Relations, University of Oxford under the supervision of Prof. Derrick A Wyatt, September 2002, p. 24 (henceforth cited as: *Andreșan-Grigorio*, 2002).

268 *Kerr/Teng*, 2010, loc. cit. Fn. 57, p. 12.

269 See in detail Chapter 9.8 on safe harbor regimes in place.

on a global level. The regulations for the enforcement of data privacy provisions are also open questions.[270] The costs resulting from this conflict of objectives is leveraged to the level of private ordering where the players on the market are forced to find detailed contractual regulations to close those compliance gaps.

7.2 Costs of privacy and data protection terms of contract

The uncertainty of the applicable law and the numerous legal provisions possibly applicable means that the contractual agreement between the cloud client and the cloud provider needs to be as detailed as possible with regard to data privacy and the use cases of the data. This is to minimize the costs resulting from a missing contractual clause. The jurisdictional conflict already shows in the following hypothetical: Assume a cloud facility based in Iowa with a client accessing from Germany and a contractual relationship concluded in France for contract data processing. The applicable law must be determined in accordance with conflict of laws. Applicable regulations can possibly be stipulated in the German Federal Data Protection Act, the U.S. Stored Communications Act, provisions of European Law and the French Data Protection Act.

Providing a high level of data privacy and data protection is a cost factor. The risk of high expenses for data privacy is reduced in a first step by opting for a contractual agreement with detailed terms on data privacy. The quality of the terms on data privacy is the next step to cost reduction. Long-term contractual relationships always suffer from the increased risk of ex post opportunism.[271] An ex ante contractual relationship found ex post incomplete is a chance for a player to alter the agreement to its own benefit.

Furthermore, the cloud providers have the possibility to distinguish themselves from each other by providing more extensive clauses for data privacy.[272] The element of data availability to cloud providers is the linchpin of the cloud facility as such. Competition amongst cloud providers with clauses stipulating the self-limitation of the cloud provider touches the core of the cloud's profitability. For example, Google runs an advertisement placement service called AdSense operating on the basis of matching the information of the consumer (behavioral advertising).[273] This concept makes data valuable as every viewed ad-

---

270 *Andreşan-Grigorio*, 2002, loc. cit. Fn. 267, p. 33.

271 *Kirchner/Käseberg*, 2011, loc. cit. Fn. 64.

272 An example is the German provider GMX, who placed TV advertisements in German television for GMX, Email made in Germany.

273 See: www.google.com/adsense/login/en_US/.

vertisement is generating revenue of Google.[274] Not having to compete with other cloud providers for clients with data privacy awareness would simplify access to information needed by the cloud service providers for their revenue-generating branch of behavioral advertisement. It is in the market players' interest to establish such a uniform level to relief the competitive pressures associated with different privacy standards. But an association of undertakings that explicitly coordinates its activities is also a cartel.[275]

7.2.1 Data privacy standardization under European law

Data privacy standards are governed by dense regulation under EU law as well as by the individual EU Member States in particular in comparison to the U.S.[276] One option is to join forces with other competitors limiting the costs of compliance with data privacy standards on the EU internal market.

Art. 101 para. 1 TFEU stipulates that any agreement or decision of association of undertakings and concerned parties shall be automatically void if an agreement between undertakings may affect trade between Member States and which have as their object or effect the prevention, restriction or distortion of competition within the internal market. In particular, agreements which directly or indirectly aim to fix purchase or selling prices or any other trading conditions are considered void pursuant to Art. 101 para. 1 lit. a TFEU and Art. 1 para. 1 Regulation 1/2003[277].[278] An agreement between the cloud providers for the standardization of data privacy is an agreement on the trading conditions as prohibited by Art. 101 para. 1 lit. a TFEU. The economies of scale and scope are able to realize significant cost reductions but would simultaneously weaken the competitive forces in the market through standardized agreement structures. The competition between data privacy standards would be weakened substantially. On the other hand, there would be a widely accepted consensus on a standard for the benefit of the consumer. The boundaries of cooperation and coordination become relevant for

274 *Picker*, 2009, loc. cit. Fn. 191, p. 3.

275 For the definition of "cartel" see *Carlton/Perloff*, 2005, loc. cit. Fn. 196, p. 112.

276 See in particular Chapter 5.

277 Council Regulation (EC) No 1/2003 of 16 December 2002 on the implementation of the rules on competition laid down in Articles 81 and 82 of the Treaty, O.J. L 1 dated 4 January 2003, p. 1–25.

278 *EU Commission*, Communication Notice from the Commission, Guidelines on the application of Article 81 (3) of the Treaty, O.J. C 101/97 dated 27 April 2004, Ref. 10 (henceforth cited as: *EU Commission*, Guidelines on the application of Article 81 (3)).

examining the exposure to Art. 101 para. 1 TFEU.[279] No prior decision of the Commission is required for triggering the legal consequence of Art. 101 para. 1 TFEU.[280] It is therefore the responsibility of the parties involved in the agreement to self-assess their behavior. The Commission is given the liberty to reasonably, flexibly and individually apply the guidelines to every set of circumstances with discretionary power.[281]

7.2.2 Individual exemption pursuant to Art. 101 para. 3 TFEU

Art. 101 para. 1 TFEU may be declared inapplicable pursuant to Art. 101 para. 3 TFEU and Art. 1 para. 2 Regulation 1/2003 if the agreement contributes to improving the production or distribution of goods or to promoting technical or economic progress whilst allowing consumers a fair share of the resulting benefit.[282]

There is no block exemption regulation for the cloud computing market. Hence, the ***criteria for individual exemption*** under Art. 101 para. 3 TFEU are the benchmark. The parties of the agreement arguing for the application of an individual exemption for the data privacy standardization agreement are faced with comprehensive amount of evidence they are required to provide. Also, the line of argumentation must account for the discretionary power the regulatory authorities have in the case of individual exemption. This also includes the possibility to take goals pursued by other TFEU provisions into account[283] when applying Art. 101 para. 3 TFEU. In the following, I present the possible path for such an individual exemption under Art. 101 para. 3 TFEU and the procedural burden of proof associated with it.

7.2.2.1 Overview of the criteria of Art. 101 para. 3 TFEU

In order to avoid the consequences of Art. 101 para. 1 and para. 2, the criteria for the inapplicability of the prohibition clause must be met. Art. 101 para. 3 TFEU stipulates four cumulative, two positive and two negative, conditions: efficiency gains and a fair share for consumers as positive criteria and an indispensability

279 The relevance of this distinction needs further assessment from the perspective of contract law, there the law of the General Terms and Conditions, see in detail Chapter 10.

280 *EU Commission*, Guidelines on the application of Article 81 (3), loc. cit. Fn. 278, Ref. 1.

281 *EU Commission*, Guidelines on the application of Article 81 (3), ibd, Ref. 6.

282 *EU Commission*, Guidelines on the application of Article 81 (3), ibd, Ref. 10.

283 *EU Commission*, Guidelines on the application of Article 81 (3), ibd, Ref. 42.

of the restriction and no elimination of competition as negative criteria.[284] If the conditions stipulated in Art. 101 para. 3 TFEU are met, the agreement enhances competition within the relevant market. Due to the agreement subject to Art. 101 para. 1 TFEU, the consumers are offered cheaper or better products and are also compensated for the anticompetitive effects of this agreement to a sufficient degree as stipulated in Art. 101 para. 3 TFEU.

The exemption regulation has the legal nature of a defense.[285] Pursuant to Art. 2 Sent. 2 Regulation 1/2003, the burden of proof lies on the undertakings invoking the benefit of the exemption regulation of Art. 101 para. 3 TFEU. If cloud service providers are found to have a cartel agreement in place pursuant to Art. 101 para. 1 TFEU, it is the cartel members' burden to stipulate to Art. 101 para. 3 TFEU. In order to fall under an individual exemption, the involved parties must undergo a self-assessment carrying the burden of proof for the four criteria. The quality of the reasoning brought forward must meet the parameters set out in the Commission's guidelines. Special attention must be paid to the ***economic approach*** stipulated by the Commission in assessing the criteria of Art. 101 para. 3 TFEU.[286] The burden of proof with regard to each of the four criteria of Art. 101 para. 3 TFEU may be approached in two steps: Is the legal (positive or negative) criterion met? And does the way the legal criterion is met benefit the consumers? These are the steps for the individual exemption of data privacy standardization agreements between cloud operators.

7.2.2.2 Criterion #1: Efficiency gains

The burden of proof commences with showing that the agreement subject to Art. 101 para. 1 TFEU results in efficiency gains. Efficiency gains are defined by the Commission as follows:

> „*In general,* **efficiencies** *stem from an integration of economic activities whereby undertakings* **combine their assets to achieve what they could not achieve as efficiently on their own** *or whereby they entrust another undertaking with tasks that can be performed more efficiently by that other undertaking.*"[287] *[emphasis added]*

The Commission has provided a circular definition. An efficiency analysis is in essence a comparison. One must ask how the output from a given set of resources can be maximized. Two approaches may be measured against each other. In result,

284 *EU Commission*, Guidelines on the application of Article 81 (3), ibd, Ref. 34 et seqq.
285 *EU Commission*, Guidelines on the application of Article 81 (3), ibd, Ref. 41.
286 *EU Commission*, Guidelines on the application of Article 81 (3), ibd, Ref. 38.
287 *EU Commission*, Guidelines on the application of Article 81 (3), ibd, Ref. 60.

the method producing the smaller amount of economic waste is the approach with the higher level of efficiency. Efficiency is not scalable. A singular performance can never be ‚more efficient', since efficiency in itself is a comparison by concept. Also, there are different approaches to efficiency: ***productive*** efficiency, ***allocative*** efficiency, ***utility maximization*** and many more. To that, the Commission states:

> *„There is considerable overlap between the various categories mentioned in Article 81 (3) and the same agreement may give rise to several kinds of efficiencies. It is therefore not appropriate to draw clear and firm distinctions between the various categories."*[288]

This statement of the Commission is the gateway to a possibly significant problem: The burden of proof on the undertakings with regard to efficiency gains is in economic terms. The assessment of the provided evidence for Art. 101 para. 3 TFEU is of legal nature and not strictly bound to economic principles.

An efficiency gain surfaces if the amount of economic waste produced decreases. To stay in line with the Commission's overriding criterion of enlarging the amount of consumer surplus, the economic waste reduced must also relate back to the consumer on the relevant market. Efficiency gains need not always be in the form of cost efficiencies. The Commission also recognizes qualitative efficiencies. Qualitative efficiencies may be the main motivator for an agreement between undertakings.[289] The verification of efficiency gains is a two-step process: The defendant must illustrate that there is a ***direct causal link*** between the agreement and the claimed efficiency[290] and then he must show the ***value of the efficiency gain.***[291] With regard to the value, the Commission does not mention here that the value of the efficiency gain is assessed in light of increasing consumer surplus. The burden of proof is substantial. The guidelines stipulate that the nature of the claimed efficiency, a direct causal link between the agreement and the efficiencies, the likelihood and magnitude of each claimed efficiency and how and when each claimed efficiency would be achieved must be demonstrated to meet the burden of proof.[292] In the case of efficiencies in the form of new or improved products and other non-cost based efficiencies, it must be

---

288 The Commission differentiates between cost efficiencies and efficiencies of qualitative nature, see: *EU Commission*, Guidelines on the application of Article 81 (3), ibd, Ref. 59.

289 *EU Commission*, Guidelines on the application of Article 81 (3), ibd, Ref. 59 and 69.

290 *Glaxo Welcome* – Case IV/36.957/F3, Ref. 178 and 179; *EU Commission*, Guidelines on the application of Article 81 (3), loc. cit. Fn. 278, Ref. 54.

291 *EU Commission*, Guidelines on the application of Article 81 (3), ibd, Ref. 50.

292 *EU Commission*, Guidelines on the application of Article 81 (3), ibd, Ref. 51.

shown what the nature of the efficiency is and how and why it constitutes an objective economic benefit.[293]

Elevating the standard of data privacy may fall under the scope of application of Art. 101 para. 3 TFEU. Efficiency gains through an agreement for data privacy standardization may be realized by promoting technical or economic progress in the form of elevated data privacy standards. For cloud computing, this thought was first articulated by *Kirchner/Käseberg*.[294] The underlying argument is based on the assumption that competition policy also encompasses data protection and data privacy as a part of relevant competition law policy parameters as a quality parameter protected by competition law.[295] Similarly, product safety and product improvement concerns may serve as a parallel for data privacy standards.

Once efficiencies are identified, the next step is to prove efficiency gains to the Commission. But also, the Commission can investigate independently. Pursuant to Art. 18 para. 1 Regulation 1/2003, the Commission may require undertakings to provide all necessary information in order to carry out its duties and investigations as empowered by Regulation 1/2003. The Commission is also entitled to define the scope and the format of requests for information.[296] Data may be obtained from parties involved in the investigating procedure or third parties, trade associations, the press, other independent consultants, governmental sources or survey information.[297] The Commission considers data on costs, output, sales, prices, capacity, product characteristics, delivery flows, customer characteristics, tender details, entry barriers, business strategies and market shares of the parties involved and information about other market participants necessary:[298]

---

293 *EU Commission*, Guidelines on the application of Article 81 (3), ibd, Ref. 57.

294 *Kirchner/Käseberg*, 2011, loc. cit. Fn. 64.

295 *TomTom/Tele Atlas* – Case COMP/M.4854 dated 14 May 2008. The Decision was a competition law merger case, not a unilateral conduct proceeding.

296 *EU Commission, DG COMP*, Best Practices for the submission of economic evidence and data collection in cases concerning the application of Articles 101 and 102 TFEU and in Merger Cases, Ref. 46, also available at: http://ec.europa.eu/competition/consultations/2010_best_practices/best_practice_submissions.pdf, last accessed 12 April 2011 (henceforth cited as: *EU Commission, DG COMP*, Best Practices for the submission of economic evidence).

297 *EU Commission, DG COMP*, Best Practices for the submission of economic evidence, ibd, Ref. 56.

298 *EU Commission, DG COMP*, Best Practices for the submission of economic evidence, ibd, Ref. 55.

For the economic reasoning of an efficiency gain, the submitted data must be defined and tested for sensitivity and robustness. Especially in the case of incomplete data, the substitute calculation must be shown and tested. Furthermore, the applied economic models and the underlying assumptions and conditions must be explained to the Commission. Due to the small number of proceedings against cloud service providers initiated so far, it is to be expected that the data required by the Commission will be extensive in order to get a better understanding of the market.

7.2.2.3 Criterion #2: Increase of consumer benefit

To meet the economic nature of the individual exemption, the Commission's understanding of the term "economic approach" is important. The Commission establishes a consumer-welfare approach:

> *„The aim of the Community competition rules is to protect competition on the market as a means of* ***enhancing consumer welfare*** *and of ensuring an efficient allocation of resources. (...) The net effect of such agreements is to promote the very essence of the competitive process, namely to win customers by offering better products or better prices than those offered by rivals."*[299] *[emphasis added]*

The focus on consumer welfare is an overriding criterion in European competition law.[300] For instance, the consumer welfare approach is a core value in European merger control, since effective competition is defined as such that brings benefits to the consumers.[301] The goal is to spare the consumers costs, such as switching-supplier-costs[302] and higher product prices[303] caused by mergers maximizing the consumer surplus. The Commission will assess whether the pro-competitive beneficial effects of the agreement outweigh the anti-competitive effects – with

---

299 *EU Commission*, Guidelines on the application of Article 81 (3), loc. cit. Fn. 278, Ref. 33 and 43.

300 *EU Commission, DG COMP*, Best Practices on the conduct of proceedings concerning Articles 101 and 102 TFEU, Ref. 9, 103 and 116, also available under: http://ec.europa.eu/competition/consultations/2010_best_practices/best_practice_articles.pdf, last accessed 12 April 2011.

301 *EU Commission*, Guidelines on the assessment of horizontal mergers under the Council Regulation on the control of concentrations between undertakings, 2004/C 31/03, O.J. C 031 dated 5 February 2004, pp. 5–18, Ref. 8 (henceforth cited as: *EU Commission*, Horizontal Merger Guidelines).

302 *EU Commission*, Horizontal Merger Guidelines, ibd, pp. 5–18, Ref. 31.

303 *EU Commission*, Horizontal Merger Guidelines, ibd, pp. 5–18, Ref. 24.

a positive balance for the consumer.[304] Hence, the cloud operators entering into a standardization agreement for data privacy protection must provide the Commission with an in-depth analysis of the pro-competitive and therefor beneficial effects of the agreement accounting for the consumer. Furthermore, the benefit obtained must be linked to enlarging the absolute value of consumer surplus. The net effect of the agreement subject to Art. 101 para. 1 TFEU must at least be neutral from the point of view of those consumers directly or likely affected by the agreement[305] and the claimed efficiencies must create real value for consumers in that market to compensate them for the adverse effects of the restriction of competition.[306]

7.2.2.4 Criterion #3: Indispensability of the restriction

The Commission evaluates the criterion of indispensability of the restriction in two steps. First, the restrictive agreement as such must be reasonably necessary to achieve efficiencies and second, the individual restrictions of competition resulting from the agreement must be reasonably necessary for the attainment of the efficiencies.[307] The restriction is indispensable if its absence would eliminate or significantly reduce the efficiencies that follow from the agreement or make it significantly less likely that they will materialize.[308] The indispensability of the agreement is therefore determined via a comparison of the hypothetical situation with the agreement subject to Art. 101 para. 1 TFEU and the situation without the agreement. The question is under which conditions the competitive activity is performed more effectively.[309] The Commission will assess under the aspect of plausibility whether there is any other economically practicable and less restrictive means of achieving efficiencies through an agreement subject to Art. 101 para. 1 TFEU.[310]

---

304 Case T-65/98, Judgment of the Court of First Instance (5th Chamber) dated 23 October 2003 – *Van den Bergh Foods,* Ref. 107; *EU Commission,* Guidelines on the application of Article 81 (3), loc. cit. Rn. 278, Ref. 11 and 32 et seqq.

305 *EU Commission,* Guidelines on the application of Article 81 (3), loc. cit. Fn. 278, Ref. 85.

306 *EU Commission,* Guidelines on the application of Article 81 (3), ibd, Ref. 104.

307 *EU Commission,* Guidelines on the application of Article 81 (3), ibd, Ref. 73.

308 *EU Commission,* Guidelines on the application of Article 81 (3), ibd, Ref. 79.

309 *EU Commission,* Guidelines on the application of Article 81 (3), ibd, Ref. 74.

310 *EU Commission,* Guidelines on the application of Article 81 (3), ibd, Ref. 75.

7.2.2.5 Criterion #4: No elimination of competition

The Commission views that short-term efficiency gains are outweighed by longer-term losses stemming from reduced innovation, higher prices and misallocation of resources.[311] Again, the Commission works with a comparison, here between the degree of competition prior to the agreement and the degree of competition under the agreement.[312] Furthermore, the Commission assesses the impact of the agreement on competition with regard on its influence on „*the various parameters of competition*"[313].The following parameters are considered: the general regulatory framework, the cost of entry and sunk costs, minimum efficient scale, competitive strengths of potential entrants, the position of buyers and their ability to innovate, the incumbent's response to attempted new market entries, past market entries and the economic outlook for the industry sector.[314]

7.2.3 Data privacy standardization under U.S. law

In order to put the EU standardization possibilities into perspective, I henceforth give an overview of data privacy standardization options under U.S. law.

The fast development of the cloud aggrandizes the gap between the policy framework provided as public ordering and the standard of technology in the U.S.[315] Compliance with the data privacy regulations under U.S. law is challenging, since the different provisions demand distinct degrees of security standards and stipulate different ways of handling the data.[316]

The most relevant with regard to cloud computing are the Patriot Act, the Health Insurance Portability and Accountability Act (HIPAA), the Stored Communications Act[317]. All in all, data privacy is a legal matter dealt with in

311 *EU Commission*, Guidelines on the application of Article 81 (3), ibd, Ref. 105.

312 *EU Commission*, Guidelines on the application of Article 81 (3), ibd, Ref. 107.

313 *EU Commission*, Guidelines on the application of Article 81 (3), ibd, Ref. 110.

314 *EU Commission*, Guidelines on the application of Article 81 (3), ibd, Ref. 115 (i) to (viii).

315 *Kerr/Teng*, 2010, loc. cit. Fn. 57, p. 8.

316 *Kerr/Teng*, 2010, ibd, p. 10. For an overview of U.S. data privacy laws, see in detail Chapter 5.1.1.

317 The Stored Communications Act distinguishes between two categories of computer networks: (1) electronic communication services (ECS) for data transmissions and electronic mail and (2) remote computing services (RCS) for outsourced computer processing and data storage, both are relevant categories for cloud computing services, see: *William Jeremy Robinson*, 2010, loc. cit. Fn. 60, p. 1205.

fragments and sector-dependently in comparison to the EU. In the case *Google/DoubleClick*[318], due to data privacy concerns, the FTC was asked by third parties to intervene. Google and DoubleClick's combined assets of consumer data was identified as a threat to privacy in light of behavioral advertising.[319] This transaction requesting merger clearance for Google's acquisition of DoubleClick has been tackled by both the FTC and the EU Commission. The finding of the FTC did consider the competitive effects of consumer privacy issues as a non-price attribute but did not see sufficient ground to challenge the transaction on this basis.[320]

For the purposes of the analysis of data privacy standardization between cloud providers under U.S. law, *Google/DoubleClick* clearly illustrates one key issue to consider. The IT-sector for internet services is globally operating and the cooperation of U.S. and EU authorities is necessary. This may also lead to a spill-over effect of different data privacy standards of both systems of law influencing each other. For the assessment of a standardization agreement, this FTC finding is a positive signal if elevating the standard of data privacy is considered a non-price attribute of competition and whose absence is negatively valued by the FTC.[321] Data privacy has become an element of antitrust policy and is a parameter to determine the quality of the market. The amount of emphasis laid

318 *Google/DoubleClick* – FTC File No. 071–0170 (Federal Trade Commission) and Case COMP/M.4731 – *Google/DoubleClick* (European Commission). The case may be viewed as a parallel decision to the European decision *TomTom/Tele Atlas* – Case COMP/M.4854.

319 With each "google search" the user makes a declaration of interest. Providing advertisement that is linked to the declaration of interest is in its essence behavioral advertising.

320 *Google/DoubleClick* – FTC File No. 071–0170 (Federal Trade Commission), Statement of the FTC, p. 3. Dissenting opinion of *Commissioner Pamela Jones Harbour* emphasizes the strong network effects this merger created and acknowledges data privacy standards as a factor to antitrust assessments with a higher standard than the majority of the votes in this decision. In her view, this case must be seen as a data merger, where the FTC should have seized the opportunity to evaluate the merger implications with a consumer protection and a competition perspective.

321 *Harbour/Koslov*, 2010, loc. cit. Fn. 194, p. 773 with references *Averitt/Lande*, Consumer Sovereignity: A Unified Theory of Antitrust and Consumer Protection Law, 65 Antitrust Law Journal 713, 1997 and *Waller*, In Search of Economic Justice: Considering Competition and Consumer Protection Law, Chicago Law Review, 2005, p. 631 – for consumer protection and antitrust law goals as being complementary concluding to data privacy as a policy goal under antitrust law.

on consumer protection will most likely remain smaller in comparison to the EU because antitrust law follows the total welfare approach. But the gap was getting bridged. Following the lines of *Commissioner Pamela Jones Harbour* and her Dissenting Opinion[322], her train of thought for the incorporation of privacy standards into an antitrust case analysis is comparable to an EU trained lawyer's possible line of argumentation. In particular, she questioned the sole power of private ordering to solve this conflict of interest without any interference from public ordering[323] This is a very European argument to make. Her intention of enhancing the cooperation between the two largest competition and antitrust law authorities was clearly stipulated:

> *„For example, the Commission (*FTC*) should learn more about the extent to which these principles are consistent with privacy regulations and principles adopted elsewhere in the world. Any final set of principles that emerges must respect the privacy regimes established in other jurisdictions, in order to foster international trust and facilitate global commerce.*"[324]

Her term at the FTC expired in September 2009.

7.3 Summary

Consumers may make privacy concerns, the density of privacy regulation and data security as a factor for choosing a product. This in consequence influences the cloud service provider's behavior and possible strategies for data privacy solutions and their compliance with competition and antitrust law. Even though cloud providers may be based outside the EU, as soon as the EU common market is touched, the rules of competition law are applicable. With the consumer welfare approach, the possibilities of an efficiency defense are limited, since the efficiency gains must be directly related back to the benefit of the consumer.

Providing a high privacy and data protection standard to customers is a large cost factor. Ensuring a better standard is more expensive than a lower one as several protection layers are in place. Sharing the burden by collaboration and for example joint declarations could ease the financial burden. But striking data privacy standardization agreements as a sign of higher quality cloud service

---

322 *Google/DoubleClick* – FTC File No. 071–0170, Dissenting Statement of *Commissioner Pamela Jones Harbour*, p. 10 et seqq (henceforth cited as: *Commissioner Pamela Jones Harbour* in *Google/DoubleClick*).

323 *Commissioner Pamela Jones Harbour* in *Google/DoubleClick*, ibd, p. 12.

324 *Commissioner Pamela Jones Harbour* in *Google/DoubleClick*, ibd, p. 11.

is also a cartel as stipulated in Art. 101 para. 1 TFEU. Art. 101 TFEU liability can be avoided if the cartel members stipulate to Art. 101 para. 3 TFEU. The pro-competitive effects of a data privacy standardization cartel must outweigh the anticompetitive effects and link to a direct consumer benefit. The burden of proof for this falls on the cloud service operators. There are precedents that show that this could be an acceptable course in the future. Especially in light of strong political forces that have successfully pushed for uniform and EU-wide data privacy regulations, as implemented in the GDPR, the chances to successfully claim Art. 101 para. 3 TFEU on the basis of an individual exemption is increasing.

8 Interoperability and innovation

> *„The most difficult case I had to decide was certainly Microsoft. I am sure that it is Microsoft not just for the technical complexity but because there was a rather dramatic trade off to be made after the long investigation and after the three days intensive final negotiations with the CEO of Microsoft in order to achieve a settlement. That was a very good phase, but I concluded that we needed for the benefit of legal certainty and of competition enforcement, to have a binding precedent. To me the biggest cost associated with getting to a decision had to do with our transatlantic relationship“ - Mario Monti (2008)*[325]

Interoperability plays a large role in database management systems. It is determining factor whether data can be migrated and integrated into an existing cloud platform. It also is the decisive factor for potentially high switching costs and for the pursuits of a standardization agreement between technology companies. Interoperability and innovation are linked. The following chapter illustrates the nexus between interoperability and innovation by examining different types of innovation and its impact on competition law and policy. The question that cases before U.S. and EU courts and competition agencies have raised remains unanswered. The compulsory disclosure of interoperability information can either lead to an additional incentive to innovate because the competitive pressures have been heightened by government agencies. Or, the incentive to innovate will drop substantially because the reason for innovation is void once competition law compulsory disclosure renders leveraging the competitive power of using this innovation abusive.

8.1 Definition of interoperability

Interoperability is context-related. The category of information that may be qualified as an interoperability information must be identified, e.g. information regarding server-to-server, server-to-client, client-to-server.[326] The ***interfaces*** are the communication port for configuration, controlling and provisioning the virtualized server units.[327] Interfaces may be seen as a gate. Whether the gates of two components are compatible is a question of interoperability.

---

325 *Mario Monti* quoted in *Reynolds/Best,* Article 102 and innovation: the journey since Microsoft, 39th annual Fordham Conference on International Antitrust Law and Policy, 20–21 September 2012.

326 *Microsoft*, COMP/C-3/37.792, loc. cit. Fn. 82, Ref. 567.

327 *BITKOM*-Leitfaden, 2009, loc. cit. Fn. 249, p. 43.

8.1.1 EU definition

Council Directive 91/250/EEC of 14 May 1991 on the legal protection of computer programs provides a definition of the term interoperability as follows:

> *„Whereas the function of a computer program is to communicate and work together with other components of a computer system and with users and, for this purpose, a logical and, where appropriate, physical interconnection and interaction is required to permit all elements of software and hardware to work with other software and hardware and with users in all the ways in which they are intended to function;*
>
> *Whereas the parts of the program which provide for such interconnection and interaction between elements of software and hardware are generally known as 'interfaces';*
>
> *Whereas this functional interconnection and interaction is generally known as 'interoperability'; whereas such interoperability can be defined as the ability to exchange information and mutually to use the information which has been exchanged;*"[328]

The Directive's definition is technical and focused on the interaction of hardware and software components. With regard to DBMS, the definition can be transferred to the cloud sector. This would include data organizational patterns.

8.1.2 U.S. definition

Gasser/Palfrey from the *The Berkman Center for Internet & Society* at Harvard Law School provided the following definition of interoperability in November 2007:

> *„At the definitional core of the multi-layered and multifaceted concept „ICT (Information & Communications Technology) interoperability" is what we might describe as the ability to transfer and render useful data and other information across systems (which may include organizations), applications, or components. (...) The working definition needs to be concretized for each context and use case separately.*"[329]

By *Gasser/Palfrey*, the question of interoperability is context specific, a technical issue and also a matter of work flow management, the involved personal and the legal framework. It is not built around solely technical factors but also considers the pursuit of interoperability for a specific output goal.

---

328 Recitals 10 to 12 of the Council Directive 91/250/EEC as also quoted in *Microsoft*, COMP/C-3/37.792, loc. cit. Fn. 82, Ref. 21.

329 *Gasser/Palfrey*, 2007, loc. cit. Fn. 13, p. 4.

8.2 Interoperability and the IBM cases

In 1974, more than three decades prior to the *Microsoft* cases, the Commission initiated another case revolving around the disclosure of interoperability information. IBM held a dominant position on the market for supplying operating systems and CPUs. This statement was inferred from IBM's comments on the case, but the Commission never took stance. The Commission said that it does not "*divulge information on cases in which it has not yet adopted a final position*"[330]. In *IBM Corp. v Commission*[331], the case revolved around the disclosure of interface information with regard to periphery hardware and software products. IBM's proprietary System/370 controlled the interface information that manufacturers needed in order to interface their components to the system. An example for this would be a printer that needs an interface in order to receive print jobs.

The reason why *IBM Corp. v Commission* has not reached the level of media coverage and academic discourse is because IBM and the Commission concluded a settlement prior to a finding. Consequently, the case never became a formal legal precedent. The content of the settlement was comparable to *Microsoft*. The technical difference between the two cases is the nature of the interfacing object of the plaintiff. IBM was ordered to disclose a sufficient degree of information under FRAND-terms so that competitors are enabled to interface with System/370 with their software and hardware products. Similarly, in *Microsoft*[332], the case dealt with the disclosure of work-group server interoperability information. In both cases, the refusal to disclose the application programming interface information lead to the ability of the proprietary to leverage its dominant position into an abusive conduct. Interestingly, in both cases there was a parallel American proceeding. In 1969, the U.S. DoJ filed a complaint for *U.S. v. IBM*[333] on 17 January 1969 for the violation of Sec. 2 Sherman Act with regard to the monopolization of the electronic digital computer system market in the business segment. However, that case was dismissed as "without merit".[334]

---

330 *Terrance L Bessey*, Comity and Computers in the Common Market: The IBM Case, Northwestern Journal of International Law & Business, Vol. 4 No. 2, 1982, p. 626 et seqq., referencing the reply of the Commission of the European Communities to Written Question No. 2033/80, submitted by Mrs. Scrivener, Member of the European Parliament, C.M.Rep. CCH 10303.

331 *IBM Corp. v. E.C.Commission*, 32 C.M.L.R. 93, 1981.

332 *Microsoft Corp. v. Commission*, Case T-201/04 R, CFI [2007], CMLR 11, (henceforth cited as: *Microsoft I*, 2007); *Microsoft*, COMP/C-3/37.792, loc. cit. Fn. 82.

333 *United States v. IBM*, Action No. 69–200 (S.D.N.Y.) (D.N.E.) dated 17 January 1969.

334 *In re International Business Machines Corp.*, 687 F.2d 591 (2d Cir 1982), Ref. 594.

Again in 2007 to 2011, IBM faced competition and antitrust law scrutiny for restricting interoperability information. The complaint was filed by Platform Solutions, Inc., a company that has developed a competing computer mainframe product. Shortly after the complaint was filed, IBM acquired its competitor in exchange for dropping the complaint.[335] Lastly in 2011, IBM faced tying investigations, but proceedings were not followed through and complaints were withdrawn.[336]

8.3 Interoperability and the Microsoft cases

In the U.S., Microsoft faced numerous investigations based on anticompetitive tying of the internet explorer with the Windows operation system, exclusive dealing and monopolization. With the *Microsoft-Case*[337] initiated by Sun Microsystems in 1998, the Commission has dealt with the question of interoperability and competition law for the IT-sector (work group servers) for over 13 years. If the criteria of a refusal to deal situation were given, the EU Commission can order the remedy of third party access in the form of a compulsory license. This means that interoperability information must be given to a competitor and the competitor must be enabled to interface with the incumbent's facility. As seen above[338], interoperability of DBMS is an integral part of the cloud infrastructure. Without interoperability, it is not possible to migrate, integrate and coherently process data within the data center. Once interoperability arises as a concern in the cloud market due to standardization efforts or lock-in effects, the *Microsoft-Case* will be a cornerstone of the assessment with regard to legal exposure under Art. 101 and 102 TFEU. For this purpose, I present the key takeaways of the *Microsoft* cases.

The Commission conducted an investigation against Microsoft under Art. 102 TFEU for a number of factors involving PC operating system software and workgroup server operating systems for several years. Particular attention was given to the ***proprietary protocols allowing interoperability*** of PC and server. The

335 *Financial Times* news report, available at: http://www.ft.com/cms/s/0/085a371e-36e5-11df-bc0f-00144feabdc0.html, last accessed 29 December 2014.

336 Case COMP/C-3/39.692 – *IBM Maintenance Services*, Commission Decision dated 13 December 2011.

337 *Microsoft I*, 2007, loc. cit. Fn. 332; *Microsoft*, COMP/C-3/37.792, loc. cit. Fn. 82: Microsoft. Sun's initial complaint regarded the interface information necessary to develop products that operate with Microsoft Windows products.

338 See in detail Chapter 2.3.

Commission saw competitors being handicapped by the lack of interoperability information[339] to fully compete on the client-server vendor markets. The competing products shall obtain the same level of interoperability as Microsoft's own products. Hence, the Commission ordered Microsoft to the compulsory licensing of interoperability information on the basis of Art. 102 TFEU under FRAND-conditions.[340] The Art. 102 TFEU analyses is a mixture of several elements. It heavily relied in its assessment on previously established criteria in *Volvo Veng*[341], *Magill*[342], *IMS Health*[343], *Bronner*[344] and *Ladbroke*[345].[346] However, the criteria for duty to license are not exhaustively established in precedents and other criteria may apply.[347]

In this case, the Commission used ***eight factors*** in total to ***establish a duty to license.***[348] Firstly, the authorities established that the conduct of no disclosure of the interoperability information is part of a tying conduct also examined for abusive unilateral conduct.[349] Secondly, it found that Microsoft discriminated

339 Interoperability information is defined by Article 1 Sec. 1 of the decision as *"the complete and accurate specifications for all the protocols implemented in Windows work group server operating systems and (…) used by Windows work group servers to deliver file and print services and group and user administration services, including the Windows domain controller services, Active Directory services and "Group Policy" services to Windows work group networks."*.

340 *Microsoft*, COMP/C-3/37.792, loc. cit. Fn. 82 was appealed at the CFI.

341 *Volvo v. Erik Veng (UK) Ltd.*; Case 238/87, 1988 E.C.R. 6211, 1989, 4 C.M.L.R. 122 (henceforth cited as: *Volvo v. Veng)*.

342 *Magill*, loc. cit. Fn. 81.

343 *IMS Health GmbH & Co. OHG v. NDC Health GmbH & Co. KG*, Case C-418/01, CFI [2000] ECR I-5039, [2004] 4 C.M.L.R. 28 (henceforth cited as: *IMS Health*).

344 *Oscar Bronner GmbH & Co. KG v. Mediaprint Zeitungs- und Zeitschriftenverlag GmbH & Co. KG*; Case C-7/97 [1998] E.C.R. I-7791, [1999] C.M.L.R. 112 (henceforth cited as: *Oscar Bronner*).

345 *Tierce Ladbroke SA v. Commission*; Case T-504/93, CFI [1995] E.C.R. II-923, [1997] 5 C.M.L.R. 309.

346 *Microsoft I*, 2007, loc. cit. Fn. 332; *Microsoft*, COMP/C-3/37.792, loc. cit. Fn. 82, Ref. 548–554.

347 *Microsoft*, COMP/C-3/37.792, ibd, Ref. 555 and 557 referencing *Micro Leader Business v Commission,* Judgment of the Court of First Instance (3rd Chamber) dated 16 December 1999, Case T-198/98, E.C.R. 1999 p. II-03989 whereas abuse cannot be restricted to one particular set of circumstances.

348 As also listed in *O'Donoghue/Padilla*, 2006, loc. cit. Fn. 222, p. 431.

349 *Microsoft I*, 2007, loc. cit. Fn. 332 and previously *Microsoft*, COMP/C-3/37.792, loc. cit. Fn. 82.

against certain vendors but not all.[350] Thirdly, it is a factor that past voluntary interoperability information disclosure was terminated and not engaged in in the future.[351] This means that there had to be a change in the market player's behavior on the relevant market. Fourthly, the authorities saw a significant competitive importance of interoperability information of client-server hardware that was predicted to lead to elimination of competition.[352] Next, the refusal to license has an adverse impact on consumer welfare and the technical development rate in the market. This is strengthened by the fact that the IT sector in particular the software industry should practice interoperability information disclosure on a regular basis as market standard.[353] However, even under a duty to license, the source code information shall not be disclosed under the remedy.[354] With that, disclosure of interoperability information shall be consistent with EU legislation on software program protection with EU secondary law regulations.[355]

In light of this case, it has become clear that one of the key characteristics of compulsory interoperability information disclosure is indispensability. Competing with the work group server Microsoft product is not possible without the ability of the competing product to interoperate with the proprietary domain architecture.[356] Consequently, a competitor cannot build up enough leverage to exert competitive power on the dominant firm to suppress an abusive conduct opportunity. A second key finding of this case is that the new product criterion as introduced by *IMS Health*[357] has been modified in its interpretation by this decision:

> *"The circumstance relating to the appearance of a new product, as envisaged in Magill and IMS Health, cited in paragraph 107 above*, **cannot be the only parameter** *which determines whether a refusal to license an intellectual property right is capable of causing prejudice to consumers within the meaning of Article 82(b) EC. As that provision states, such prejudice may arise where there is a limitation not only of production or markets, but also of technical development."*[358] *[emphasis added]*

This means that the refusal to license of an IPR is no longer benchmarked to a previously known criterion. With that, the scope of liability is now highly case-

350 *Microsoft*, COMP/C-3/37.792, ibd, Ref. 574 et seqq.
351 *Microsoft*, COMP/C-3/37.792, ibd, Ref. 578 et seqq.
352 *Microsoft*, COMP/C-3/37.792, ibd, para. 586.
353 *Microsoft*, COMP/C-3/37.792, ibd, Ref. 730 et seqq.
354 *Microsoft*, COMP/C-3/37.792, ibd, Ref. 714.
355 *Microsoft*, COMP/C-3/37.792, ibd, Ref. 743 et seqq.
356 *Microsoft I*, 2007, loc. cit. Fn. 332; *Microsoft*, COMP/C-3/37.792, ibd, Ref. 369 to 436.
357 *IMS Health*, loc. cit. Fn. 343.
358 *Microsoft I*, 2007, loc. cit. Fn. 332; *Microsoft*, COMP/C-3/37.792, loc. cit. Fn. 82, Ref. 647.

dependent and subject to the discretionary interpretation of the facts by the courts and the Commission. With that, these competition authorities have received more room to assess on an individual basis whether or not an elimination of effective competition[359] has occurred.

> *"In this case, the Commission had all the more reason to apply Article 82 EC before the elimination of competition on the work group server operating systems market had become a reality because that market is characterised by significant network effects and because the elimination of competition would therefore be difficult to reverse (see recitals 515 to 522 and 533 to the contested decision)"*[360]

In 2008, Microsoft has again been under competition law investigation by the Commission. This time, it was with regard to unilateral anticompetitive conduct by demanding anticompetitive royalty payments for interoperability information. This is the follow-up case to where Microsoft had been previously found to be subject to a duty to supply and authorize the use of interoperability information by competitors. In 2012, the court upheld the Commission's decision and merely adjusted the amount of the fines.[361] This is the last wave of *Microsoft*[362] with regard to interoperability information. The legal proceedings between Microsoft, its competitors, the EU Commission, the Monitoring Trustee[363] and U.S. Courts[364] and the FTC have been exhaustive. One must ask why this proceeding in particular was so resource-demanding. Furthermore, players on the market for cloud computing services may regard the *Microsoft* cases as a precedent from which best practice courses of action can be extracted with regard to the Commission's possible future proceedings on the IT sector. Pursuant to *Microsoft*, the burden of proof needs to be met by the defendant as to why the proprietor of the interoperability information is justified to non-disclosure to competitors.[365] Following the

---

359 *Microsoft I*, 2007, ibd; *Microsoft*, COMP/C-3/37.792, ibd, Ref. 560 to 563.

360 *Microsoft I*, 2007, ibd; *Microsoft*, COMP/C-3/37.792, ibd, Ref. 562.

361 *Microsoft Corp. v. Commission*, Case T-167/08, Judgment of the General Court (Second Chamber) dated 27 June 2012, Ref. 233 et. seqq. (henceforth cited as: *Microsoft II*, 2012).

362 *Microsoft I*, 2007, loc. cit. Fn. 332; *Microsoft*, COMP/C-3/37.792, loc. cit. Fn. 82.

363 The appointment of the Monitoring Trustee shall be considered unlawful due to lack of competence.

364 *Microsoft*, Supplemental Response 21 December 2005 stating violations of transparency, lack of legal certainty. Microsoft also applied to US-American courts to achieve disclosure of its fiercest competitors regarding its correspondence with the European Commission (*NYTimes*, 4 March 2006).

365 *Microsoft*, COMP/C-3/37.792, loc. cit. Fn. 82, Ref. 554.

IMS Health[366] and *Magill*[367] findings, the Commission considers the principles of refusal to deal applicable in exceptional circumstances. However, the Commission withholds Art. 102 TFEU defendants more precise information:

> *„On a general note, there is no persuasiveness to an approach that would advocate the existence of an exhaustive checklist for exceptional circumstances and would have the Commission disregard a limine other circumstances of exceptional character that may deserve to be taken into account when assessing a refusal to supply.“*[368]

For the Art. 102 TFEU defendants, this statement is of great effect for dynamic and static competition in need of impact analysis. Compulsory licensing is an instrument of competition law that strongly intervenes in the proprietary structure of the Art. 102 TFEU defendants. With this large scope of discretion reserved for the Commission regarding IPRs, Art. 102 TFEU defendants are burdened in two ways: Firstly, the legal boundaries of the refusal to deal and essential facilities doctrine are watered down. The exceptional circumstance criterion may include any patent, trade secret, technical know-how or other proprietary possession henceforth. Hinged to that, the scope of interoperability information that needs to be disclosed is unclear.[369] Secondly, by imposing a burden of proof on the Art. 102 TFEU defendant, a significant ***danger of free-riding*** is given. The competitor relying on the bottleneck resource will make a third party access-claim as substantial and exhaustive as possible relying on the Commission to dismiss the claim as much as regarded overarching. This economic calculus is illustrated in the letter dated 15 September 1998 from Richard Green of Sunsoft, Inc. to Paul Maritz, Microsoft demanding the

> *„full set of Active Directory technologies currently on the market [thinking that it is] necessary that such information be provided in a timely manner and on a continuing basis for Active Directory technologies which are to be released to the market in the future.“*.[370]

8.3.1 Application programming interfaces as essential facilities

Application Programming Interfaces (API) is a resource that enables the sending and receiving of data through a platform or operating system and is thus the channel of communication of the software system. API information is protected as a business secret and other IPRs and is a cornerstone of valuable property of a company in this

366 *IMS Health*, loc. cit. Fn. 343.

367 *Magill*, loc. cit. Fn. 81.

368 *Microsoft*, COMP/C-3/37.792, loc. cit. Fn. 82, Ref. 555.

369 *Microsoft*, COMP/C-3/37.792, ibd, Ref. 563 – „discloses ***enough*** interface information“.

370 *Microsoft*, COMP/C-3/37.792, ibd, Footnote 247.

relevant market. The mere refusal to grant technology licenses does not per se constitute an abuse of a dominant position pursuant to Art. 102 TFEU.[371] Nevertheless, exercising the exclusive right granted by an intellectual property right is considered an abusive conduct under Art. 102 TFEU in exceptional cases.[372] This leaves the owner of an essential facility in a dilemma situation. An API is easily protected under IPRs such as a copyright and most certainly as a business secret. With this in mind, the statement of then-Commissioner Kroes goes rather far:

> *„Normally speaking, the source code is not ultimate documentation to anything. (…) This is precisely the reason why programmers are required to provide comprehensive documentation to go along with their source code.“*[373]

The key criterion of an essential facility is the impossibility to duplicate it at reasonable costs. It is of fundamental importance to recognize that an IPR shall only be categorized as such if the information is not duplicable. If a company can access knowledge by generating it, even if with higher internal generation costs than potential licensing costs, the desired information is not an EF but merely a competitive advantage protected by an IPR stipulating exclusivity to the owner.[374]

In light of the Commission's conduct up to date, in particular the strong influence of the precedents *Magill*[375], *Bronner*[376] and *IMS Health*[377] remains. For a potential defendant, it is important to see that the findings of the precedents may be applied in a directional sense. If projecting into the future an elimination of competition may occur that already gives rise to proceedings under Art. 102 TFEU.[378]

---

371 *Volvo v. Veng*, loc. cit. Fn. 341.

372 *Magill*, loc. cit. Fn. 81.

373 *BBC News* dated 26 January 2006 available under: http://news.bbc.co.uk/2/hi/business/4649348.stm, last accessed 29 December 2014.

374 With different opinion: *Antonelli*, Technological Knowledge as an Essential Facility, Working paper No. 04/2005 of the Dipartimento di Economia, S. Cognetti de Martiis, Laboratorio di Economia dell'Innovazione, Franco Monigliano, 2005.

375 *Magill*, loc. cit. Fn. 81.

376 *Oscar Bronner*, loc. cit. Fn. 344.

377 *IMS Health*, loc. cit. Fn. 343.

378 *Microsoft I*, 2007, loc. cit. Fn. 332; *Microsoft*, COMP/C-3/37.792, loc. cit. Fn. 82, Ref. 561 and *Ahlborn/Evans*, The Microsoft Judgment and its Implications for Competition Policy Towards Dominant Firms in Europe, Antitrust Law Journal Vol. 75 No. 3, 2009, also available at http://papers.ssrn.com/sol3/papers.cfm?abstract_id=1115867##, last accessed 23 October 2012.

8.3.2 Adequate remuneration for interoperability information

Determining the adequate remuneration for interoperability information, the charged amount for access must allow "*its users to compete viably with Microsoft's work group server operating system. Moreover, according to recital 1008(ii) to the 2004 decision, **such remuneration should not reflect the strategic value** stemming from Microsoft's market power in the client PC operating system market or in the work group server operating system market.*"[379] *[emphasis added]* With this, the question of value calculation is raised. The value of the information considered an essential input in light of Art. 102 TFEU may have a strategic value or an intrinsic value.[380] In result, the court found that the remedy compelling the defendant to make interoperability information available and with that allow the development and distribution of work group server related products. This must simultaneously exclude the possibility of the defendant to make earnings that are comparable to those made based on the unilateral conduct infringing Art. 102 TFEU.[381]

8.3.3 New product test and objective justification

It is noteworthy that the analysis in *Microsoft*[382] does no longer rely on the criterion of a limitation of technical development within the scope of the new product test.

> *"In that regard, it should be recalled that, in order for the refusal by an undertaking which owns a copyright to give access to a product or service indispensable for carrying on a particular business to be regarded as abuse, it is sufficient that three cumulative conditions be satisfied, namely that that refusal is preventing the emergence of a new product for which there is a potential consumer demand, that it is unjustified and that it is such as to exclude any competition on a secondary market (Case C-418/01 IMS Health [2004] ECR I-5039, paragraph 38).*"[383]

With regard to *Microsoft I*[384], the decision in *Microsoft II*[385] states the satisfaction of the cumulatively required conditions based on the findings of *IMS Health*[386] and the new product test. In contrast, *Microsoft I* explicitly allow other criteria alongside the new product test for the Art. 102 TFEU assessments.

---

379 *Microsoft II*, 2012, loc. cit. 361, Ref. 29 with reference to *Microsoft I*, 2007, loc. cit. Fn. 332; *Microsoft*, COMP/C-3/37.792, loc. cit. Fn. 82.

380 *Microsoft II*, 2012, loc. cit. 361, Ref. 138.

381 *Microsoft II*, 2012, ibd, Ref. 141.

382 *Microsoft II*, 2012, ibd, 361.

383 *Microsoft II*, 2012, ibd, Ref. 139.

384 *Microsoft I*, 2007, loc. cit. Fn. 332; *Microsoft*, COMP/C-3/37.792, loc. cit. Fn. 82.

385 *Microsoft II*, 2012, loc. cit. 361.

386 *IMS Health*, loc. cit. Fn. 343.

„In this case, it has been found that, since the three cumulative condItions mentioned in paragraph 139 above were satisfied, Microsoft's refusal to give access to the interoperability information and to authorise its use was abusive (see, to that effect, Microsoft v Commission, paragraph 18 above, paragraphs 711 and 712).“[387]

This unsystematic interpretation of the new product test raised a total of three objecting arguments in Microsoft's appeal against the Commission's decision. The defendant argued that the complaint issued by Sun Microsystems never requested the disclosure themselves. Secondly, the criteria of the new product test were not followed through and applied in the case before the Commission and thirdly, TRIPS regulations were not followed.[388] Most importantly, the Commission never explicitly identified what product was hindered from emerging due to the undisclosed interoperability information.

Even if the hurdle of the new product test is cleared, the refusal to deal must have an objective justification in order to avoid Art. 102 TFEU liabilities. The core argument for a justification is that the interoperability information is protected by IP. And with that, a refusal to share IP is necessary in order to safeguard incentives to innovate:

"The objective justification for Microsoft's refusal to disclose its intellectual property rights is self-evident: those rights are meant to protect the outcome of billions of dollars of R&D investments in software features, functions and technologies. This is the essence of intellectual property right protection. Disclosure would negate that protection and eliminate future incentives to invest in the creation of more intellectual property."[389]

This argumentation did not persuade the Commission and its finding was in essence upheld by the CFI. Stipulating an obligation to disclose does not only hinder innovation by competitors,[390] it on top also enhances innovation because it reestablishes a level playing field for competitive pressure[391]. Basically, competitive forces were reintroduced to the relevant market by taking away the advantage Microsoft has worked for through R&D and business performance.

387 *Microsoft II*, 2012, loc. cit. 361, Ref. 140.

388 *Microsoft I*, 2007, loc. cit. Fn. 332.

389 *Microsoft*, COMP/C-3/37.792, loc. cit. Fn. 82, Ref. 709, quoting NERA report to Microsoft's submission on 17 October 2003.

390 *Microsoft*, COMP/C-3/37.792, ibd, Ref. 712.

391 *Microsoft*, COMP/C-3/37.792, ibd, Ref. 725.

8.3.4 Summarizing Comments on Microsoft I and Microsoft II

In total, the fines and penalty payments[392] stemming from the cases *Microsoft I* and *Microsoft II*[393] amount to over 1.6 billion EUR (497 million EUR[394] + 280.5 million EUR[395] + 860 million EUR[396]).

> *"It's not about the money for Microsoft, it's not about the money for the commission or the other applicants (...)" – Nicolas Petit, Professor of Law, University of Liege.*

If it is not about the money – what is it about? This case is concerned with ***interoperability information***, the ***methodological aspects*** of the cases with regard to the effects-based approach and the ***consequences for investment security***. The higher the market considers the value of the information, the more important the handling of the interface information with regard to value determination becomes. On the value of interoperability information, the case states:

> *"As to the merits of this plea, it should be made clear, as a preliminary point, that the distinction between the strategic value and the intrinsic value of the technologies covered by the contested decision is a basic premise of the assessment of the reasonableness of any remuneration charged by Microsoft for allowing access to, and use of, the interoperability information."*[397]

The process of information disclosure is not clear. Specific computer engineering skills may become necessary for the process of disclosure. Secondly, the scope of information compelled to disclose is unclear. During the disclosure, information fragments and tranches of information that is not subject to disclosure must be separated for compliance with the verdict. Next, it must be determined to whom information is disclosed. Linking to this, access to disclosed information must be administered. Lastly, it must be determined how the recipient of the information must compensate the disclosing defendant and calculate the adequate amount of remuneration under FRAND terms. Applying both *Microsoft I* and *II* simultaneously raises questions of legal certainty. As illustrated above, *Microsoft I* and *II*

392 Interestingly, the court does not see a given cause to methodologically distinguish between the concept of a 'fine' and a 'penalty payment', see *Microsoft II*, 2012, loc. cit. 361, Ref. 94.

393 *Microsoft II*, 2012, ibd.

394 Tying and Interoperability fines – *Microsoft I*, 2007, loc. cit. Fn. 332; *Microsoft*, COMP/C-3/37.792, loc. cit. Fn. 82.

395 Interoperability information not provided accurately and lacking completeness, penalty payment related to *Microsoft I*, 2007, loc. cit. Fn. 332; *Microsoft*, COMP/C-3/37.792, loc. cit. Fn. 82.

396 The second penalty payment of 899 million EUR has been reduced to 860 million EUR regarding royalty payments for interoperability information.

397 *Microsoft II*, 2012, loc. cit. 361, Ref. 138.

have incorporated several components into their analysis that may be categorized as either form-based or effects-based. The following overview chart briefly illustrates ***the methodological category of the criterion*** and whether they have been applied consistently throughout the cases:

Fig. 14: Microsoft I and II methodology comparison

Criterion	*Microsoft I*	*Microsoft II*	*Application*
Market share as a decisive component	☒[398]	☐	The acquisition of a high market share on the relevant market is a classic form-based approach tool to establish dominance of the defendant. It disregards the possibility of market dominance out of a small market share position and is strongly rooted in the Structure-Conduct-Performance-Paradigm.
The new product test	☒[399]	☒[400]	The new product test is used as a precedent in both cases, but in rather different context. The reference in *Microsoft II* is more static and does not account for the more open interpretation provided by *Microsoft I* allowing to examine the limitations of technical development as a factor.
Strong reliance on EFD and RTD precedents	☒[401]	☐	*Microsoft I* references *Volvo v. Veng, Magill*[402], *IMS Health, Bronner*[403] *and Ladbroke.* *Microsoft II* only relies briefly on *IMS Health*[404] and formally on the new product test.
Elimination of effective competition	☒[405]	☒[406]	The criterion of Art. 102 TFEU has been extended by both decisions. *Microsoft I* saw cause given for a pre-empt interference through the Commission by seeing a hypothetical and future elimination of competitors on the market. *Microsoft II* established the criteria for adequate remuneration linked to the dominance of the defendant.

398 *Microsoft I*, 2007, loc. cit. Fn. 332; *Microsoft*, COMP/C-3/37.792, 2004, Ref. 664.

399 *Microsoft II*, 2012, loc. cit. Fn. 361, Ref. 647.

400 *Microsoft II*, 2012, ibd, Ref. 139.

401 *Microsoft I*, 2007, loc. cit. Fn. 332; *Microsoft*, COMP/C-3/37.792, 2004, Ref. 548–554.

402 *Magill*, loc. cit. Fn. 81.

403 *Oscar Bronner*, loc. cit. Fn. 344.

404 *IMS Health*, loc. cit. Fn. 343.

405 *Microsoft I*, 2007, loc. cit. Fn. 332; *Microsoft*, COMP/C-3/37.792, 2004, Ref. 562.

406 *Microsoft II*, 2012, loc. cit. 361, Ref. 29.

The incongruous methodological approach in both cases illustrates the lack of a clear preference and consistent application of the effects-based approach. With regard to legal certainty and the clarity of the law, this set of cases illustrates how the transition form the form-based approach to the effects-based approach is particularly sensitive. The decisions must evolve to adopting the new method but most not deviate from precedents in an unmethodical way to safeguard the predictability and reliability of the law and with that, the defendant's ability of risk calculation.

Investment security has been an overriding concern of the cases by the defendant and the parties in support[407] of the defendant. The most problematic concern of the defendant – dismissed by the court in *Microsoft II*[408] – is the lack of clear instructions claimed by the defendant: *"First, the Commission infringed its obligation to specify positively what Microsoft had to do in order to comply with Article 5(a) of the 2004 decision."*.[409] In consequence, *Microsoft II* also incorporated a procedural complaint regarding the Commission's infringement of Art. 24 Directive 1/2003, the right of defense.[410] Complaints regarding a lack of clarity of how to comply with a decision are a risk. As the supporting party *CompTIA*[411] established in the case, the uncertainty poses a risk of discouraging innovation to the detriment of consumers.[412]

The verdict in *Microsoft I* has been revealed to have been a decision ***voted 6 to 7***.[413] This does not only illustrate the very controversial decision's nature amongst the judges, but also that it indicates a lack of a clear majority position with regard to predicting future outcomes of lawsuits. It also shows that the Directorate-Generale for competition will apply an increasingly firm hand regard to Art. 102 TFEU enforcement to the IT sector. In 2012, new investigations of the Commission with regard to browser choice commitments made in 2009 were launched.[414]

---

407 Most notably CompTIA, see *Microsoft II*, 2012, loc. cit. 361, Ref. 77.

408 *Microsoft II*, 2012, loc. cit. 361.

409 *Microsoft II*, 2012, ibd, Ref. 74.

410 *Microsoft II*, 2012, ibd, Ref. 179 et seqq.

411 CompTIA stands for The Computing Technology Industry Association, Inc.

412 *Microsoft II*, 2012, ibd, Ref. 77.

413 *Bodoni/Newman*, at *Bloomberg*, Microsoft Settled EU Case Not Knowing Vote Was 7 to 6, dated 5 September 2008, also available at http://www.bloomberg.com/apps/news?pid=newsarchive&sid=avY9xtzrv2Zs&refer=e, last accessed 19 October 2012 2008.

414 *EU Commission*, press release dated 17 July 2012 and available at: http://europa.eu/rapid/pressReleasesAction.do?reference=IP/12/800.

8.4 Interoperability as a sound policy goal

Pursuant to *Gasser/Palfrey*, interoperability contributes to innovation, increased number of consumer choice through low switching costs, ease of use and access to content and diversity on the product market. Nevertheless, *Gasser/Palfrey* could not identify a causal link between interoperability and innovation due to lack of empirical proof.[415] The policy for the incentive structure for the degree of interoperability shall be based on the specific market structure analyzing the strength of the market, the density of network effects and the likelihood of lock-in effects. This raises the subsequent question of what type of innovation is desired on the market.

Radical innovation is fostered by a low level of interoperability, ***incremental innovation*** fostered by high level of innovation and may set network effects free.[416] The vast majority of innovative achievements are of incremental nature. A product is improved step-by-step through innovation and follow-up innovation. The best example for this is the development of the motorized vehicle, like commercial cars. Thousands of patents link together to always marginally improve the product further for a better overall product. Radical innovation seldom occurs. It represents a leapfrog innovation that does not build upon previous incremental steps, it rather overhauls the systematics of follow-up innovation with a new idea. An example is the iPod after the portable CD-players. With regard to cloud computing, the level of interoperability is relevant for two reasons. Firstly, a high level of interoperability may compromise the security and defense mechanisms of the IT infrastructure from a technical perspective. Secondly, interoperability is a relevant legal criterion for consumer switching costs and lock-in effects. The two goals are opposing each other in this sector. Consequently, we must ask whether interoperability is a sound policy goal for the cloud computing market from a competition law perspective. Making a high level of interoperability a policy priority must be made subject of a cost-benefit analysis. We must ask what we can obtain by a low level of interoperability and with a high level of interoperability:

---

415 *Gasser/Palfrey*, 2007, loc. cit. Fn. 13, p. 12.

416 *Gasser/Palfrey*, 2007, ibd, p. 13.

Fig. 15: Degrees of interoperability

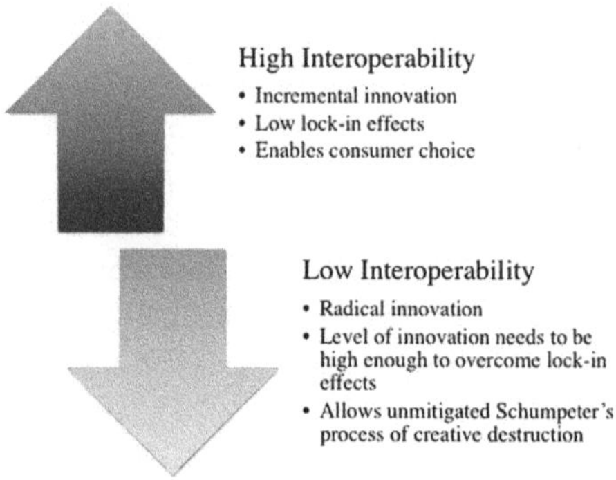

From a competition law perspective, low interoperability may channel a virtual monopolist. The creation and control of an interface or any other IP protected by a patent, copyright or trade secret makes it difficult for a competitor to erode network effects of the incumbent through duplication. A viable chance of competitive survival is an innovation in the form of a superior technology replacing the former standard and becoming the new leader.[417] This struggle is currently visible on the basis of patent packages. In the mobile devices industry, patent packages and licenses are at the heart of patent litigation proceedings enabling interoperability with other components of mobile devices and broadband internet access.

So far, the regulatory problem of fostering incremental or radical innovation has been seen as alternatives to one another. Either a mechanism is introduced to establish incentive mechanisms for incremental or radical innovation in the market. If improvement in existing product markets through incremental innovation may exist parallel to innovative forces in a new product market, the resources need not be allocated exclusively for one or the other type of incentive mechanism. In consequence, the trade-off decision would be shaped differently. There are relatively few cases touching upon radical innovation and also have transatlantic bearing. But if that occurs, the policy understandings between the EU and the U.S. play an important role. In the U.S. and in particular in Silicon Valley, the emphasis on individual accomplishment and economic freedom is comparatively higher than in the EU. Also, the private sector's needs for govern-

417 *Giffordal/Kudrle*, Antitrust Approaches to Dynamically Competitive Industries in the United States and the European Union, Journal of Competition Law & Economics, September 2011, p. 5.

mental regulation on the level of public ordering are substantially lower in the U.S. The policy cultures are different. The U.S. business mentality favors and values the overhauling forces of radical innovation. In the EU, the basis of policies is to provide the market a strong basic frame in which the market players may act within the rules. The consequence of this historically shaped policy culture is an automatic lean towards incremental over radical innovation in the EU.[418] The cases *Microsoft I* and *II* illustrate the preference of high interoperability and small and incremental innovation within EU competition law policy:

> *"In Microsoft, the Commission and the General Court refused to follow Microsoft's line of argumentation, which would have privileged breakthrough innovation and competition for the market at the expense of incremental innovation and competition in the market."*[419]

An additional layer to this regulatory problem is the source of interoperability information. The source of the information may be a patent but also a trade or business secret of the company. Antitrust or competition law obliging the owner to disclose this information is an intrusion into the sphere of the owner on different levels depending on the nature of the right protecting the information:

Fig. 16: Circles of intrusion for interoperability information

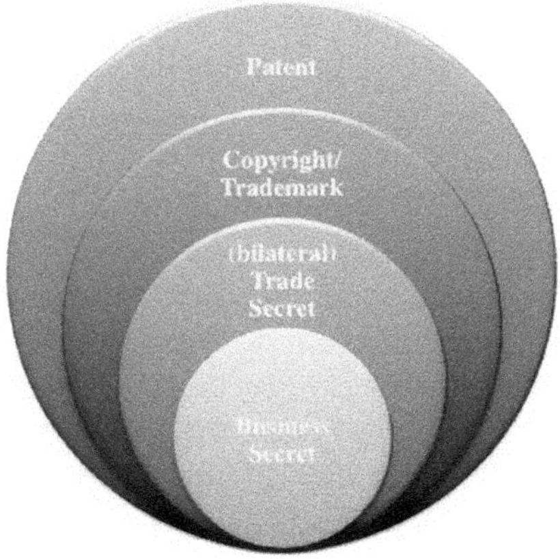

418 An early example on interoperability information and the incremental innovation nature of the policy is EC Directive 91/250/EEC dated 14 May 1991, Art. 5 para. 3 and Art. 6.

419 *Sluijs/Larouche/Sauter*, 2012, loc. cit. Fn. 3, p. 23.

Interoperability can only be made possible if information is shared. The cost-benefit-analysis must account for the source of this information. Only that way can a trade-off be made, considering a balancing test of the interests that must be incorporated into the decision. Having competition law oblige the owner to disclose information via a compulsory license is the outer circle of intrusion. Copyright and trademark information may also be a source of interoperability information, i.e. the basis of an individual design for cable plugs or other synchronizing interfaces. Trademark and copyright is a more internal company value given its brand value and product identification value on the market. It links the product to an identity on the market. Business and trade secrets are at the innermost of the circle that a company wishes to protect. Hence, an intrusion through competition/antitrust law will be seen as a violation of the core of the company.

As discussed by *Gasser/Palfrey* for other sectors[420], interoperability can be achieved via numerous mechanisms. They may be clustered into the operating levels of public and private ordering and a unilateral or cooperative approach.[421] *Gasser/Palfrey* concludes that interoperability issues are best solved by private actors. Governmental interferences through public ordering is generally not necessary – with the explicit exception of Art. 102 TFEU proceedings.[422]. Interoperability information allows the owner to leverage the scope of the proprietary right beyond the legal boundaries of IP. As *Välimäki/Oksanen* pointed out, the incentive structures can be handled via IP law, competition law or consumer protection law.[423]

Examining the incentive mechanisms, we must distinguish between static and dynamic competition incentives. The following scenario based on Google's search algorithm shall provide an example of incentive mechanism analysis that would favorably respond to dynamic competition incentives: Google's search engine algorithm is self-reinforcing itself with every search request run through the program perpetuating the strong position with every additional search conducted. This is especially beneficial for behavioral advertising. The incentive to compete with this algorithm is not very high since establishing a comparable data basis to Google's is a significant barrier to entry. The incentive to invent a

420 The paper by *Gasser/Palfrey* presented three case studies on (1) DRM-protected music distribution, (2) digital identity systems and (3) mash-up web services.

421 *Gasser/Palfrey*, 2007, loc. cit. Fn. 13, p. 20 et. seqq.

422 *Gasser/Palfrey*, 2007, ibd, p. 27.

423 *Välimäki/Oksanen*, DRM Interoperability and Intellectual Property Policy in Europe, European Intellectual Property Review 11/2006, Vol. 26 No. 11, pp. 562–568, p. 567.

new form of search engine is high with the prospect of a temporary monopoly on this market.

On the level of choice of rules, it must be weighed whether static or dynamic competition incentives shall be encouraged by the law to be implemented. The goal of the decision-making process must be incorporated into the concrete market scenario. Whether the purpose of a legal intervention is to foster a long-term policy objective or to overcome a short-term market failure, it matters for the correct choice of legal tool. Furthermore, it matters to what degree the potential mechanism to be implemented trespass the barriers of property rights granted to the owner. This interference can consequently lead to a diminished property right value. With focus on disclosure obligations, it must be subject to empirical research whether an obligation to disclose constitutes a causal link to a higher level of interoperability in the relevant market. Equally so, it must be subject to empirical assessment whether and to what degree an *ex ante* obligation to disclose eliminates the benefits of radical innovation.

8.5 Summary

For cloud service providers, interoperability is a two-edged sword. On the one hand, it ensures that data migration is easy for customers and that lock-in effects are kept low. On the other hand, interoperability of the systems poses a data security risk. If systems cannot interface, the system has better defense mechanisms against attacks.

The definition of interoperability is in flux and depends on the jurisdiction in question. The definition can be extensively applied to cover a vast amount of scenarios. With that, the EU Commission has room for discretion in assessing the cases individually. Special attention must be paid to the possibility of a compulsory license remedy through Art. 102 TFEU for application programming interfaces. Even though such license is linked to remuneration on FRAND-terms, the foregone temporary monopoly and the value of having to assist your competitor in linking to your product is a large risk. Furthermore, FRAND-compensation does not cover losing the competitive advantage of having exclusive information in the race of innovations. Targeting interoperability information as a potential subject to compulsory licensing is also an indicator for the type of innovation competition law preferences. The policy mentalities across the Atlantic are different and with that, the type of market behavior that is fostered changes too. Incremental innovation is a mirror of the way business is done in Continental Europe. Progress is embedded in social and economic security to the highest degree possible. As a general observation, EU policies assume a more risk adverse business behavior. Especially in comparison to the start-up culture in Silicon Valley, this understanding of innovation and risk taking is hard to stomach because of its vast difference in business culture. But by mutually understanding these preferences and underlying policy assumptions the transatlantic dialogue will gain quality.

Part III: Cloud computing and data privacy law

9 Cloud computing and the new EU data privacy regulation

The new data privacy regulations are heavily intertwined with innovations driven by cloud computing. Cloud computing affects business in the way information is structured, organized, stored and accessed worldwide. This chapter examines the key provisions of the newly enacted General Data Protection Regulation[424] ("GDPR") dated 27 April 2016 and their impact on European and U.S. business. The GDPR will come into effect on 25 May 2018. Compliance with these new provisions requires restructuring efforts, new notification and reporting lines as well as an active engagement with the data subject. With sanctioning fines at a record high, compliance has become more and more important.

9.1 The legislative process of the GDPR

On 25 January 2012, the EU Commission proposed a comprehensive reform of the EU's 1995 data protection rules set forth in the Directive 95/46/EC[425]. The aim of the reform is to adjust the existing legal framework for technological progress, globalization and consolidate the legal landscape to one set of rules for the EU internal market. One of the main objectives of the EU is to reinforce consumer confidence in online services. On 12 March 2014, the European Parliament voted in very strong favor of the proposed new Directive[426] and Regulation[427]. The GDPR targets data processing operations in the context of civil use. The new Directive stipulates general data protection principles and rules for police and judicial. The GDPR has been adopted on 27 April 2016 and was published in the Official Journal of the European Union on 4 May 2016.[428] Its rules will enter into effect on 25 May 2018, giving the addressees of the Regulation two years to place their data

---

424 For the final version of the GDPR see O.J. L 119/1 dated 4 May 2016, available at: http://eur-lex.europa.eu/legal-content/EN/TXT/PDF/?uri=CELEX:32016R0679&from=EN, last accessed 22 May 2016.

425 Directive 95/46/EC, loc. cit. Fn. 182, p. 31–50.

426 The draft for the Directive is available at: http://eur-lex.europa.eu/legal-content/EN/TXT/PDF/?uri=CELEX:52012PC0010&from=en, last accessed 16 July 2014.

427 The draft for the Regulation is available at: http://ec.europa.eu/justice/data-protection/document/review2012/com_2012_11_en.pdf, last accessed 16 January 2014.

428 See for the full source loc. cit. Fn. 424.

protection and privacy practices into compliance with the GDPR. The following analysis will focus solely on the new data privacy regulations stipulated by the GDPR. The laws of data privacy standards for criminal investigation stipulated by the new Directive are not considered in this analysis.

9.2 Overview of key amendments

The following chapter gives a brief introduction to the main amendments the GDPR proposes.

The territorial scope of the GDPR will be expanded. EU data privacy rules shall apply to non-EU companies as well. The rules of the GDPR shall apply if personal data is handled abroad by companies that are present with business in the EU market and offer their services to EU citizens. A single set of rules on data protection shall be valid across the EU and do not require transposition into national laws. Organizations will only have to deal with a single national data protection authority in the EU country where they have their main establishment. Likewise, people can refer to the data protection authority in their country, even when a company based outside the EU processes their personal data. Independent national data protection authorities will be strengthened so they can better enforce the EU rules in their home countries. They will be empowered to fine companies that violate EU data protection rules. This can lead to penalties of up to €20 million or up to 4 % of the global annual turnover of a company, whichever is higher (Art. 83 GDPR). Before the GDPR, data protection authorities' fining competence was mostly limited to administrative fines capped as a misdemeanor offence. This level of sanctioning gives data controllers and data processors[429] a strong compliance incentive. Corporations will face increasing responsibility and accountability for processing personal data. They must be compliant with notification and reporting structure requirements as stipulated by the GDPR for increasingly strict requirements. The GDPR places large emphasis on consumer protection. From a technical perspective, data portability will be a key element of the new laws. Consumers will have easier access to their own data and be able to transfer personal data from one service provider to another more easily. A 'right to be forgotten' gives consumers the option of having their data deleted if there are no legitimate

429 The data controller is the entity that determines the purposes and means of the data processing activities; the data processor is the entity that processes the data on behalf of the data controller and per the data controller's instructions (Art. 4 para. 7 and 8 GDPR).

grounds for retaining it. Wherever consent is required for sensitive data to be processed, it is clarified that it has to be given explicitly, rather than assumed. Non-sensitive personal data processing has to be based on the data subject's unambiguous consent. The following chapters analyze the key new provisions in greater detail.

9.3 Right to be forgotten

On 13 May 2014, the Court of Justice of the European Union ruled in favor of the right to be forgotten.[430] The decision is highly controversial and has added traction to the discussion on data privacy reforms. The CJEU ruling still applies the standards of the Directive 95/46/EC. In this case, a Spanish citizen lodged a complaint against a Spanish newspaper, Google Spain and Google Inc. with the national data protection agency in Spain in 2010. The newspaper article reported about the plaintiff's home and an auction notice of repossession. He claimed that these events have been completely resolved for years. Consequently, reference to these past events is irrelevant and infringes his privacy rights. The plaintiff requested that the newspaper removed information that makes him personally identifiable so that he would no longer appear in the article and that Google Spain or Google Inc. be obligated to remove his personal data so he would no longer appear in the search results list.[431]

The Spanish court referred the case to the CJEU. The CJEU confirmed a Spanish court's decision. The ruling was that hyperlinks to approximately 100 newspaper articles to be removed from the search engine. The newspaper articles itself did not have to be changed, i.e. the content of the articles remained intact.[432] This means that the right to be forgotten triggers the obligation to de-index or de-list content from the search engine. The CJEU argued with three main points in its ruling.

On territoriality:

> *"Even if the physical server of a company processing data is located outside Europe, EU rules apply to search engine operators if they have a branch or subsidiary in a Member State which promotes the selling of advertising space offered by the search engine."*[433]

430 *Google/Costeja,* C-131/12, loc. cit. Fn. 4.

431 *Google/Costeja,* C-131/12, loc. cit. Fn. 4., Ref. 14–19.

432 *Google/Costeja,* C-131/12, ibd, Ref. 88.

433 *EU Council,* press release No. 10578/14), loc. cit. Fn. 5, Ref. 56 to 59.

On applicability of EU data protection rules to search engines:

> *"Search engines are controllers of personal data. Google can therefore not escape its responsibilities before European law when handling personal data by saying it is a search engine. EU data protection law applies and so does the right to be forgotten."*[434]

On the right to be forgotten:

> *"Individuals have the right – under certain conditions – to ask search engines to remove links with personal information about them. This applies where the information is inaccurate, inadequate, irrelevant or excessive for the purposes of the data processing."*[435]

> *"(...) the right to be forgotten is not absolute but will always need to be balanced against other fundamental rights, such as the freedom of expression and of the media. (...) A case-by-case assessment is needed considering the type of information in question, its sensitivity for the individual's private live and the interest of the public in having access to that information and the role of the person requesting the deletion plays in public life."*[436]

The ruling has stirred controversial discussion and numerous aspects of the ruling raise subsequent questions. In the following, I examine the legislative process of the right to be forgotten by Art. 17 GDPR in the Commission Proposal and compare it to the proposed text of the European Parliament Vote. Furthermore, I examine the burden of proof established in the right be forgotten and examine the defendants' rights and the technical feasibility of the claim.

9.3.1 The legislative process of Art. 17 GDPR

Art. 12 Directive 95/46/EC does not stipulate an explicit right to be forgotten. It merely gives the person a right to demand that personal data be deleted once the data is no longer necessary. Art. 17 GDPR explicitly states that an EU citizen has a right to be erased from the internet under certain conditions. The Commission Proposal[437] and the European Parliament Vote[438] drafted the right to be forgotten with different nuances. The differences are highlighted below:

---

434 *EU Council*, press release No. 10578/14, ibd, Ref. 20.

435 *EU Council*, press release No. 10578/14, ibd, Ref. 93.

436 *EU Council*, press release No. 10578/14, ibd, Ref. 85.

437 *EU Commission*, General Data Protection Regulation, loc. cit. Fn. 6.

438 *European Parliament*, Draft Report on the proposal for a regulation of the European Parliament and of the Council on the protection of individual with regard to the processing of personal data and on the free movement of such data (General Data Protection Regulation); (COM(2012)0011–C7-0025/2012–2012/0011(COD); dated 17 December 2012 (henceforth cited as: *European Parliament*, European Parliament Vote).

Commission Proposal[439]	**European Parliament Vote**[440]
Article 17: Right to be forgotten and to erasure	*Article 17: Right to erasure*
1. The data subject shall have the right to obtain from the controller the erasure of personal data relating to them and the abstention from further dissemination of such data, especially in relation to personal data which are made available by the data subject while he or she was a child, where one of the following grounds applies:	1. The data subject shall have the right to obtain from the controller the erasure of personal data relating to them and the abstention from further dissemination of such data, where one of the following grounds applies:
2. Where the controller referred to in paragraph 1 has made the personal data public, it shall take all reasonable steps, including technical measures, in relation to data for the publication of which the controller is responsible, to inform third parties which are processing such data, that a data subject requests them to erase any links to, or copy or replication of that personal data. Where the controller has authorised a third party publication of personal data, the controller shall be considered responsible for that publication.	2. Where the controller referred to in paragraph 1 has transferred or made the personal data public without a justification based on Article 6 (1), it shall take all necessary steps to have the data erased, without prejudice to Article 77. 2a. Any measures for erasure of published personal data shall respect the right to freedom of expression, as referred to in Article 80.
4. Instead of erasure, the controller shall restrict processing of personal data where:	4. Instead of erasure, the controller shall restrict processing of personal data in such a way that it is not subject to the normal data access and processing operations of the controller and can not be changed anymore, where:
(d) the data subject requests to transmit the personal data into another automated processing system in accordance with Article 18(2).	(d) the data subject requests to transmit the personal data into another automated processing system in accordance with Articlel 5(2) and 2a.

439 Available at: http://ec.europa.eu/justice/data-protection/document/review2012/com_2012_11_en.pdf, last accessed 16 January 2014.

440 Available at: http://www.europarl.europa.eu/meetdocs/2009_2014/documents/libe/pr/922/922387/922387en.pdf, last accessed 20 July 2014.

5. Personal data referred to in paragraph 4 may, with the exception of storage, only be processed for purposes of proof, or with the data subject's consent, or for the protection of the rights of another natural or legal person or for an objective of public interest.	5. Personal data referred to in paragraph 4 may, with the exception of storage, only be processed for purposes of proof, or with the data subject's consent, or for the protection of the rights of a natural or legal person or for compliance with a legal obligation to process the personal data by the Union or national law to which the controller is subject.
9. The Commission shall be empowered to adopt delegated acts in accordance with Article 86 for the purpose of further specifying:	9. The Commission shall be empowered to adopt, after requesting an opinion of the European Data Protection Board, delegated acts in accordance with Article 86 for the purpose of further specifying:
(b) the conditions for deleting links, copies or replications of personal data from publicly available communication services as referred to in paragraph 2;	(b) the conditions for deleting personal data from publicly available communication services as referred to in paragraph 2;

The main discussion revolves around the question of balancing the data subject's right to be forgotten against the freedom of speech and expression. Furthermore, the *European Parliament Vote* emphasizes that the right to be forgotten must apply to all data subjects equally and not just to adults.[441] Also, the *European Parliament Vote* emphasized that the right to be forgotten must be balanced against other rights. A data subject exercising this right must be benchmarked against how the publication of the personal data took place. If personal data was initially published on legal grounds "*a 'right to be forgotten' is neither realistic nor legitimate*"[442]. Legal grounds for a third party processing this personal data must exist. But nevertheless, exercising the right to be forgotten under the premise of an initially lawful disclosure shall be linked to stricter criteria. The second mayor point of discussion is the data controller's duties.[443] The data controller's action is the result of the decision after weighing public interest against the data subject's right to be forgotten. The data controller's duties shall include manag-

441 *European Parliament*, European Parliament Vote, Justification for amendment at Art. 17 para. 1.

442 *European Parliament*, European Parliament Vote, Justification for amendment at Art. 17 para. 2.

443 *European Parliament*, European Parliament Vote, Justification for amendment at Art. 17 para. 2 and 4.

ing the data subject's data and handle the procedure after a privacy breach has been detected. The data controller enables the data subject to get in touch with any third parties to remedy the situation. For corporations, the discussion between the European Commission and the European Parliament vote illustrates two things: Firstly, the ***data controller*** will hold a key position with regard to data privacy law compliance and will remain the key responsible entity for the data processing activities. This function is further highlighted by the fact that Art. 17 GDPR is linked to Art. 3 GDPR, detailing the GDPR's territorial scope. The physical location of the server is irrelevant for the application of Art. 17 GDPR. This means that corporations must spend additional resources to get non-EU data controllers up to speed with EU data privacy laws as well. An additional administrative burden will be Art. 7 GDPR, stipulating the consent requirements.[444] Their notification and process compliance will be key under the new laws. Secondly, the ***burden of proof*** for a right to be forgotten-claim is hard to crystalize. It is clear that these cases will be individual ones and that the ECJ intends to decide on a case-by-case analysis. It is also clear that the right to be forgotten will be balanced against the freedom of expression and speech. The final version of Art. 17 GDPR is a relatively strict de-indexing obligation with few caveats for the balancing text described above. It remains unclear how the parties can underscore their position with evidentiary support to meet their respective burden of proof.

9.3.2 The burden of proof: When will the internet forget you?

The *Google Decision* based its findings on Directive 95/46/EC. The judgment allocated the burden of proof in favor of the plaintiff. The company must demonstrate that the data cannot be deleted because it is still needed or is still relevant. It is not upon the data subject to show that the personal data can be deleted because it is no longer needed or no longer relevant. The emphasis of individual justice in Art. 17 GDPR-proceedings shows that the factors established in the *Google Decision* will likely function as precedent. The fact that this ruling is still based on the Directive 95/46/EC is not a concern. Art. 17 GDPR explicitly states a right to be forgotten. The *Google Decision* based on Art. 12 Directive 95/46/EC does not stipulate data erasure explicitly. The Commission perceived the *Google Decision* as a supportive force behind the Art. 17 GDPR proposal. The verdict still holds under the new GDPR rules.

444 See below 9.4 for how the data controller obtains consent from the data subject to process personal data.

The factors considered in the analysis of the right to be forgotten are (i) the emphasis on individual justice, (ii), the nature of the information in question, (iii) the sensitivity of information for the person's private life, (iv) the personality in question, (v) the public's interest in having that specific information available and (vi) how much time passed since the original reference to the person.[445] Consequently, the balancing test distributes the burden of proof along these five criteria.

9.3.3 The defendant: Content provider or search engine?

One of the most surprising twists of the *Google Decision* is that the Spanish newspaper did not have to change any of its articles that included information about the plaintiff. But the court obligated Google – being the search engine and not the content provider itself – to take down the newspaper articles from the search result list.

The *Google Decision* press release states: *"The Spanish citizens' data may still be accessible but is no longer ubiquitous."*[446] This is a very nebulous understanding of the right to be forgotten. If the plaintiff's personal data shall be completely inaccessible, the content provider is the primary defendant to enforce the plaintiff's claim. But if the court finds that – after considering freedom of expression and speech against the plaintiff's right to privacy – there is a remaining interest in accessibility, the search engine is the correct defendant. The search engine has no initial stakes in the published information. The search algorithm makes no value-based judgment against the data subject. It is merely a tool to find potentially valid "hits" for a search and rank the result by relevance. The *Google Decision* sends a strong signal in favor of the plaintiff claiming Art. 17 GDPR. If the case-by-case assessment results in the plaintiff's all-encompassing right to have the information removed, sue the content provider. If the case is persuasive but not sufficiently so to target the content provider, sue the search engine. For the plaintiff, it is a procedural tactic to collect as many defendants as possible. If the claim against the content provider does not come through, plaintiff can use the search engine as a catch basin. Incentivizing plaintiffs this way is detrimental for public interest. Information that is factually correct is now harder to find. Search engines' job is to filter information correctly by relevance and cater to a search query with high quality. The bilateral dispute between the con-

445 *Google/Costeja*, C-131/12, loc. cit. Fn. 4, Ref. 91 to 99.

446 *EU Commission*, Factsheet on the "Right to be Forgotten", loc. cit. Fn. 5, p. 4.

tent provider and the data subject is shifted to an initially unrelated third party, namely the search engine.

9.3.4 Technical compliance: How does the internet forget?

Technical compliance with the requirements of the right to be forgotten is unclear. The core of this question means that we have to define "*How does the internet forget*?". For information technology companies, the answer to this question directly translates into a cost factor.

Under the ruling, it could be sufficient to disable the hyperlink to the information itself. A hyperlink is a reference. It is the internet's citation. By following the hyperlink, the reader follows the road to the source he desires to read. This means that – in this case – the newspaper article is still stored on a server but it can no longer be accessed once the hyperlink is disabled. By removing the link to the information, the road is not in service. Alternatively, technical compliance with the right to be forgotten could mean that the information itself needs to be removed from the servers. In that case, the road (the hyperlink) leads nowhere.

The right to be forgotten is currently limited to the EU jurisdiction.[447] For example, U.S. data subjects do not have the right to claim the right to be forgotten under a comparable constellation under U.S. jurisdiction and laws. If technical compliance with the right to be forgotten means that the hyperlink to the information must be disabled, the information itself remains accessible from jurisdictions the enforcement of the right to be forgotten does not apply to. If on the other hand, the information itself must be deleted at the back end (data center), the information is lost no matter where the front end access query comes from. Information technology companies have an incentive to ensure that their data sets are as complete as possible. The quality of the search result depends on the database the search algorithm can run on. An algorithm is nothing but a program that automates a step-by-step calculation.

Consider the following example: We have a set of numbers (n). They are presented in an unsorted list. The goal is to find out which number is the largest one in the list. For that, we must look at each number in the unsorted list, one at a time. The algorithm for this solution is built with the following parameters:

---

447 The French Data Protection Authority is called the Commission nationale de l'informatique et des libertés ("CNIL") fined Google 100.000 EUR in May 2016 for not complying with the right to be forgotten on a global scale, including the search results displayed on www.google.com, see: http://www.reuters.com/article/us-google-france-privacy-idUSKCN0WQ1WX, last accessed 22 May 2016.

- If our set of numbers has no number in it, there is no highest number.
- If there is one or more numbers in our set, we first assume that the first number is the largest one.
- Now, for each following number in the set, if that number is larger than the current largest one, consider this number the largest one in the set.
- Once there are no more numbers in our set, consider the last largest number to be the largest one of the set.

We have a result showing us that $n_2 > n_4 > n_1 > n_3 > n_m$.

Now, the right to be forgotten ruling requires us to remove the value n_2 from our set. Consequently, asking the same question *{Largest number in the set of n numbers}*, we will receive a different answer: $\mathbf{n_4} > n_1 > n_3 > n_m$. The search algorithm has failed to produce a complete result leaving n_2 unconsidered. Even though n_2 fits the search parameters and would be an element of the set as defined by the search parameters.

Let us alter the example and now as for *{Unusual disease; treatment by Dr. X; considered not curable; test results study 2014 promise cure}*. Our set of numbers is rather small because patients with this disease are scattered across the globe and in multiple treatment facilities. One treatment facility had a breakthrough with patient n_x. The studies based around this patient's case are by far the most valuable information. For extending circumstances, the physician and the patient are difficult to identify, but there is a reference in a local newspaper. Patient n_x resides in the EU and enforces the right to be forgotten. Patient n_m resides a small town and is eager to network and cooperate with others sharing this rare condition. But he cannot find n_x:

$\underline{\mathbf{N_x} \gg} n_1 > n_3 > (\ldots) > n_m$. N_x will not appear in the search result.

If solely the hyperlink to the information were removed, a person entering the same search parameters in a different jurisdiction would find this additional piece of information. If on the other hand, the information itself had to be deleted, the information value itself was lost.

The right to be forgotten is not a binary question. But its enforcement is. Technology companies like Google are built on the philosophy that information shall be accessible for everyone from anywhere. Information and internet access are powerful tools. Access to the most remote and unique fact may be a game-changing factor for some individuals in search of something specific. Creative back-up options such as a data center in international waters are an (expensive) work-around possibility. But the situation should not escalate this far. The technical parameters of the right to be forgotten must account for the value of the targeted information and the technical feasibility of a court ruling.

9.4 Consent

Pursuant to Art. 4 para. 11 GDPR, consent means any freely given specific, informed and unambiguous indication of the data subject's wishes by which the he or she, by a statement or by a clear affirmative action, signifies agreement to the processing of personal data relating to him or her.

Art. 7 GDPR stipulates the conditions for consent. Pursuant to Art. 7 para. 1 GDPR, the data controller bears the burden of proof that the data subject has given consent to the processing of personal data for specific purposes. Art. 7 para. 2 GDPR distinguishes between written an oral consent. Art. 7 para. 3 GDPR gives the data subject the right to withdraw consent at any time. But the withdrawal of consent bears no effect on the lawfulness of data processing based on the initial consent prior to its withdrawal. Lastly, Art. 7 para. 4 GDPR stipulates the critera for assessing whether consent has been given freely. Unambiguous consent does not equal assumed or circumstantial consent. With the new Art. 4 para. 11 and Art. 7 GDPR, the transaction costs for obtaining the data subject's initial permission to gather and process data will increase substantially. "One click consent" is no longer an option, especially when it comes the to collection and re-composition of data sets. The new best practice will include clearly distinguishable check boxes that the data subject has to tick, indicating consent. Pre-checked boxes that the data subject can opt-out from are not sufficient to meet the requirements of Art. 7 GDPR. Considering that Art. 7 para. 1 GDPR places the burden of proof on the data controller, Art. 7 para. 2 GDPR is a formality that no risk-averse controller will adopt. Providing proof of consent without a written agreement can only be provided through circumstantial evidence. In light of the threat of high non-compliance fines, companies are not incentivized to accept the risk of non-compliance. And gathering personal data without the data subjects' prior consent is a serious infringement.[448] Consequently, the ToS and SLAs will very likely account for this legal responsibility through more explicit clauses. With regard to Art. 7 para. 3 Sent. 2 GDPR, it is unclear how the withdrawal of consent affects the data controller's duty. It is clear that an ongoing act of data processing is compliant if consent initially covered this activity. But presumably, at any given time after consent has been

448 See below at 9.8.4 for fines for infringements of GDPR requirements.

withdrawn, the same processing activity starting anew is no longer covered. If these are automated processes, the data controller is in charge of stopping and altering these procedures in order to remain compliant with the data subject's current choices.

9.5 Data portability

Data portability is a central issue of the data privacy reform efforts. Data portability requirements are stipulated in Art. 20 para. 1 to 4 GDPR, and have two elements. On the one hand, the data subject has the right to obtain a copy of the dataset the data controller is processing (Art. 20 para. 1 GDPR). On the other hand, the data subject has the right to transmit personal data and any other information provided by him based on consent (Art. 20 para. 2 GDPR). This means that the data subject can transfer (or have the data transferred by the company) any data retained by an automated processing system from one system to another. For a company processing such datasets, this means that the software design must allow for the transfer of the customers' data set. The data subject to portability must be interoperable and readable for the customer and a third-party service provider once the relationship with the data subject is terminated. For the addressee of the obligation stipulated in Art. 20 GDPR, the crucial question is the one about the technical specifications for data portability. An example of a platform is SAP's Customer Relationship Management (CRM) or Haufe's human resources talent management platform. The regulation with the potential of incurring high compliance costs for corporations is Art. 20 para. 3 GDPR. The Commission may specify the electronic format referred to in Art. 20 para. 1 and the technical standards, modalities and procedures for the transmission of personal data in accordance with Art. 20 para. 3 GDPR.[449] This means that there shall be a uniform electronic format in place. Consequently, companies must adopt this format in order to remain compliant with the new data privacy laws. Art. 20 para. 3 Sent. 2 GDPR in connection with the procedural requirements of Art. 93 para. 2 GDPR and Art. 5 Regulation (EU) No. 182/2011 allow the Commission to act in a standard-setting capacity with regard to the electronic format, technical standards, modalities and procedures for the transmission of personal data. The worst-case scenario for companies is a complete redesign of data processing platforms.

449 The implementing acts will be adopted in accordance with the examination procedure stipulated in Art. 93 para. 2 GDPR, see: Art. 20 para. 3 Sent. 2 GDPR.

9.6 Privacy by design

The protection of personal data has been elevated to a new level. The GDPR requires a privacy by design approach. This is best illustrated by Art. 25 GDPR. Pursuant to Art. 25 para. 2 GDPR, the controller must make sure that only those personal data are processed that are necessary for each specific purpose. No collection or data retention is permissible beyond the minimum absolutely necessary to meet the purpose of data collection. In terms of platform architecture and algorithm design, this means that a fundamental change in IT design may need to occur. The revolution cloud computing and big data analysis introduced is the ability to collect and analyze data on unprecedented scale. This is illustrated and explained by the following slides that have been made public by *Edward Snowden* via the journalist *Glenn Greenwald* in his book "*No Place to Hide*".

Fig. 17: Bandwidth capacity

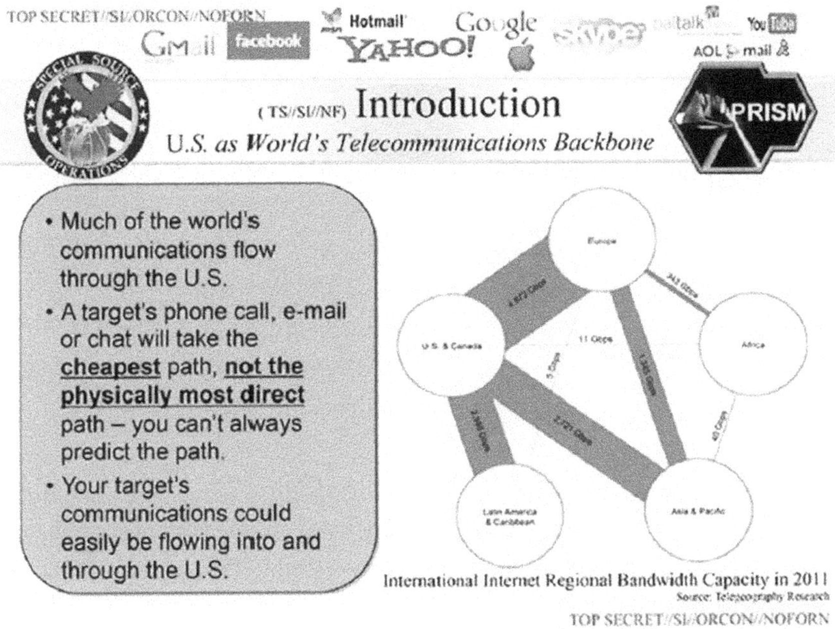

This figure[450] shows the bandwidth capacity of the telecommunications backbone in 2011. It illustrates the amount of traffic in Gigabits per second. It illustrates that the flow of communication takes place through the U.S. with comparably much higher traffic rates than any other hub. This slide alone does not provide sufficient contextual understanding for Art. 25 GDPR. The following image illustrates that the utility of data sets for governmental and non-governmental use is based on the same sets of information.

Fig. 18: PRISM collection details

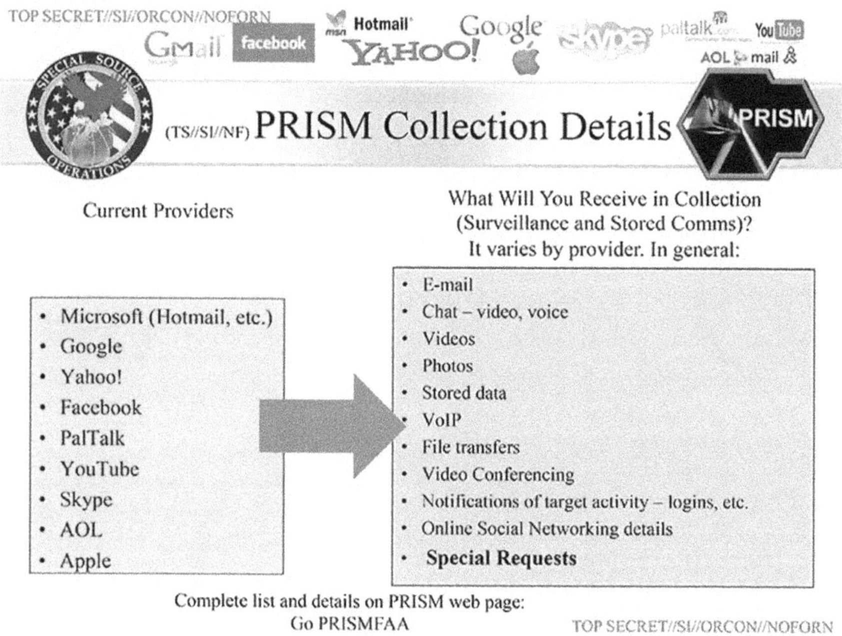

This image[451] illustrates that non-governmental entities operate as content providers. The content provider is – in all the cases listed on this side in the green box

450 The slide is available on Wikipedia at: http://en.wikipedia.org/wiki/PRISM_%28surveillance_program%29, last accessed 15 August 2014. All files are publicly available free of charge on *Der Spiegel Online* at: http://www.spiegel.de/netzwelt/web/snowdens-deutschland-akte-alle-dokumente-als-pdf-a-975885.html, last accessed 15 August 2014.

451 Also available at: http://en.wikipedia.org/wiki/PRISM_%28surveillance_program%29, last accessed 15 August 2014.

to the left – also a platform that provides content-based information previously provided by customers of the services offered by the company.

The two images combined allow the deduction that the vast majority of internet traffic is routed through the U.S and stored for content analysis. The content of this traffic is subject to the data gatherings illustrated by Fig. 18: PRISM collection details. The data used for i.e. targeted advertising may be the same raw data that is of interest to government entities and that the PRISM algorithms are designed to analyze. For example, a user may be searching for flights from location A to location B. For the purposes of non-governmental corporate use, this information is useful to show advertisements of passenger airline carriers operating at those locations. For the purposes of intelligence, this information is an indicator that the person is looking into changing his or her physical location from A to B. The system can retain the complete traffic for a day to a couple of days, running sophisticated algorithms to determine whether the information collected bears any importance on intelligence purposes. In light of this systematic information gathering and overlapping intelligence and corporate non-governmental interests, Art. 25 para. 2 GDPR shines in a different light. Privacy by design is a legal requirement stipulating the principle of scarce data collection and also a political response to recent transatlantic tensions.

9.7 Notification obligations

If a personal data breach occurs, the data protection authority must be notified without delay. A notification requirement is not new to data privacy laws. But with Artt. 33 and 34 GDPR, the burden for notification requirements is shifting to the disadvantage to the company processing personal data. A violation of notification reporting lines can also lead to fines.[452] If a personal data breach occurs, the controller must notify the data protection authority (Art. 33 GDPR) and the data subject (Art. 34 GDPR) without undue delay . Pursuant to Art. 33 para. 1 GDPR, a late notification 72 hours after an occurred breach must be justified. Data breach shall not result in economic loss and social harm, such as identity fraud, physical harm, significant humiliation or damage to reputation. Individuals must be enabled to take necessary precautions against dangers. Appropriate technological protection and organizational measures need to be in place to immediately notify data protection authorities and the data subject of a personal data breach. The notification requirement vis á vis the data protection authority of Art. 33 para. 3 lit. a to lit. d GDPR must entail the following details of the data breach:

452 See Chapter 9.8.4.

- Describe the nature of the personal data breach including the categories and number of data subjects concerned and the categories and number of data records concerned (Art. 33 para. 3 lit. a GDPR);
- Communicate the identity and contact details of the data protection officer or other contact point able to provide more information (Art. 33 para. 3 lit. b GDPR);
- Describe the likely consequences of the personal data breach (Art. 33 para. 3 lit. c GDPR) ; and
- Describe the measures taken or proposed to be taken by the controller to address the personal data breach, including measures to mitigate its possible adverse effects (Art. 33 para. 3 lit. d GDPR).

The new notification requirements focus on the protection of the data subject. An undertaking's software and platform that is processing personal data must accommodate the technical ability to comply with the notification requirements regarding customer data. Consent for the processing of personal data is no longer assumed but must be declared explicitly.[453] The outline, whether this consent has to be given in writing and how specific the declaration needs to be is still subject to discussion.

9.8 Compliance of international data flows

The proposed changes are EU-extraterritorial in scope. If a non-EU company is present on the EU market, the company's activities must be compliant with EU data privacy laws, even if data is handled on servers located outside of the EU. A presence on the EU market is sufficient to establish the applicability of EU privacy and data protection laws. A possible solution is to keep the U.S. business separate from its EU business. This must be arranged as such that the subsidiaries do not interact with the company's European data as a whole. Data stream management, access to EU citizens' personal data and data transfers must not occur for EU privacy and data protection laws not to apply. This is a very high threshold and would be extremely difficult to achieve, given technical, corporate and antitrust law hurdles. Hence, a globally active company must set itself up for EU privacy and data protection law compliance under the GDPR. The deadline is 25 May 2018, the day the GDPR comes into effect.

Chapter V of the GDPR stipulates the principles for the transfer of personal data to third countries and international organizations. As a general rule, Art. 44

453 See Chapter 9.4 on consent.

GDPR requires that any transfer of personal data that is processed upon transfer to a third country or international organization may only take place if the data controller and processor comply with this regulation. For practical purposes, this means that Artt. 44 et seqq. GDPR stipulate EU-external rules. If EU citizens' personal data leaves the EU via a transfer, further data processing may only take place in compliance with the rules of the GDPR that would apply had the personal data been processed within the EU.

The data transfer takes place between two entities, the data exporter (located in the EU) and the data importer (located outside the EU). The EU Commission can declare jurisdictions as offering an adequate level of protection to EU citizens' data. If that is determined, the EU Commission issues an adequacy decision (Art. 45 GDPR) and the data may flow freely without additional compliance requirements for the transfer.

If the country of the data importer is not deemed to offer an adequate level of protection to EU citizens' data, the data transfer must be based on a data transfer mechanism. The United States are not considered to be a country offering this adequate level of privacy and data protection laws.

Before the EU-U.S. Safe Harbor Framework ("Safe Harbor") was declared invalid[454], it was considered one of these data transfer mechanisms. Currently, data transfers either rely on Standard Contractual Clauses or Binding Corporate Rules ("BCRs").[455] Companies who do not have an entity in the EU cannot use these mechanisms, as both of them need an EU entity acting as the data exporter. Therefore, the invalidation of the Safe Harbor leaves small companies without an EU corporate presence in a compliance vacuum. The Safe Harbor filled this gap because companies did not need an EU corporate affiliate to self-certify to the Safe Harbor. The EU Commission and the U.S. Department of Commerce recently finished negotiating the successor of the Safe Harbor, the EU-U.S. Privacy Shield, which went live on 1 August 2016.[456]

---

454 See below Chapter 9.8.1.4.

455 The Data Protection Authorities do not consider the data subject's consent as a legitimate basis for systematic and regular data transfers. See for example the regional authority of Scheswig-Holstein: https://www.datenschutzzentrum.de/artikel/967-Positionspapier-des-ULD-zum-Safe-Harbor-Urteil-des-Gerichtshofs-der-Europaeischen-Union-vom-6.-Oktober-2015,-C-36214.html, last accessed 10 July 2016.

456 Since then companies can complete the self-certification process on www.privacyshield.gov, last accessed 10 August 2016.

To trace the developments of this fragile element of data protection law, we must look at why the Safe Harbor was invalidated, what other data transfer mechanisms between the EU and the U.S. remain available, and how this affects the cloud computing sector.

9.8.1 The invalidation of the Safe Harbor

The Safe Harbor between the EU and the U.S. was a bilateral agreement based on the Safe Harbor Privacy Principles[457]. Companies can sign up to the Safe Harbor List[458] of the U.S. Department of Commerce and with that, they obligate themselves to abide by an "adequate data privacy standard" compared to the EU. More than 4100 U.S. companies had up to date registrations in October 2015, when Safe Harbor was invalidated by the CJEU.[459] Increasing political pressures made cross border data transfers more difficult. A report[460] by the EU articulated discontent with the current Safe Harbor rules, even before the transfer mechanism was invalidated on 6 October 2015. The discussion became more heated after the surveillance-related disclosures of the National Security Agency (NSA). Data transfer mechanisms, such as the Safe Harbor, are vital for the business because of different privacy approaches between the EU and the U.S. Adequacy decisions and data transfer mechanisms, such as what the Safe Harbor represented, help businesses bridge this gap and harmonize compliance approaches.

9.8.1.1 The U.S. data privacy regime and the Safe Harbor principles

The privacy system of the U.S. is based on the idea that a U.S. citizen shall be protected from government action. A privacy right is a "negative" right. It obligates the government or a third party to not take certain actions. The U.S. Constitution does not grant a right to data privacy that is directly derived from the

457 Available at: http://www.export.gov/safeharbor/eu/eg_main_018476.asp, last accessed 31 August 2014.

458 The list is available here: http://safeharbor.export.gov/list.aspx, last accessed 31 August 2014.

459 *CJEU* judgment C-362/14 dated 6 October 2015 – *Maximillian Schrems v Data Protection Commissioner* (henceworth cited as: *Maximillian Schrems v Data Protection Commissioner)*

460 *EU Commission*, Communication on the Functioning of the Safe Harbour, loc. cit. Fn. 9.

constitution. American courts only once mentioned "privacy" stating that there is "*a penumbra where privacy is protected from governmental intrusion.*"[461] Since then, U.S. courts have not mentioned a right to privacy directly derived from the U.S. constitution. More so, courts are pedaling back and limiting the scope of the aforementioned "penumbra".[462] Data privacy laws in the U.S. are found scattered across many laws. There are state and federal laws and those that regulate private and governmental use. Many industries have no data privacy regime in place at all because privacy and data protection laws are mostly sectoral. Even if there is a right to privacy stipulated in the law, the scope of this right is limited to the data covered by the law and the specific circumstances associated with it. To illustrate the range and density of regulation, HIPAA[463] is an example where the overall structure of the law resembles an EU law. In addition to federal and state laws, the U.S. data privacy system heavily relies on companies pursuing a self-regulatory approach. Companies make commitments about how they will gather and work with data. Also, the FTC's powers are in general limited to checking this self-proclaimed commitment. In 2012, the FTC published data security guidelines.[464] These guidelines stipulate that data collection of personal identifiers should be minimal. Also, data should not be stored longer than necessary for the business purpose it was initially collected for. However, companies follow these guidelines on a voluntary basis.

9.8.1.2 EU data protection law and Safe Harbor rules

Art. 8 of the European Convention on Human Rights grants a basic human right to privacy. "*Everyone has the right to respect for his privacy and family life, his home and his correspondence.*"[465] Additionally, Art. 8 of the Charter of Fundamental Rights of the European Union also stipulates a right to privacy: "*Everyone has the*

461 *Griswold v. Connecticut*, 381 U.S. 479, 483 (1965).

462 *United States v. Jones*, 132 S. Ct. 949 (2012).

463 Health Insurance Portability and Accountability Act, Pub.L. 104–191, 110 Stat. 1936, enacted 21 August 1996.

464 *FTC*, Protecting Consumer Privacy in an Era of Rapid Change: Recommendations for Businesses and Policymakers, March 2012, also available at: http://www.ftc.gov/reports/protecting-consumer-privacy-era-rapid-change-recommendations-businesses-policymakers, last accessed 31 August 2014.

465 Art. 8 European Convention on Human Rights, available at: http://www.echr.coe.int/Documents/Convention_ENG.pdf, last accessed 31 August 2014.

right to the protection of personal data concerning him or her."[466] There is an EU a right to privacy that is codified on a constitutional level.[467]

Data privacy in the EU is an affirmative right. The state or the government has an affirmative duty to protect the data subject from an unjust infringement of their privacy. Even if data privacy laws do not apply directly, the constitutionally codified law makes data privacy a general principle of law. Even if there is no specific source of law obligating someone to specific data privacy standards, the general principle must be upheld.[468]

With the new GDPR, EU privacy and data protection laws will be harmonized. The GDPR is uniformly applicable on the EU internal market across all sectors. This will help the implementation process of Art. 8 ECHR.

9.8.1.3 *Safe Harbor in the balance: Revoke or reform?*

Even before the invalidation of the Safe Harbor, the EU had expressed great concern and dissatisfaction in two reports. The *Commission Communication on the European Parliament and the Council on the Functioning of the Safe Harbour from the Perspective of EU Citizens and Companies Established in the EU*[469] dated 27 November 2013 noted that it is dissatisfied with the FTC regarding Safe Harbor violation enforcements. In the last four years, the FTC had prosecuted only 10 cases of violation.[470] The report concluded that the Safe Harbor principles are not actively enforced. This is rooted in the fact that companies are self-certified and hence, the standards cannot be effectively controlled. The report said that the Safe Harbor must be revised, suspended or completely revoked by summer

466 Charter of Fundamental Rights of the European Union, 7 December 2000, O.J. L C 364/01, available at: http://www.europarl.europa.eu/charter/pdf/text_en.pdf, last accessed 31 August 2014. This provision remained valid in its meaning after the Treaty of Lisbon amending the Treaty on the European Union and the Treaty Establishing the European Community.

467 As another example for an EU member state, German law acknowledges the right to informational self-determination as a constitutional right. This is the so-called „*Recht auf informationelle Selbstbestimmung*“ (right to informational self-determination), German Federal Constitutional Court ruling; *BVerfG*, Urteil des Ersten Senats vom 15. Dezember 1983, 1 BvR 209/83 u. a. – *Volkszählung*; BVerfGE 65, 1.

468 *Internationale Handelsgesellschaft v. Einfuhr- und Vorratsstelle für Getreide und Futtermittel*, 1970, ECR 1125, Case 11/70.

469 *EU Commission*, Communication on the Functioning of the Safe Harbour, loc. cit. Fn. 9.

470 *EU Commission*, Communication on the Functioning of the Safe Harbour, ibd, p. 10.

2014 if improvements were not made in time. The Commission made 13 recommendations in total. This shows that the most relied-upon data transfer mechanism was standing on shaky legs more than a year before it was declared invalid. The most important recommendations for the cloud computing sector were the following:[471]

Firstly, self-certified companies must disclose their privacy policies and their website must contain a link to the U.S. Department of Commerce Safe Harbor Website.[472] Secondly, "*self-certified companies should publish privacy conditions of any contracts they conclude with subcontractors, e.g. cloud computing services. Safe Harbour allows onward transfers from Safe Harbour self-certified companies to third parties acting as "agents", for example to cloud service providers. According to our understanding, in such cases the Department of Commerce requires from self-certified companies to enter into a contract. However, when entering such a contract, a Safe Harbour company should also notify the Department of Commerce and be obliged to make public the privacy safeguards.*"[473] This illustrates that a much higher level of transparency should have been implemented than the business practice had been to date. Thirdly, the Department of Commerce must have flagged companies that were not currently compliant with the label "not current" on the list.[474] Also, companies must have had to explicitly state their caveats. Self-certifying companies should have indicated in their policies if and when they applied exceptions to the Safe Harbor principles for national security, public interest or law enforcement reasons.[475]

The second report is the *Draft Report of European Parliament Committee on Civil Liberties, Justice and Home Affairs on the U.S. NSA surveillance Programme*[476] dated 21 February 2014. This report had been released in direct response to the NSA surveillance program. It asked for an immediate suspension of data transfers

---

471 *EU Commission*, Communication on the Functioning of the Safe Harbour, ibd, p. 18–19.

472 http://www.export.gov/safeharbor/index.asp, last accessed 29 December 2014.

473 *EU Commission*, Communication on the Functioning of the Safe Harbour, loc. cit. Fn. 9, p. 18, No. 3.

474 *EU Commission*, Communication on the Functioning of the Safe Harbour, ibd, p. 18.

475 *EU Commission*, Communication on the Functioning of the Safe Harbour, ibd, p. 18.

476 *European Parliament*, Draft Report of European Parliament Committee on Civil Liberties, Justice and Home Affairs on the U.S. NSA surveillance Programme, 21 February 2014, (2013/2188(INI)), available at: http://www.europarl.europa.eu/sides/getDoc.do?type=REPORT&reference=A7-2014-0139&language=EN#title1, last accessed 31 August 2014 (henceforth cited as: *LIBE Report)*.

and the end of the Safe Harbor program. Data transfer to self-certified U.S. companies should have been immediately stopped. The report also clearly identified the mechanisms through which surveillance was made possible:[477]

- The PRISM program as an enabler to mass surveillance of EU citizens through direct access to central servers of U.S. technology companies
- The Xkeyscore program for the analysis of content and metadata
- The BULLRUN program to circumvent online encryption
- The Tempora program gives access to computer and telephone networks, and access to location data, as well as to systems of the UK intelligence agency GCHQ such as the upstream surveillance activity
- Edgehill is a decryption program
- Quantumtheory and Foxacid programmes target the 'man-in-the-middle attacks' on information systems
- The Dishfire program collects and retains more than 200 million text messages daily

The internet is ubiquitously available through mobile devices, the front end devices. They enable us to access cloud services. Without omnipresent computing power and everyone's every day relying on cloud-based services, these surveillance tools would not be so powerful. Our online behavior is what feeds the machine. Many business models are built on concepts around processing personal data for specific use cases. This is what makes this situation unprecedented – the computing capability and the availability of information.

9.8.1.4 The Safe Harbor invalidation on 6 October 2015

The ongoing political discussion about the Safe Harbor's fate came to an abrupt stop when the CJEU spoke the final word in this debate in *Maximillian Schrems v. Data Protection Commissioner*[478], a preliminary ruling requested by the Irish High Court.

Schrems is an Austrian Facebook user who claimed that the Safe Harbor did not adequately protect his personal data because it allowed disclosures of EU citizens' data to the U.S. National Security Agency ("NSA"). Facebook relied on the Safe Harbor for data transfers taking place between its Irish entity and the U.S. parent company. In 2013, Schrems requested that the Irish DPA investigate Facebook's practices and suspend data transfers to its U.S. data centers. How-

477 All of the itemized points listed in *LIBE Report*, ibd, main reason Ref. 2.

478 *Maximillian Schrems v. Data Protection Commissioner*, loc. cit. Fn. 459.

ever, the Irish DPA considered itself bound by the EU Commission's decision of 26 July 2000, which formally recognizes Safe Harbor as a legal basis for transferring data from the EU to the U.S. Schrems appealed the DPA's ruling to the Irish High Court, which asked the CJEU to clarify whether or not a national DPA is bound by the European Commission's Safe Harbor decision.

The CJEU's ruling went beyond the scope of the preliminary ruling requested by the Irish High Court. The CJEU found the EU Commission's adequacy decision on Safe Harbor invalid.[479] This means that all data transfers based on the Safe Harbor taking place after the CJEU judgment had been issued were illegal because they relied on an invalid data transfer mechanism. According to the CJEU, the broad national security exception contained in the Safe Harbor allowing for disclosures of personal data to law enforcement authorities does not satisfy the standards of fundamental rights in the EU. In particular, the CJEU held that this exception enables disproportionate interference with the privacy rights of EU individuals. In addition, the CJEU emphasized the lack of judicial remedy or redress for EU individuals, including the right to have the data accessed, rectified, or erased, and the lack of oversight powers by EU national DPAs.

9.8.1.5 The EU-U.S. Privacy Shield

The CJEU's arguments for invalidating the Safe Harbor as a data transfer mechanism go far beyond pure privacy and data protection law concerns. It is a political power play between two regions whose information gathering practices enable them to gather unprecedented quantity and quality of intelligence.

The EU-U.S. Privacy Shield ("Privacy Shield") is the successor of the Safe Harbor and is supposed to address the concerns the CJEU addressed in *Maximillian Schrems v. Data Protection Commissioner*. The first draft of the Privacy Shield adequacy decision was made public on February 29, 2016,[480] but was met with criticism by the Working Party 29.[481]

---

479 *Maximillian Schrems v Data Protection Commissioner*, loc. cit. Fn. 459.

480 See the press release at: http://europa.eu/rapid/press-release_IP-16-433_en.htm, last accessed 4 June 2016.

481 *Article 29 Working Party*, Opinion 01/2016 on the EU – U.S. Privacy Shield draft adequacy decision, dated 13 April 2016, available here: http://ec.europa.eu/justice/data-protection/article-29/documentation/opinion-recommendation/files/2016/wp238_en.pdf, last accessed 10 July 2016.

In early July, the Article 31 Committee voted for the adoption of the Privacy Shield, marking the last step of the legislative process under Directive 95/46/EC.[482] It was then on the EU Commission to issue its adequacy decision and for the U.S. Department of Commerce to implement the certification mechanism. The self-certification website was opened on 1 August 2016 on www.privacyshield.gov.

9.8.1.6 Impact for startups and cloud computing business

As discussed below, other data transfer mechanisms require an EU entity to set up the data transfer mechanism for transatlantic data flows. The EU entity acts as the data exporter and the foreign-based entities as data importers. Those data transfer mechanisms rely on a bilateral agreement between the data importer and data exporter.

Safe Harbor was an exception and vastly relied upon by SME companies. Startups and medium size companies able to attract business from the EU, but do not have an established entity in the EU. Most of them operate from one headquarter office in Silicon Valley or another hub. The Privacy Shield will fill this void. This data transfer mechanism, like the Safe Harbor, does not require an EU-based entity to act as the data exporter.

9.8.2 Standard Contractual Clauses

Since the invalidation of the Safe Harbor on 6 October 2015[483], Standard Contractual Clauses ("SCCs") have become the most commonly used data transfer mechanism for international data flows between the EU and the U.S. The SCCs are template contracts[484] that exist in two variations:

- Controller-to-controller SCCs, where the data exporter and the data importer both act as data controllers, meaning that both determine the purposes and means of the data processing activity; and
- Controller-to-processor SCCs, where the (EU-based) data exporter is the data controller and instructs the (U.S.-based) data importer to process the data on its behalf.

---

482 See the press release at: http://europa.eu/rapid/press-release_STATEMENT-16-2443_en.htm, last accessed 10 July 2016.

483 *Maximillian Schrems v Data Protection Commissioner*, loc. cit. Fn. 459 and see Chapter 9.8.1.4.

484 The EU Commission makes the SCCs publicly available as template agreements. The word documents are available here: http://ec.europa.eu/justice/data-protection/international-transfers/transfer/index_en.htm, last accessed 10 July 2016.

Originally, Art. 26 para. 4 Directive 95/46/EC authorized the EU Commission to adopt the SCCs to offer sufficient safeguards for international data transfers. As required by Art. 26 para. 2 Directive 95/46/EC, the SCCs provide adequate safeguards with respect to the protection of the privacy and fundamental rights and freedoms of individuals and as regards the exercise of the corresponding rights.[485] The GDPR continues to recognize SCCs as a data transfer mechanism (Art. 46 para. 3 lit. c GDPR).

In comparison to Binding Corporate Rules ("BCRs"), SCCs are much quicker to adopt. Whilst BCRs take several months to implement, SCCs are complete once the parties complete the template agreement blanks. Even though some national jurisdictions have SCCs registration or authorization requirements, the transaction costs are still substantially lower in comparison to BCRs.

In practice, the parties may use the SCCs template by downloading them from the EU Commission's website.[486] The material clauses of the agreement must be kept as is. Changing the language of the clauses means that they will lose their validity as an approved data transfer mechanism. The only parts that the parties may draft themselves are the language of the annexes. The annexes describe the data transfer, including the purpose of the data transfer and the categories of data that are transmitted.

Maximilian Schrems' first mark on the data protection law was his proceeding that led to the invalidation of the Safe Harbor. In most recent developments, he has launched new proceedings, this time seeking the legal review and invalidation of the EU-U.S. SCCs that Facebook has put into place.[487] If that proceeding is successful, Maximilian Schrems will be responsible for invalidating two of three widely used data transfer mechanisms that the technology sector relies on. The only mechanism showing robustness to date are the BCRs, examined next below.

9.8.3 Corporate restructuring for Binding Corporate Rules

BCRs are an internal Code of Conduct of a multinational company. The BCRs define its global policy with regard to international data transfers that are necessary for the company's day-to-day operations. Specifically, they apply for personal

485 See EU Commission, Directorate-Generale Justice, available at: http://ec.europa.eu/justice/data-protection/international-transfers/transfer/index_en.htm, last accessed 22 May 2016.

486 As made available above, loc. cit. Fn. 485.

487 See *Facebook v. Europe*, the privacy activist platform operated by Maximilian Schrems, press release dated 25 May 2016, available here: http://www.europe-v-facebook.org/PA_MCs.pdf, last accessed 10 July 2016.

data transfers outside of the EU (Art. 47 GDPR). For example, BCRs cover the multinational company's international HR data, customer relationship management data or payroll data transfers.

One of the key reasons why BCRs are showing so much robustness in light of the ongoing challenges to data transfer mechanisms is the co-review process performed by more than one data protection authority. Whilst the review process takes an average of 18 months, the BCRs are drafted with a full compliance approach in mind.[488]

According to Art. 47 para. 2 lit. a to lit. n GDPR, corporate rules must indicate, amongst others,

- the structure and contact details of the group handling personal data outside the EU
- the set of data transfers including the categories of personal data, the type of processing and its purposes, the type of data subjects affected and the identification of the third country in question
- the internally and externally legally binding nature of the corporate rules
- the general data protection principles (i.e. purpose limitation, data quality, legal basis for processing, processing sensitive personal data, measures to ensure data security, requirements for further data transfer)
- the rights of the data subjects and their means to exercise their rights
- the acceptance of the outside data controller by a controller or processor established on the territory of an EU member state
- the mechanisms to ensure the verification of compliance with the binding corporate rules
- the cooperation mechanism with the supervising authorities.

Particularly noteworthy is Art. 47 para. 2 lit. f GDPR stipulating that the controller or processor of personal data outside the EU must be tied to a data controller or data processor located within the EU. This means that there is always an entity within EU jurisdiction that can be held responsible for any data privacy non-compliance that occurs outside the EU. Similar to the questions regarding data portability,[489] Art. 47 para. 3 GDPR stipulates that the Commission is empowered to adopt secondary acts to further specify the criteria and

488 See for example the FAQs of the UK Information Commissioner's Office, advising that a straightforward approval process may take at least 12 months. The FAQs are available here: https://ico.org.uk/for-organisations/guide-to-data-protection/binding-corporate-rules/, last accessed 10 July 2016.

489 See Chapter 9.5.

requirements for BCRs. This de facto enables the Commission to set EU-wide standards and beyond regarding the structure of controller and processor reporting lines.

9.8.4 Conclusion

As described above, one of the core elements of offering cloud services is connecting a front end device with the back end performing the computations. The communication of the front end and the back end elements is the data transfer taking place. Without data transfers, cloud-based services cannot function.

If the data transfer is governed by an adequacy decision, data may flow freely. If the EU Commission has not issued an adequacy decision for a jurisdiction of the data importers' place of establishment, a data transfer mechanism must be put in place.

Before the invalidation of the Safe Harbor, data transfers were neatly organized in three business case scenarios. If the data controller was solely established in the U.S., the only available mechanism was the Safe Harbor because it does not require an EU corporate entity to act as the data exporter. Multinational companies, and especially large corporations, work with SCCs until they have worked through the BCRs approval process with their lead and co-supervising DPAs. Since the BCRs approval process is time consuming, companies tend to rely on SCCs as an interim solution. Lastly, SCCs can be concluded between two entities of the same corporation (as an intra-group agreement) or between an EU-based data controller and an independent third party company.

After 6 October 2015, data transfer mechanisms are being systematically scrutinized. At the forefront is the privacy activist Maximilian Schrems, who had already announced his intention to challenge the Privacy Shield and is currently pushing to have the SCCs invalidated.[490]

The discussion around government surveillance is in flux and lawmakers have an obligation to make sure that data transfer mechanisms are not used to infringe EU citizens' rights. However, a solution must be found that also considers cloud-based services and their business models, since international data flows are at the core of their business operations.

490 See his announcements on http://europe-v-facebook.org/EN/en.html, last accessed 20 August 2016.

9.9 Fines for infringements of GDPR requirements

The fines for non-compliance are the highest ever set for data privacy law infringements. Pursuant to Art. 83 (2) GDPR, the amount of administrative sanctions is determined by the nature, gravity and duration of the breach, the intentional or negligent character of the infringement, the degree of responsibility of the natural or legal person and of previous breaches by this person, the technical and organizational measures and procedures implemented pursuant to Art. 32 GDPR and the degree of cooperation with the supervisory authority in order to remedy the breach. Art. 25 GDPR stipulates data protection by design and default in the system. The controller must implement appropriate technical and organizational requirements for data processing and must ensure that only those personal data are processed that are necessary for each specific purpose and are not utilized or stored beyond immediate necessity. The exact amount of penalty payment will depend on the type, length, severity and general scope of the infringement. The maximum administrative fine may be up to 20.000.000 EUR or 4 % of the total worldwide annual turnover of the preceding financial year, whichever is higher (Art. 83 (6) GDPR). The Commission is expected to have high discretionary power in establishing the appropriate penalty payment on a case-by-case basis.

9.10 Conclusion

The GDPR is a response to many issues. Firstly, the current data privacy regime is based on Directive 95/46/EC, a set of rules that is 21 years old. In the world of IT technology, this translates into ancient history. The adoption of cloud solutions is an IT innovation that has taken place in the past eight years. The technological abilities must be accounted for in the new provisions. Secondly, global businesses rely on data processing to an unprecedented degree. Physical or geographical barriers are largely irrelevant for IT solutions. The laws must reflect this through rules that do not act prohibitively on transatlantic business relationships.

The EU and the U.S. have very different approaches to privacy and liberty as well as their governing laws. Safe heaven provisions are a necessity for SMEs as well as global conglomerates to operate efficiently. During the course of research for this section, I interviewed several Silicon Valley based startup company CEOs. I asked them how they would navigate the issue of data privacy compliance in the EU. Across the board, two main strategies seem to prevail: i) They will refrain from entering the EU internal market or ii) they plan to duplicate their facilities and keep the two businesses completely separate from each other in order to avoid data transfers and overlaps if compliance with EU laws cannot be reached or financially afforded otherwise. Compliance with ever-changing laws and requirements is expensive. Especially for small start-ups, the unpredictable nature of EU legislation is a large concern. Above all other issues stands the question of organizing international data flows in a compliant way. Communication has to be constructive. Companies approach the EU internal market with the desire to place themselves and their practices into full compliance. But they need to be told how. Especially with the legal assessment of data transfers so much in flux right now, it is important to say what is still reliable and compliant in the authorities' eyes.

Thirdly, the proposed new regulation is a response to recent political developments. As mentioned in the LIBE Report[491], the transatlantic relationship has been profoundly shaken. There is a lack of trust between governments, the functioning of democratic institutions, the security of IT services and communication systems as well as the respect for the rule of law.

The highest priority of the law is to protect data subjects from abusive and unlawful personal data use that could harm the individual's right to privacy. But any legal provision that is not strongly rooted in what is technically possible, economically realistic and politically balanced will have negative external effects on the EU internal market and with that, also on the consumers.

491 *LIBE Report*, loc. cit. Fn. 477, main reason Ref. 4.

10 Contracts and certifications for cloud service providers

The contractual relationship between cloud service providers and customers is governed by several agreements. Sometimes in combination, as a general rule there are four primary documents: the Service Level Agreement (SLA), the Terms of Service (ToS), the Acceptable Use Policy (AUP), the Privacy Policy. If applicable, there also is an End-User-Licensing Agreement (EULA).

10.1 Content of agreements and standardization

The SLA is the contractual agreement that specifies the level and kind of service that the customer will receive in exchange for the remuneration of the cloud service provider. The ToS are the accompanying general contractual framework. It stipulates the general contractual clauses that are not subject to individual negotiation. These include the choice of jurisdiction and governing law and liability disclaimers. The AUP is also a general supplement to the SLA. It stipulates the allowed and forbidden types of service usage. Lastly, the privacy policy states how the cloud service provider deals with data privacy, data security and information management questions vis á vis its customers. These contractual agreements would fall under the German provisions of General Terms and Conditions – *Allgemeine Geschäftsbedingungen* – whereby Sec. 305 et seqq. German Civil Code are applicable. Furthermore, there may be a general framework agreement, the Master Service Agreement (MSA), governing all types of SLAs issued by the cloud service provider. Also, sometimes there are separate agreements solely on the service and maintenance, called Service Agreements with an accompanying Service Description. Furthermore, there may be a Business Continuity Policy in place.[492]

Unfortunately, a uniform code of security guidelines does not exist nor is its speedy adoption likely. Standardization agencies such as the International Organization for Standardization (ISO), the National Institute of Standards and Technology (NIST), the Cloud Security Alliance or the government agencies like ENISA have so far not come up with a proposal for a uniform security guideline. In terms of voluntary guidelines, cloud service operators can submit to voluntarily abiding

492 *EU Commission*, Cloud Service Level Agreement Standardization Guidelines dated 24 June 2014, available at: http://ec.europa.eu/digital-agenda/en/news/cloud-service-level-agreement-standardisation-guidelines, last accessed 29 December 2014, p. 9 (henceforth cited as: *EU Commission*, SLA Guidelines).

by the *Cloud Security Alliance's Security Guidelines for Critical Areas of Focus for Cloud Computing*[493]. The Cloud Select Industry Group (CSIG) is a working group organized by the EU Commission. In June 2014, the CSIG published the *Cloud Service Level Agreement Standardization Guidelines*[494]. The guidelines stipulate recommended clauses for performance service level objectives[495], security service level objectives[496], data management service level objectives[497], and personal data protection service level objectives[498]. The guidelines highlight two key points, data portability and the principle of data minimization. Within data portability, the guidelines consider three main aspects. Firstly, the data portability format must specify the electronic format in which cloud service customer data can be accessed and transferred from the cloud service.[499] Secondly, the data portability interface must comply with the required characteristics. This means that it must specify the mechanisms that can be used to transfer cloud service customer data in- and outbound. This may also include specifying transport protocols and APIs.[500] Lastly, the data transfer rate must be at a minimum rate at which cloud service customer data can be transferred in- and outbound using the data interface provisions.[501] Data minimization is a principle that requires that only the minimum personal data necessary is collected and retained and solely as long as it is needed. Erased personal data must be irretrievable.[502]

10.2 ISO/IEC 27001, PS 980, ISO 19600 and ISO/IEC 27018

In addition to obeying by the CSIG guidelines, cloud service operators may seek certification pursuant to multiple standards. Information management systems are not governed by a custom tailored standardization process. Hence, the characteristics of information management systems must be identified and then made to fit under the different standardization options.

---

493 Available at: https://cloudsecurityalliance.org/download/security-guidance-for-critical-areas-of-focus-in-cloud-computing-v3, last accessed 29 December 2014.

494 Available at: http://ec.europa.eu/digital-agenda/en/news/cloud-service-level-agreement-standardisation-guidelines, last accessed 29 December 2014.

495 *EU Commission*, SLA Guidelines, loc. cit. Fn. 493, p. 15 to 19.

496 *EU Commission*, SLA Guidelines, ibd, p. 20 to 43

497 *EU Commission*, SLA Guidelines, ibd, p. 44 to 50.

498 *EU Commission*, SLA Guidelines, ibd, p. 51 to 61.

499 *EU Commission*, SLA Guidelines, ibd, p. 30.

500 *EU Commission*, SLA Guidelines, ibd, p. 30.

501 *EU Commission*, SLA Guidelines, ibd, p. 30.

502 *EU Commission*, SLA Guidelines, ibd, p. 33.

Information management systems must entail a number of criteria within a company. Firstly, the implementing company must identify its core data privacy risks in a structured fashion. This means that each company must internally identify its data privacy exposures. This can range from customers' data in the health insurance business to banking data for portfolio management. Secondly, data privacy standards must be implemented and its upkeep and compliance must be monitored. For that, the rights of the data subjects need to be clearly defined and enforceable through the means of raised objections, blocking, deletion, correction and frugal data collection. If contract data processing occurs[503], the contractor must be selected in accordance with the company's own data protection regime and contractually obligated to comply. Next, the company itself must entail an organizational structure such as reporting lines and a data protection officer. Within the company, there must be internal educational programs such as privacy workshops, notifications in case of breach and the handling of external data requests. Controls over the implemented standards can happen via an ex ante privacy impact assessment, IT audits and certification procedures.

In terms of certification procedures, four main frameworks are available, ISO 19600, IDW PS 980, ISO/IEC 27001 and ISO/IEC 27018. Firstly, there is ISO 19600.[504] Its documents have been last revised in 2014 and they provide *"guidance for establishing, developing, implementing, evaluating, maintaining and improving an effective and responsive compliance management system within an organization. (…) ISO 19600:2014 is based on the principles of good governance, proportionality, transparency and sustainability."*[505] It is designed to ensure that leading employees of a company conduct themselves obeying the laws. Secondly, the Institute for Public Auditors in Germany (Institut für Wirtschaftsprüfer, IDW) issued a standard titled *Principles for the Proper Performance of Reasonable Assurance Engagements Relating to Compliance Management Systems* (Grundsätze ordnungsgemäßer Prüfungen von Compliance Management Systemen), IDW PS 980.[506] However, this standard is geared to corporate compliance with the laws for corporations. It is designed to place compliance mechanisms into corporations to oversee the

503 In Germany pursuant to § 11 BDSG (Auftragsdatenverarbeitung).

504 Available at: http://www.iso.org/iso/catalogue_detail?csnumber=62342, last accessed 29 December 2014.

505 Description of ISO 19600 at: http://www.iso.org/iso/catalogue_detail?csnumber=62342, last accessed 29 December 2014. The download of the document is charged at 132 CHF for corporations.

506 Available at: http://www.idw.de/idw/portal/n589244/n589350/n611308/index.jsp, last accessed 29 December 2014.

board of directors and the supervisory board.[507] Its bearing on information risk management and data privacy management systems is limited. Thirdly, the ISO 27k-family is an information security standard for Information Security Management Systems (ISMS).[508] It describes a total of 12 fields of tasks and how risk analysis and risk management can be conducted in this field. Within that, there are a total of 123 checkpoints with implementation suggestions for the ISMS. The suggestions are neutral with regard to the sector. Consequently, they can be adopted by a variety of sectors but need custom-tailoring. However, the available certification options do not satisfy the full bandwidth of legal requirements in terms of data privacy and security requirements.

But working with the ISO 27k-series alone was not sufficient until recently. ISO 27k was not targeted at setting a standard for the management of personal data. Its focal point is to standardize and ensure information security. Consequently, a certification alone was insufficient to ensure that a company is compliant with data privacy requirements.

In recent developments, there is a new ISO/IEC 27018 standard. ISO/IEC 27018 is designed to establish a code of practice for the protection of personally identifiable information (PII) in public clouds processing PII data.[509] Companies can now certify to ISO/IEC 27018 in combination with ISO/IEC 27001 and 27002. This standard builds on ISO/IEC 27002 for information security of PII and considering the regulatory requirements for contract data processing. This is an important leap because the vast majority of public clouds' business is based on contract data processing, i.e. on § 11 of the German Bundesdatenschutzgesetz. ISO/IEC 27018 is suitable for the public and private sector as well as SMEs and non-profits.[510] With that, ISO/IEC closed an important and large certification gap.

10.3 Control over contractual partners

The cloud customer shifts the maintenance burden of the IT infrastructure to the cloud operator and the service provider is entrusted with the clients' data in ex-

---

507 *Institute for Public Auditors in Germany*, Principles for the Proper Performance of Reasonable Assurance Engagements Relating to Compliance Management Systems, 2011, Executive summary p. 1.

508 Available at: http://www.iso.org/iso/home/store/catalogue_tc/catalogue_detail.htm?csnumber=63411, last accessed 29 December 2014.

509 *ISO/IEC* 27018:2014 is available at: http://www.iso.org/iso/catalogue_detail?csnumber=61498, last accessed 29 December 2014.

510 *ISO/IEC* 27018:2014 executive summary, available at: ibid.

change for a pay-for-use remuneration model.[511] In addition to costs, an enterprise using cloud computing products must comply with other factors as well, such as protecting customer relationships, the public image of the enterprise, business flexibility and compliance regulations.[512] The most concerning point for 'conscious' customers is monitoring the cloud operator. Through the data collected, the contractual parties shall be able to monitor each other whether the SLA has been violated. As mentioned by *Patel/Ranabahu/Seth*, the customer may express three main monitoring demands.[513] Firstly, the customer may demand the raw metric numbers of how the data is exposed by the service provider. Secondly, the customer may desire a collection of data composited into meaningful context. Thirdly, the customer may ask for the collection of certain customized data sets and may specify the criteria for data collection. The layers of interest that must be organized by a SLA are illustrated in the following image:

Fig. 19: Service level agreement contractual rule needs

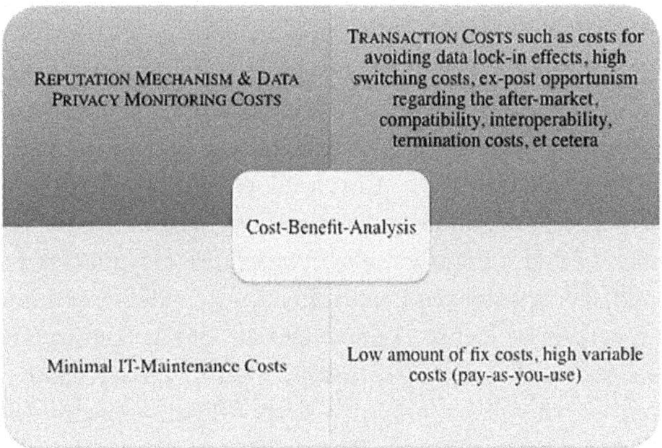

Transaction costs must be held low enough to maintain cloud computing outsourcing as an option. The interest structure varies depending on whether the contractual parties are the cloud service provider and a SaaS-user, or the could service provider and an application software developer (PaaS). The reputation

511 *Patel/Ranabahu/Sheth*, Service Level Agreement in Cloud Computing, Knoesis Center, Wright State University, USA and DA-IICT, Gandhinagar, India, 2010, p. 1.

512 *Khajeh-Hosseini/Sommerville/Sriram*, 2010, loc. cit. Fn. 42, p. 2.

513 See for instance Amazon CloudWatch: http://aws.amazon.com/de/cloudwatch/ and http://aws.amazon.com/ec2-sla/.

mechanism mentioned in the figure above refers to possible irreversible costs of a data breach incident. One „negative" act is sufficient to destroy a long-established positive reputation leading to higher costs in contractual security measures due to lacking trust of the contractual party. Lowering transaction costs could be achieved by a public ordering approach comparable to the CISG or GATT-regulations[514] for cloud computing services in order to handle the problems of territoriality of the law and the question of applicable law and data protection standards.

The equilibrium of forces between the contractual parties before and after closing of the contract changes to the disadvantage of the customer. Once the long-term contractual relationship is concluded, the customer's leverage is minimalized due to data lock-in, information barriers and high switching costs forming a higher threshold to terminate the existing contract.

10.4 Conclusion

The contractual agreements between cloud service providers and its customers carry a very large weight in data protection law compliance. Lacking a uniform compliance standard for cloud service providers and with no certification available that fully meets the scope of the law, it is left to the contractual parties to find a legal solution to the requirements of U.S., EU and EU Member State laws. There is a systematic imbalance of power in favor of the cloud service providers who draft the contracts. Hence, if the terms and conditions of the agreement are imbalanced, the risk will remain with the cloud service provider. For example, under Sec. 307 German Civil Code, the imbalanced contractual clause will be rendered nill and void should it be a surprising clause to the detriment of the customer or infringe mandatory provisions; and data protection provisions are mandatory laws. Because of that, cloud service providers must show diligence in drafting the contractual frameworks and protect the customers' interests equitably. Also in light of a potential Art. 102 TFEU exposure, a more detailed and explicit contractual landscape will help prevent liability under tying and bundling.[515]

Cloud service providers must show that they are trustworthy on the EU internal market in order to conduct successful business relationships. An ISO/IEC 27018 certification and stipulating to the Cloud Service Level Agreement Standardization Guidelines are two cornerstones that can help build this trust.

---

514 Including GATT-regulations into a Service Level Agreement to lower transaction costs has already been suggested by *Kerr/Teng*, 2010, loc. cit. Fn. 57, p. 15.

515 See above Chapter 6.3.

11 Society and public service use of cloud services

In September 2012, the EU adopted a new strategy in the IT-sector called *Unleashing the Potential of Cloud Computing in Europe*[516]. The proposal targets a net gain of 2.5 million new jobs within the EU and a 1 % boost to the EU GDP at an estimated 160 billion EUR.[517] The main points of this EU strategy are based on establishing a higher level of trust in cloud computing with regard to privacy and data protection, setting standards for interoperability, data portability and reversibility for cloud users in the form of technical standards and creating safe and fair contract terms and conditions within the cloud computing sector for both private and governmental use.

The EU is recognizing the effect of the reputation mechanism in the cloud computing sector by identifying the necessity of the "*right technology to protect [itself]*"[518]. Five components are laid down as a mechanism to establish the EU as a competitive market for cloud computing services.[519] Firstly, the European cloud should be "*supporting the key building blocks for pan-European services*".[520] Secondly, the initiative should boost the demand of the public sector for cloud services.[521] Thirdly, more means should be spent on research and innovation funding security and privacy in the cloud sector to boost supply.[522] Next, the initiative wants to establish a higher level of transparency and recover lost trust through

516 *EU Commission*, Unleashing the Potential of Cloud Computing in Europe, loc. cit. Fn. 175.

517 See: http://ec.europa.eu/digital-agenda/en/telecoms-and-internet/cloud-computing, last accessed 3 December 2013.

518 See: http://ec.europa.eu/commission_2010-2014/kroes/en/content/making-europe-natural-home-safe-cloud-computing, last accessed 3 December 2013.

519 See: http://ec.europa.eu/digital-agenda/en/telecoms-and-internet/cloud-computing and http://ec.europa.eu/commission_2010-2014/kroes/en/content/making-europe-natural-home-safe-cloud-computing, last accessed 3 December 2013.

520 *EU Commission*, Unleashing the Potential of Cloud Computing in Europe, loc. cit. Fn. 175, p. 3.

521 See the project launched in Berlin called „Cloud for Europe" (C4E) on 14 November 2013, i.e. at http://ec.europa.eu/digital-agenda/en/news/cloud-europe-stage, last accessed 3 December 2013.

522 *EU Commission*, Unleashing the Potential of Cloud Computing in Europe, loc. cit. Fn. 175, p. 3.

informing users about i.e. whether the data leaves the EU.[523] Lastly, the initiative aims to realize the EU internal market for personal data and the corresponding rules of protection by introducing a uniform set of privacy and data protection standards.[524]

Since the question of mandatory or voluntary cooperation has entered the public domain, the EU has been more articulate about establishing a competing market that investors can forum shop. The European cloud computing strategy aims to promote the "*rapid adoption of cloud computing in all sectors of the economy in order to boost productivity*". A cornerstone of this project is the establishment of "*Safe and Fair Contract Terms and Conditions*" that include the following elements not covered by the Common European Sales Law:

- *"data preservation after termination of the contract,*
- *data disclosure and integrity,*
- *data location and transfer,*
- *ownership of the data,*
- *direct and indirect liability change of service by cloud providers and subcontracting."*[525]

All in all, these measures are all directed at establishing transparent rules in order to gain the EU market's trust in cloud services. In Fall of 2013, a former NSA-contractor Edward Snowden broke into global media with information about the governmental use of private communication information. The uncovering of the ability of the United States' National Security Agency and other national governments to gather and process vast amount of telecommunication data and metadata is a testimony to the power of cloud computing. The ability to store, evaluate and reassemble data has opened up a new dimension of data processing that was a generally unknown aspect of citizen-state and intra-government interaction.

When it is the interaction with a private company handling big data, our approach to data as a consumer is "consent and use". Uncountable times has each and every person using services provided by e.g. Google, Yahoo, Microsoft, Apple, etc. clicked "I Agree to the Following Terms and Conditions". The quality of this agreement changes with the involvement of the government. Marisa Meyer, CEO

---

523 See: http://ec.europa.eu/commission_2010-2014/kroes/en/content/making-europe-natural-home-safe-cloud-computing, last accessed 3 December 2013.

524 See in detail Chapter 9.

525 See: https://ec.europa.eu/digital-agenda/en/european-cloud-computing-strategy, last accessed 3 December 2013.

of Yahoo was clear about her duty to cooperate with the NSA on the scope of providing specific sets of data at a conference held by *TechCrunch* in San Francisco in 2013. '*Non-cooperation would result in a charge of treason*', she said.[526] The type of data sets needed for commercial and governmental use are very similar. The same sets of data can be used for i.e. targeted advertising and creating a profile on a suspect. Big data makes correlations visible and are new ways of information gathering. It is therefore an apparent step that government entities in the business of information and security are interested in vast amounts of data allowing this profiling.

In addition to the diplomatic frictions the events around Edward Snowden have lead to, the consequences for the U.S. technology sector are enormous. The potential harmful side-effects for U.S. technology companies need to be priced in to the routing of communication traffic through, to and from U.S.-based servers. A German email provider (GMX) is considering rerouting its internet traffic to not touch upon American servers.[527] If customers of U.S. technology companies reconsider their business internet traffic, the recent developments will put a price tag on Silicon Valley-provided services. The way the media around this case is handled becomes a cost-benefit calculation where one parameter must be the protection of U.S.-based technology companies that are instrumentalized to provide government-instructed auxiliary services under the Patriot Act. The value of information tech companies have for the U.S. government is linked to the cloud-based services they can provide.

Data security standards are linked to reputation. The reputation mechanism is asymmetrical. On the one hand, it takes considerable investment to build a good reputation that will eventually lower transaction costs because of an established trust. On the other hand, a single act that betrays this trust is sufficient to destroy a large fraction of the previously established relationship. The intercepted mobile phones of heads of state serve as an example. On 29 October 2013, the president

526 See i.e. coverage by The Independent: http://www.independent.co.uk/life-style/gadgets-and-tech/news/marissa-mayer-and-mark-zuckerberg-respond-to-critics-over-nsa-compliance-8812167.html or by techcrunch.com with the video footage of the interview: http://www.youtube.com/watch?v=-rL1TgCJcbU, last accessed 29 December 2014.

527 See report by the *Washington Post*: http://www.washingtonpost.com/world/europe/germany-looks-at-keeping-its-internet-e-mail-traffic-inside-its-borders/2013/10/31/981104fe-424 f.-11e3-a751-f032898f2dbc_story.html?hpid=z2, last accessed 16 November 2013 and "Email made in Germany", at http://www.telekom.com/medien/konzern/192504, last accessed 3 December 2013.

of the NSA was heard for alleged spying on German Chancellor Angela Merkel's mobile phone device.[528] The accusation was not only not denied but affirmed as a rationale practice to help predict leadership decisions of allied governments in the U.S. Rebuilding this trust is the diplomatic effort the public offices are facing now.

11.1 The mechanism of trust

The overriding problem of recent governmental trespassing on privacy rights is its effect on the IT business with regard to trust. Users must trust the device, company or cloud-based service in order to use it. With its use comes the collection, processing and transfer of personal data to the U.S.. Trust can be seen as a heuristic measure. Based on experience, a person considers certain types of transactions as reliable with regard to its outcome. We 'trust' that certain input generates a specific and anticipated output based on previous experience. Users are invested in IT-systems they rely on for their daily lives. Corporations rely on e.g. Microsoft Outlook to handle the corporate email system. Private persons rely on Google Maps to show the way from point A to point B. Certain algorithms we have come to rely on, e.g. a Google-search, gets better the more people use it. The user's click on a search result that matches the search terms to the highest degree is also a form of feedback. Next time, search results will be displayed in an order that better reflects the users' preferences. It is a self-enforcing spiral. The premise is that users trust the system enough to enter search keys. Reputation and trust are intertwined. In essence, reputation is an opinion. It is the result of an evaluation process. Reputation is also a form of checks and balances for social relations. Similar to trust, reputation is a tool to predict future outcomes based on past experience. The difference between trust and reputation is its heuristic anchor. For the purposes of the assessment of IT systems, I view 'trust' as 'individualized reputation'.

11.2 The price of missing trust and a bad reputation

To illustrate the effects of lacking trust, two scenarios for comparison:

> **Scenario #1:** A wants to sell his car to B. The transaction takes place in Germany. A offers B his car and B is interested. He takes the car for a test drive. B thinks the car lives up to his expectations. It has the right motor, is the brand he likes and as far as B can tell, the car has no mechanical problems. A and B conclude the contract on the spot.

528 See for example The Guardian: https://www.theguardian.com/us-news/2015/jul/08/nsa-tapped-german-chancellery-decades-wikileaks-claims-merkel, last accessed 10 July 2016.

Scenario #2: A wants to sell his car to B. A and B are having negotiations in the Mongolian Desert. B's travel companion C warns B that A has cheated C before by selling him a lemon car. A offers B his car and B is interested again. He takes the car for a test drive in the dunes. B thinks the car is fine, but he is not entirely sure. He takes the car, disassembles it completely and examines all the parts meticulously. He then reassembles the car and is now convinced that the car is in good order. He goes back to A and tells him, he will buy the car now. They conclude the transaction.

In scenario #1, B relies on the German legal system to catch a potential lack of trust. The statutory rights of warranties (§§ 437, 280 et seqq. German Civil Code) give B a right to claim compensatory damages for a defective car. Tying back to trust in scenario #2, B has no heuristic data on A's contractual behaviors. Additionally, C's reputation information input enforces the lack of trust in B. Also, B is unfamiliar with the Mongolian legal system. With no legal provisions in place to overcome a lack of trust and a bad reputation, the transaction costs of the same deal are substantially higher.

This behavioral pattern in scenarios #1 and #2 can be transferred to technology-based contracts. Even if there is no face-to-face negotiation taking place between a user and a technology company, the unfamiliarity and potential lack of trust is mitigated by a functioning legal order. If a legal system is in place that safeguards privacy rights and stipulates rules on how to collect and process personal data, users are more enticed to trust a technology company as their contractual partner. Even if something 'goes wrong', there are legal remedies that can rectify the situation.

In a case parallel to scenario #2, the lack of a trustworthy legal and political background can lead to skepticism. Users will raise questions more prominently, such as '*What happens to my data on your servers?*', '*Who can access what I write in an iMessage on my iPhone?*' and '*How do you protect my business data – can the government see my client list? My medical record? Does it affect my credit score?*'. Questions like these are symptoms of users' missing trust and demand for accountability. The input, here the user using a technical device entrusting it with personal data, is no longer associated with the output, here the receipt of technology-based services that safeguard privacy rights.

In the U.S., data privacy is strongly based on the principle of self-regulation.[529] Data privacy standards are largely stipulated by the industry itself. Consequently, technology companies carry a comparatively large share of responsibility in the eyes of the customer. This is reflected by the companies' reputation. A well-managed self-regulation will reflect positively on customers, who in return are building a trusting relationship associated with certain brands. An example of

529 See above Chapter 5.

shaken trust is Apple's iPhone. The iPhones of celebrities were hacked and private nude photographs circulated on the internet. The hackers attacked the phones where the pictures were stored via "Find my iPhone" through the iCloud, right before a product launch in early September 2014. The media titled that the attack could not have come at a worse time for the company. Especially given that Apple is likely to introduce a device for the first time since 2010, asking consumers to trust the device with their personal data.[530]

11.3 Cloud services and trust by example of Google location data

The following image is a screenshot of the Google Privacy & Terms webpage.[531] It illustrates the types of location data Google collects from its users. There are three main types of location data collected: (i) implicit location information, (ii) internet traffic information and (iii) device-based location services.

Fig. 20: Google location data

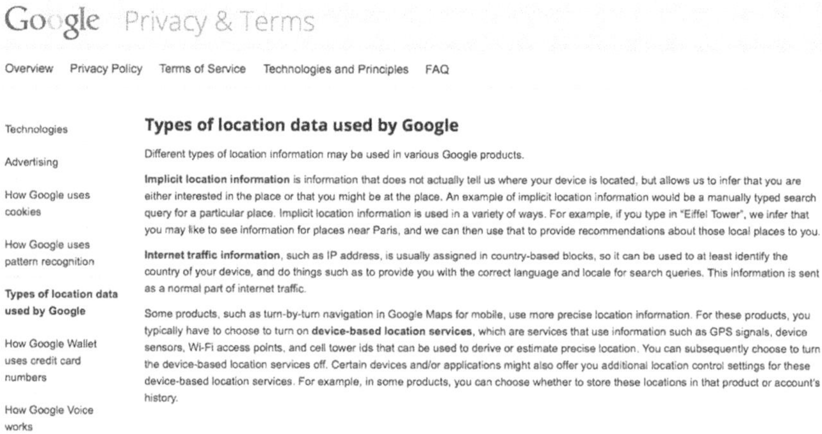
Google Privacy & Terms

Overview Privacy Policy Terms of Service Technologies and Principles FAQ

Technologies

Advertising

How Google uses cookies

How Google uses pattern recognition

Types of location data used by Google

How Google Wallet uses credit card numbers

How Google Voice works

Types of location data used by Google

Different types of location information may be used in various Google products.

Implicit location information is information that does not actually tell us where your device is located, but allows us to infer that you are either interested in the place or that you might be at the place. An example of implicit location information would be a manually typed search query for a particular place. Implicit location information is used in a variety of ways. For example, if you type in "Eiffel Tower", we infer that you may like to see information for places near Paris, and we can then use that to provide recommendations about those local places to you.

Internet traffic information, such as IP address, is usually assigned in country-based blocks, so it can be used to at least identify the country of your device, and do things such as to provide you with the correct language and locale for search queries. This information is sent as a normal part of internet traffic.

Some products, such as turn-by-turn navigation in Google Maps for mobile, use more precise location information. For these products, you typically have to choose to turn on **device-based location services**, which are services that use information such as GPS signals, device sensors, Wi-Fi access points, and cell tower ids that can be used to derive or estimate precise location. You can subsequently choose to turn the device-based location services off. Certain devices and/or applications might also offer you additional location control settings for these device-based location services. For example, in some products, you can choose whether to store these locations in that product or account's history.

These types of location data collection mechanisms work on different principles. Implicit location information is comparable to association. If a person hears the word "Big Ben", most likely the person refers to the large bell tower in London.

530 See for example *CNN News*: http://edition.cnn.com/2014/09/02/showbiz/hacked-nude-photos-five-things/, last accessed 8 September 2014.

531 http://www.google.de/intl/en/policies/technologies/location-data/, last accessed 8 September 2014.

Here again, the experience of the search algorithms matters. The number of times that the search terms "Big Ben" and "London" have correlated before is very high. Hence, the likelihood that this is the correct connection again is high. Internet traffic information can be compared to a personal v-card of a specific device. The internet protocol address (IP address) has information on who you are (the device), where you are (location of device) and contains directions on how to find you within a computer network. But this information are not precise enough on their own. The most precise location service information is the device-based location service. Here, the device checks its surroundings for available Wifi networks. The two devices identify each other. Through this mutual recognition, the location of the mobile device can be determined very precisely. Wifi-based positioning systems (WPS) allows very precise device positioning – even where other methods such as GPS fail. It is particularly good in urban areas because almost every household has a wireless internet connection installed. Hence, the density of signals is very high. The technical principle behind WPS is that the mobile device measures the intensity of the received signal. This is called "received signal strength" (RSS).[532] The quality of the information depends on the number of positions that are available simultaneously. As an example, here are the Wifi signals my mobile device receives at the moment of the screen shot in Berlin:

Fig. 21: Device-based location services based on WPS

Photo: My home Wifi area.

Fig. 22: Spider web

Photo: http://www3.artflakes.com/artwork/products/563751/poster/400178.jpg

532 Please note that there are numerous companies offering positioning services. For example, Apple uses this feature as well for „Find my iPhone".

Note that not every signal is of equal strength. Furthermore, imagine every signal as a vector whose distance to my device can be measured. The end result may be visualized like a spider web with the exact determination of the spider's location (the mobile device). The more RSS information is available, the more precise the location can be determined.

Looking at the example of Google Maps, location data feeds into the service and provides individualized results and options based on traffic. As the device moves through the streets, new RSS information becomes available. This information also allows the routing service to know whether certain roads are congested – and suggest alternatives.

These services increase in sophistication with every search query. Also, every search query has a data-related consequence because it leaves a digital footprint behind. It may be compared to a car's exhaust after the motor has burned the fuel. This data exhaust is valuable for the IT-industry offering services on this basis.

Fig. 23: Google maps routing and traffic information

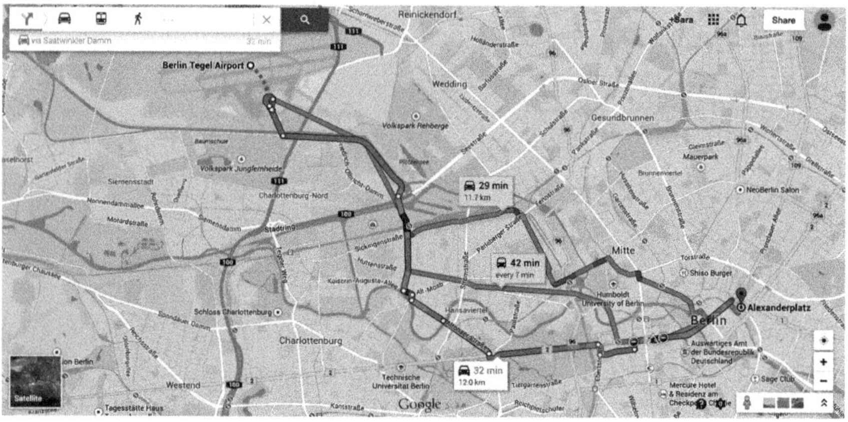

11.4 Consent requirements and the digital footprint

Big data is the foundation of a new market that emerged from so-called data mining. Each application using a smart phone, computer, laptop or tablet leaves digital footprints. Just like a car exhaust, online activities leave a trace behind in the network. These records are the foundation of the new market of data mining. The digital footprint or data exhaust encompasses all data that has been generated as an information byproduct of a digital transaction or query. Data exhaust is a platform for new products and services that build their entire business model around the existence of this information.

It gives us insights into optimizing our consumer behavior, eases consumer choices and improves products by available customer feedback. It has an inherent great potential to lead more optimized lives reaching from consumer goods shopping behaviors to medical treatment. The trade off is the technology companies' abilities of data-gathering. If the focal point of concern is the tracking-capabilities of an internet-enabled device, the technical possibilities cannot be ignored. An average phone is equipped with a dozen antennas and sensors that are permanently in operation. It contains one or two cameras, a GPS, a barometer to measure pressure for weather display, a fingerprint sensor, a gyroscope for the screen orientation in portrait or landscape mode, a Bluetooth, a brightness sensor and the usual suspects such as Wi-Fi, multi-array microphone and wireless antenna. We carry a tracking device so commonplace in our body with us. The application of information collection through sensors reach from running shoes to bridges and leading to the "internet of things", providing consumers with internet-enabled intelligent devices. In American society, there is a different understanding to data protection and privacy because of the value proposition to sharing data. The American consumer does not expect that technology companies provide a service without demanding anything in return. Online services of a company are not compensated with money, but by access to and analysis of personal data. This access is, for example, translated into behavioral advertising. Ads are automatically assigned according to the smartphone or computer user's surfing and searching behavior. This trade-off, this exchange relationship with bilateral cost-benefit analysis, the American consumer enters into willingly. Most Americans love interactive customer service. And the results prove them right: the service is better if service providers know the personal preferences of their customers.

Data exhaust can occur with or without the data subject's knowledge. A digital footprint left behind is passive if the data was collected without the data subject's knowledge, for example when the data subject is searching for a flight connection and its IP address is retained. A footprint is active if the data subject is aware of the data collection taking place, for example an uploaded photo on Facebook. The information retained about the data subject can be used to gain knowledge about the data subject's location, personal preferences, interests and distinguishing criteria of a person stipulated in Art. 3 of the German Grundgesetz such as race, religion, political views and sexual orientation. This data has been generated on the grounds of one specific business transaction, e.g. a car sensor reports to the driver that the engine needs its next maintenance checkup. The sensor has gathered data on the mileage of the car in order to report maintenance notifications in periodic frequency. The same set of information – here the mileage – may be used for a completely different business model. An example would be to provide insurance by the mile.[533] The line between a data subject's private and social space becomes fuzzy when information from one sphere is used to draw conclusions in the other. The assessment of the data subject's creditworthiness is a clear example of how the two spheres of a person become much more interrelated.[534] The credit applicant will receive a loan depending on his or her creditworthiness. The lower the creditor's score, the higher the risk for the bank to issue a loan because of an unpredictable contractual partner. This will manifest in a higher interest rate. For the credit rating, several factors play a role, such as income, debt, property or number of credit cards. But increasingly, additional information about the debtor has become available. This information may include the debtor's social circle (Linkedin, Facebook, etc.), consumer purchasing behavior (Amazon, Ebay, etc.), his political orientation (articles the debtor reads on the New York Times) and his diligence in financial matters (e.g. how fast the debtor scrolls through the disclaimer pages). This way, thousands of data points can be gathered about a credit applicant.

With regard to passive data exhaust, the data subject's consent cannot be assumed. The current legal standard of consent does not account for this systematic use of data and metadata information. Today's business models extract information from a combination of random data points. The places the data subject frequents can have an impact on him as a potential debtor, i.e. if he often visits places associated with high crime rates. Our daily routines have become subject to scrutiny, a fact many of us are not aware of. But not all use of the digital footprint is commercial. Society has powerful benefits to gain, which is the subject of the next chapter.

---

533 A company that does so is called Metromile: https://www.metromile.com/, but they install their own GPS device.

534 This issue has received large media coverage in the past 3 years. Samples from 2008 to 2014 include *CNN Money* (http://money.cnn.com/2013/08/26/technology/social/facebook-credit-score), *Bloomberg Business Week* (http://www.businessweek.com/stories/2008-01-02/measuring-your-digital-footprint), *The Guardian* (http://www.theguardian.com/media-network/media-network-blog/2014/aug/28/social-media-facebook-credit-score-banks), all last accessed 26 December 2014.

11.5 The utility of big data for society

There is more to the utility of big data than an increased individual benefit. I do not argue in favor of an unbalanced use of personal data. The protection of the private sphere of each individual and its personal data is a right that must not be infringed without legal cause and appropriate measures to establish data security and data integrity. However, I do argue that in certain instances, there must be a caveat for data utilization where a higher public purpose is met. This is where an administrative law balancing test between the public's benefit from the data use in contrast to the individual's infringements must be administered. Certainly, using personal data without explicit consent to resolve traffic jams stands a different proportionality test than does fighting a pandemic outbreak. The GDPR does not sufficiently account for society's potential interest in using data mining for public service goods. Certainly, it has a different legal quality whether private corporations or public agencies use the data and how its security and integrity is ensured. But that is a subsequent step to acknowledging that in certain instances, the public's interest in data mining for services outweighs the individual's interest of non-utilization.

The next two examples give insights into the population in real time that allows for better humanitarian crisis management and economic optimization. The two examples also illustrate two different types of consent given by the data subject.

11.5.1 Example #1: Spreading of a pandemic

In 2008, the project Google Flu Trend (GFT) was introduced. It is designed to track health behaviors online by analyzing Google user's search queries. The benchmark is the historic baseline influenza level and the search queries are related to that. The more the two data sets diverge from each other, the higher the influenza alert is. *Ginsberg/Mohebbi/Patel/Brammer /Smolinski/Brilliant* developed the search algorithm.[535] The first step is to compound data of the

535 *Ginsberg/Mohebbi/Patel/Brammer/Smolinski/Brilliant*, Detecting influenza epidemics using search engine query data, Nature 457 (7232) 2009, pp. 1012–1014, also available at: http://www.nature.com/nature/journal/v457/n7232/full/nature07634.html, last accessed 25 December 2014 and at the free of charge source provided by the authors at http://static.googleusercontent.com/external_content/untrusted_dlcp/research.google.com/en/us/archive/papers/detecting-influenza-epidemics.pdf, last accessed 25 December 2014 (henceforth cited as: *Ginsberg/Mohebbi/Patel/Brammer/Smolinski/Brilliant*, Google Flu Trend).

past. In the case of GFT, the developers used 2003 to 2008 and 50 million queries per week within the U.S., which was then compounded, into geographic regions using the IP addresses.[536] The second task is to collect data to compare the historic base level of influenza with the current situation. If a user is down with influenza, the user will enter search terms into the search engine that reflect on his or her current medical state, i.e. search for a doctor or influenza symptoms:[537]

Fig. 24: Search topics for influenza

	Top 45 Queries		Next 55 Queries	
Search Query Topic	N	Weighted	N	Weighted
Influenza Complication	11	18.15	5	3.40
Cold/Flu Remedy	8	5.05	6	5.03
General Influenza Symptoms	5	2.60	1	0.07
Term for Influenza	4	3.74	6	0.30
Specific Influenza Symptom	4	2.54	6	3.74
Symptoms of an Influenza Complication	4	2.21	2	0.92
Antibiotic Medication	3	6.23	3	3.17
General Influenza Remedies	2	0.18	1	0.32
Symptoms of a Related Disease	2	1.66	2	0.77
Antiviral Medication	1	0.39	1	0.74
Related Disease	1	6.66	3	3.77
Unrelated to Influenza	0	0.00	19	28.37
	45	**49.40**	**55**	**50.60**

Table 1: Topics found in search queries which were found to be most correlated with CDC ILI data. The top 45 queries were used in our final model; the next 55 queries are presented for comparison purposes. The number of queries in each topic is indicated, as well as query volume-weighted counts, reflecting the relative frequency of queries in each topic.

536 *Ginsberg/Mohebbi/Patel/Brammer/Smolinski/Brilliant*, Google Flu Trend, ibd, p. 1016.

537 *Ginsberg/Mohebbi/Patel/Brammer/Smolinski/Brilliant*, Google Flu Trend, ibd, p. 1016.

The result of the comparison can be visualized in two graphs, as done by *Ginsberg/Mohebbi/Patel/Brammer/Smolinski/Brilliant:*[538]

Fig. 25: Influenza trends in winter 2007/08

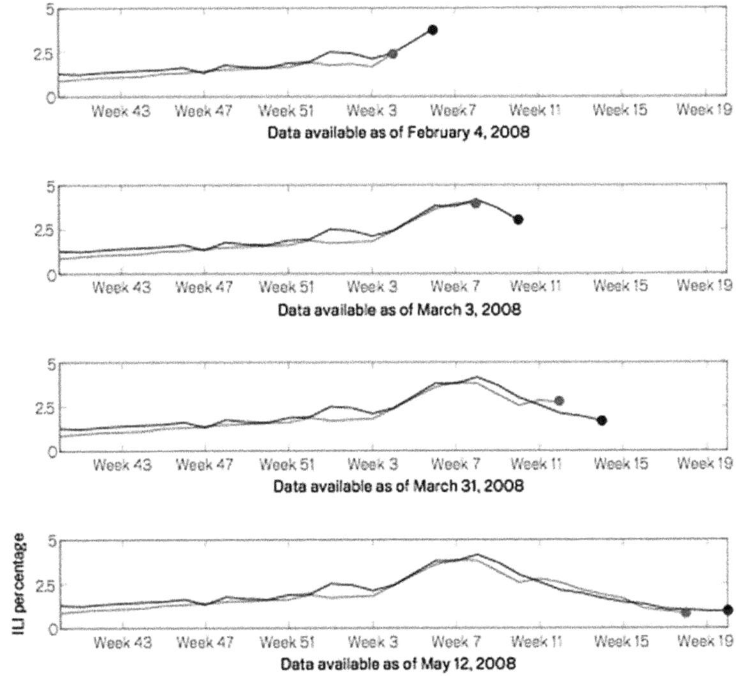

Figure 3: ILI percentages estimated by our model (black) and provided by CDC (red) in the Mid-Atlantic region, showing data available at four points in the 2007-2008 influenza season. During week 5, we detected a sharply increasing ILI percentage in the Mid-Atlantic region; similarly, on March 3, our model indicated that the peak ILI percentage had been reached during week 8, with sharp declines in weeks 9 and 10. Both results were later confirmed by CDC ILI data.

This method of comparing historic data to current influenza levels is not new. Health agencies such as the WHO have used this comparative method before.[539]

538 *Ginsberg/Mohebbi/Patel/Brammer/Smolinski/Brilliant*, Google Flu Trend, ibd, p. 1016.

539 *World Health Organization*, Influenza factsheet 2003, available at: http://www.who.int/mediacentre/factsheets/2003/fs211/en/, last accessed 25 December 2014.

However, GFT was able to take the predictions to unprecedented timeliness and scope because of its access to real time search data and very large data sets. The information that can be obtained this way is very valuable for current global crisis such as the 2014 Ebola epidemic.[540]

11.5.2 Legal implication of example #1

In this example, the search engine users agree to the Terms of Service of the service provider. Their consent is not specifically geared towards the use of their search query for this purpose. For the consent requirement pursuant to Art. 7 GDPR, the data subject must previously consent to the scope of the data gathered from the search query. This will pose a challenge for the terms of service of search engines. Systematically interpreting Art. 7 GDPR, the data subject cannot consent to a data use it does not anticipate. Even though the terms of service may include a consent clause for these purposes, the laws on the general terms of business apply. For instance, in German law, §306c Sec. 1 German Civil Code stipulates that a surprise clause that the consumer does not anticipate is void and has not become a part of the contractual relationship. For the ToS stipulated by a company vis á vis a consumer, this provision may apply in the context of Art. 7 GDPR. The consent regulation in EU regulation will have a guiding effect on the interpretation of the criterion "surprise clause". In the future, for search engines to be on the safe side of privacy and data protection compliance in the EU, they must provide a clear communication of the scope the user's personal data is used for. In line with § 305 Sec. 2 No. 1 German Civil Code, "standard business terms only become a part of a contract if the user, when entering into the contract the other contractual party refers the other party to the contract to them explicitly or, where explicit reference, due to the way in which the contract is entered into, is possible only with disproportionate difficulty, by posting a clearly visible notice at the place where the contract is entered into".[541] One possibility for this is to have an additional disclaimer when cookies are installed for the first time from a particular web page.

In any case, the EU will impose higher consent barriers on the secondary utilization of data. From the company's perspective, this data privacy policy will likely have a deterring effect. If data privacy and consent barriers are substantially

540 See the Google map to track the Ebola spreading over time: https://www.google.com/maps/d/viewer?mid=zlY48eTMIq2I.khr_OK7MUhFY, last accessed 25 December 2014.

541 This is worded after the official translation provided on www.gesetze-im-internet.de, last accessed 29 December 2014.

increased, new insights that rely on a broader scope of consent cannot be obtained, not even for highly useful services such as pandemic forecasting. Policy makers must account for the potential loss of innovative public service tools like these.[542]

11.5.3 Example #2: Traffic optimization with Google and Waze

This example illustrates how broadly available traffic information in combination with GPS based navigation services and user participation can help with real time traffic optimization. Google acquired Waze, the Israel-based company, in June 2013.[543] Waze provides a GPS-based navigation services for smartphones. It gives the user travel updates in real time and helps find the optimal route through a congested area. The following is an example for the route from Berlin to Brussels on 25 December 2014. It flags a standstill between Hannover and Braunschweig on the highway A2 and suggests alternative routes:

Fig. 26: Waze routing through highway congestion

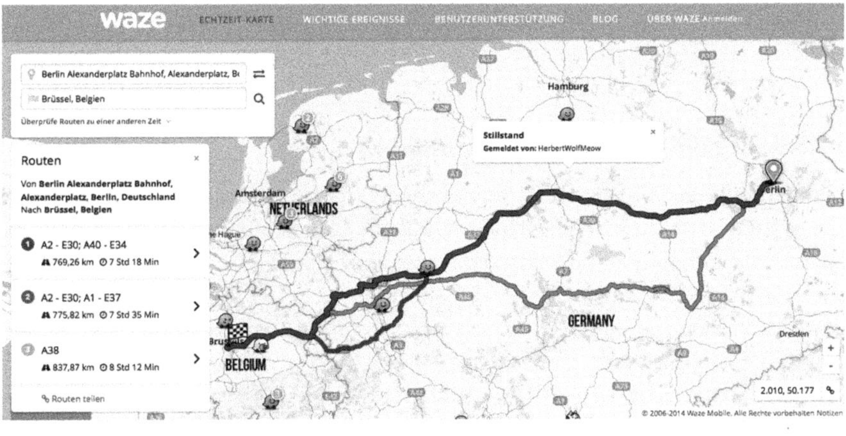

The product innovation of Waze was to deviate from the usual GPS navigation software. It relies on the user's driving time and is interactive because users can report incidents to the app, such as traffic jams, accidents or speeding cameras. It also provides information on gas prices at the different pumping stations nearby. The application's reliability of service depends on a critical mass of Waze-users

542 See in detail Chapter 11.6.1.

543 Reported by Businessweek, available at: http://investing.businessweek.com/research/stocks/private/snapshot.asp?privcapId=58203778, last accessed 25 December 2014.

to feed into the data base with location data. Waze encourages participation by using gaming features such as icons and avatars that can earn points for reporting traffic information. This application has brought the innovation of engaging users in traffic by optimizing their own route choices. It is built on the assumption that a large amount of users will consent to provide accurate location data as well as information about events and problems they observe on the road. The Waze product includes three U.S. patents, most important of which is U.S. patent 8,612,136[544], issued 17 December 2013 with a priority date of 27 August 2008 titled *system and method for road map creation* by Waze Mobile Ltd. With the merger, the intellectual property is now owned by Google Inc. The patent has been filed with the following scope of protection:

> *"The present invention provides system and method for creation of a road map, the system comprising a plurality of navigation devices; and an application server to receive from the plurality of navigation devices time series of location points, and to create a road map based on the time series of location points. The method comprising receiving location points from plurality of navigation devices, along with respective time stamps indicating the time of recordation of each of the location points; identifying at least one route according to the location points and respective time stamps; and creating a road map based on the at least one route."*[545]

11.5.4 Legal implications of example #2

Here, the application users are proactively entering data about their location into the system. If the user is informed about the use of this information, no bias against the company should exist. However, the merger raised concern regarding its anticompetitive effects under the Sherman Act. The merger gave Google a competitive edge because it was able to improve its product's real time navigation feature on Google Maps. The key asset of the merger was Waze's crowdsourced traffic information database that was integrated into Google's services[546] after the merger. The FTC initiated investigations into this merger because Waze was a viable and strong competitor in the online mapping market prior to the merger. However, there is no official record available and the case was closed rapidly because Waze's assets at 70.9 million USD did not reach the FTC investigation

544 See: http://www.google.com/patents/US8612136, last accessed 25 December 2014.

545 *Google Inc.*, Summary description of US Patent No. US8612136 B2, published 17 December 2013, date of priority 27 August 2008, available at: http://www.google.com/patents/US8612136, last accessed 25 December 2014.

546 See above Fig. 23: Google maps routing and traffic information.

threshold.[547] The transaction value threshold under the Hart-Scott-Rodino Antitrust Improvements Act of 1976 was 75.9 million USD at the time of the assessment.

11.6 Conclusion

Cloud computing is an innovation platform that has allowed society to benefit from numerous products and services that help optimizing our personal lives. Furthermore, the technical abilities can help tackle public issues in unprecedented speed through a forecasting method. The legal implications of these developments are huge and our current legal system is in urgent need to catch up with the business realities of the information technology market. The business sense and the pragmatic use of personal data to leverage its information for additional value must be appreciated for the benefits society can generate from it. Especially in the fast-paced field of the information technology sector, policy, politics and the law are hard to unmingle. Legal provisions can easily become a policy-driven tool to push politically desired issues. From a legal perspective, the two largest issues in this context are consent and the limits of data utilization.

11.6.1 Consent

Pursuant to Art. 4 para. 11 GDPR, consent refers to any freely given specific, informed and unambiguous indication of his or her wishes by which the data subject, either by a statement or by a clear affirmative action, signifies agreement to personal data relating to them being processed. Under the proposed new Art. 7 GDPR para. 1, the data controller bears the burden of proof that the data subject has expressed valid consent. This means that consent can no longer be implied. It must cumulatively be given prior to the data use and specific to the purpose the data subject has given consent to.[548] In particularly moving forward with the legal implications of public service big data-based tools, it would be very useful to implement a caveat within the Art. 7 GDPR for the use of personal data that serves a public utility purpose to counter an immanent humanitarian crisis.

The requirements for consensual data gathering and use will increase substantially. From the perspective of data protection, data security and the individual protection of the data subjects' privacy, this is a commendable step. However,

547 http://www.reuters.com/article/2013/06/24/us-google-waze-idUSBRE95N1CE20130624, last accessed 25 December 2014.

548 See in detail Chapter 9.4.

with regard to the market for cloud-based services and the sector relying on data mining, this poses a large problem. Access to datasets is the fuel of this industry. If the scope of the data subject's consent does not include the notice and additional data transfer mechanisms, numerous services and new products will not emerge or their utility and development be stifled. If the ToS and SLAs cannot be designed sufficiently broadly to accommodate the business interest of the company, the short-term consequence is that the users will not receive the quality of service within the EU internal market due to a restrictive use of personal data in comparison to the U.S. market. In the medium and long term, a too restrictive consent-policy will bear the heavier consequence of start-ups shying away from the EU internal market due to the prospect of heavy sanctions and technologically unreasonable compliance policies.

From a technical perspective, metadata oftentimes yields more utility to a company than the actual data. The law does not recognize this pattern and assumes the same consent structures and utilization patterns. This is unfortunate because an aggregate use of metadata would be a possibility to mitigate the data privacy concerns raised by EU policy makers and the data access needs of the sector.

11.6.2 Data utilization

The GDPR is lackluster with regard to one mayor issue: It does not clearly distinguish between the handling of data and metadata. Data is the actual content of the information transmitted. Metadata is information that surrounds the transmission of the information itself, it is the "data about data". The following example shall illustrate this distinction:

> A calls B to inform him that the appointment at the doctor went well and he should not be concerned. – This is the actual information that is transmitted through the call.
>
> A calls B from telephone number +1 415 XXX–XXXX and reaches B not at +49 162 XXXX XXX, but at +44 XXX XXX XX. The call lasts 38 seconds. The call is placed at cell phone cluster XYZ, approximate location Market Street, San Francisco, USA and received at cell phone cluster ABC, approximate location Oxford Circus, London, UK. – This is the metadata.
>
> In this example, there is certainly value to the information that A's medical condition is no longer critical. But from a surveillance point of view, even more valuable is the fact that A's and B's geographic location can be determined. B seems to have two international phone numbers. And B seems to be using the UK number, not the German one; and so forth.

Here the distinction between information, knowledge and data becomes important again, as outlined introducing the concepts in Chapter 2.1. The value of metadata is oftentimes higher than the value of the data itself. Metadata allows the creation of patterns. Those patterns can range from geographic location, frequency and sequence of contact information (B always calls C after having spoken to A). There is commercial as well as governmental interest associated with this information. A commercial interest may be the ride share service knowing where to pick you up, a governmental interest may lay in tracking down a suspect. Google maps knows that there is a traffic jam on I-280 at a specific intersection through the transmission of metadata. In any case, we as front end device users enable data centers to process vast amount of metadata every second. We agree to the transmission with by accepting the ToS. If the GDPR desires to strike a balance between commercial interests and privacy, it ought to differentiate clearly between these two types of data. Otherwise, one could respect privacy and data protection rules by not looking into the information that is transmitted. But the personal sphere of the data subject is not safeguarded by any means if metadata is up for grabs. On the other hand, businesses operate on the basis of using data. Jeopardizing the free flow and handling of data for the commercial sector will stifle the EU market for innovative cloud-based products.

Part IV: Cloud computing and the road ahead

12 Cyber foreign policy

Cloud service providers have recently experienced a lot of political push back because of the governmental use personal data. Cyber foreign politics is no longer a niche activity but a core concern on the international diplomatic agenda. The recent cyber security efforts are a legal recourse and a political reaction. But just because cyber security has not been at the forefront of the international political agenda before does not mean that there is no preexisting legal environment. This chapter illustrates the provisions already in place.

12.1 Introduction to the NIS Directive

The Directive of the European Parliament and of the Council concerning measures to ensure a high common level of network and information security across the Union (NIS Directive) is designed to ensure a uniform network and information security (NIS) level. The NIS Directive proposes an increased collaboration between EU Member States. It will also mandate *operators of critical infrastructures, such as energy, transport, and key providers of information society services (e-commerce platforms, social networks, etc.), as well as public administrations to adopt appropriate steps to manage security risks and report serious incidents to the national competent authorities.*[549] Data gathered from information society services such as social networks and commerce platforms as well as banking data inherently entails personal data. Since the NIS Directive mandates that risk management measures and information exchange with relevant authorities be adopted[550], the information to be exchanged may at the same time be subject to the GDPR. A leading concern the NIS Directive aims to mitigate is the unequal level of consumer and business protection in the EU internal market.[551] The NIS Directive will play an important role in the interpretation of the new GDPR. The NIS Directive has been proposed a year after the GDPR. It shows that recent political and international affairs have stirred up numerous regulatory needs in the field of IT security. This is also reflected by the proposal recitals:

> *"The magnitude and frequency of deliberate or accidental security incidents is increasing and represents a major threat to the functioning of networks and information systems.*

549 *NIS Directive*, loc. cit. Fn. 8, p. 2.

550 *NIS Directive*, ibd, p. 4.

551 *NIS Directive*, ibd, p. 4, Ref. No. 6.

Such incidents can impede the pursuit of economic activities, generate substantial financial losses, undermine user confidence and cause major damage to the economy of the Union."[552]

12.2 Pre-existing legal provisions for IT security

The NIS Directive will be embedded in a preexisting but currently still fragmented legal environment. This field ranges from the protection of critical infrastructure facilities to cybercrime combatting efforts. The European Network and Information Security Agency (ENISA) competency is rooted in Regulation (EC) No. 460/2004 and in existence since 2010. ENISA's mandate is to ensure network and information security within the EU internal market. ENISA has played an important role in the Microsoft[553] proceedings because it contributed opinion statements to the technical parameters of application programming interfaces (API). ENISA conducts numerous and diverse empirical studies for the purposes of market assessment. On 30 September 2010, a proposal was adopted to modernize the ENISA mandate.[554]

In addition, there is Directive 2002/21/EC of the European Parliament and of the Council of 7 March 2002 on a common regulatory framework for electronic communications networks and services that aims to strengthen competition by making market entry easier and by stimulating investment in the sector.[555] Art. 13a and Art. 13b Directive 2002/21/EC stipulates security requirements for electronic communication service providers that had been implemented by the Member States since May 2011.

The most important effective regulation is Directive 2002/58/EC of the European Parliament and of the Council of 12 July 2002 concerning the processing of personal data and the protection of privacy in the electronic communications sector.[556] There is an interrelation between the GDPR and the NIS Directive with regard to network and information security breaches regarding personal data. If the breach compromises personal data, the reporting and notification requirements are triggered. This is not the case if compromised services are unrelated to

---

552 *NIS Directive*, ibd, p. 4, Ref. No. 2.

553 *Microsoft I*, 2007, loc. cit. Fn. 332 and previously: *Microsoft*, COMP/C-3/37.792, loc. cit. Fn. 82 and *Microsoft II*, 2012, loc. cit. 361.

554 *EU Commission*, press release 16 April 2013, loc. cit. Fn. 12.

555 The Directive is available at: http://europa.eu/legislation_summaries/information_society/legislative_framework/l24216a_en.htm, last accessed 29 December 2014.

556 Directive 2002/58/EC, loc. cit. Fn. 183, p. 37–47.

personal data usage, e.g. a gas turbine control failure. In this case, the NIS Directive applies, but not in relation with the GDPR.

In the field of cyber security, regulation on the protection of critical infrastructure (CI) existed before. Pursuant to Art. 2 lit. a Directive 2008/114/EC of 8 December 2008[557], CI is defined as

> *„an asset, system or part thereof located in Member States which is essential for the maintenance of vital societal functions, health, safety, security, economic or social well-being of people, and the disruption or destruction of which would have a significant impact in a Member State as a result of the failure to maintain those functions".*

The distinction between CI and European critical infrastructures (ECI) is the implication of its disruption. The CI is within the boundaries of one member state of the EU whereas an ECI concerns more than one member state in its supply stability and security. Pursuant to Art. 2 lit. a of Directive 2008/114/EC 8 December 2008, ECI is defined as

> *"critical infrastructure located in Member States the disruption or destruction of which would have a significant impact on at least two Member States. The significance of the impact shall be assessed in terms of cross-cutting criteria. This includes effects resulting from cross-sector dependencies on other types of infrastructure."*

Pursuant to Annex I Directive 2008/114/EC, ECI is segmented into energy sectors electricity, gas and oil. In the electricity sector, the critical components are associated with generation and transmission. In the gas sector, the critical components include production, refining, treatment, striate, pipeline transmission and LNG facilities.[558] With regard to the oil sector, the scope covers production, refining, treatment, storage and pipeline transmission.[559] Within the transportation sector, the covered components are road, rail and air transportation, inland waterways transport and ocean and short-sea shipping including ports.[560] If the electricity grid CI and ECI fail function smoothly, the impact of a failure is severe. The electricity supply system is interconnected with many other sectors relying on the energy input to function, such

557 Council Directive 2008/114/EC of 8 December 2008 on the identification and designation of European critical infrastructures and the assessment of the need to improve their protection, O.J. L 345/75 dated 23 December 2008 (henceforth cited as: Directive 2008/114/EC).

558 Annex I of Directive 2008/114/EC, ibd.

559 Annex I of Directive 2008/114/EC, ibd.

560 Annex I of Directive 2008/114/EC. ibd.

as water pumps, the stock exchange, traffic and many more.[561] A problem in the electricity grid spreads without much buffering time to react, in real time. Maintenance has to be conducted in real time. However, there are sensitive infrastructure components in other energy networks as well. Electricity substations and interconnectors, gas compressor stations at significant pipelines, oil ports and major oil pipelines have been identified as the most sensitive components within energy supply networks.[562]

The protection of CI and ECI and the question of risk governance in the 21st century is not only a matter of physical infrastructure protection. Risk governance has become a matter that cyber security investors must be conscious about.[563] A joint effort of the EU and the U.S. to identify cyber security concerns is the European Dependability Initiative (EDI) implemented in 1998/99, followed by the Dependability Development Support Initiative (DDSI) in 2001/02[564] and the European Program for Critical Infrastructure Protection (EPCIP) in 2004[565]. Even though the protection of CI is primarily a national concern, the EU adopted enhanced responsibility for the physical and cyber security of CI and ECI. With regard to cyber crime, the Commission established a European Cyber Crime Center (EC3) on 11 January 2013 that has become part of EUROPOL, the European Police Office. Furthermore, European agencies, institutions and bodies are obligated under the NIS Directive to set up their own Computer Emergency Response Teams (CERT-EU).[566]

---

561 *AEA*, Study on Risk Governance of European Critical Infrastructures in the ICT and Energy Sector, Final Report to European Commission Directorate-General Justice, Freedom and Security, 4 September 2009, p. 5, also available at: http://ec.europa.eu/energy/infrastructure/studies/doc/2009_10_risk_governance_report.pdf, last accessed 9 May 2012 (henceforth cited as: *AEA*, 2009).

562 *AEA*, 2009, ibd, p. 5.

563 See *European Commission*, The Commission Staff Working Document on "Towards a general policy on the Fight against Cyber Crime" – SEC 2007/ 641, 642, Brussels dated 22 May setting out the future approach of the EU-wide combat against cyber crime.

564 *AEA*, 2009, loc. cit. Fn. 562, p. 12.

565 See in detail: http://europa.eu/legislation_summaries/justice_freedom_security/fight_against_terrorism/l33260_en.htm, last accessed 25 November 2012, more recent risk governance mechanisms are enlisted on this homepage as well.

566 *NIS Directive*, loc. cit. Fn. 8, p. 6

12.3 Transatlantic cooperation for cybersecurity

The EU-U.S. Summit in 2010 established the Working Group on Cybersecurity and Cybercrime.[567] The working group consists of four subgroups: i) cyber incident management, ii) public-private partnerships, iii) awareness raising and iv) cyber crime.[568] The cooperation is mostly focused on human rights and the criminal aspects of cyber security. These include the protection of human rights online and conduct rules in cyberspace. However, there is also business-related involvement when in comes to building cyber security capacity in third countries, enhancing the security of internet protocol addresses and domains and establishing a uniform guideline for commercial purpose online tracking.[569] The Brussels Summit on 26 March 2014 strengthened this collaboration by initiating a platform to work on key international cyber developments and foreign policy-related cyber issues. Foreign policy and security policy matters will be the core subjects of this platform.[570] This goes to show that joint transatlantic efforts will increasingly dominate the know-how exchange and state of the art cyber and IT-compliance.

12.4 Key provisions of the NIS Directive

On 7 February 2013, the Proposal for a Directive of the European Parliament and of the Council concerning measures to ensure a high common level of network and information security across the Union (NIS Directive) was presented.[571] The European Parliament has adopted the NIS Directive on 6 July 2016.[572]

The NIS Directive is the first legislative framework that will apply to digital platforms. Platform providers will have to take measures to ensure the safety of

567 *European Union External Action*, Factsheet EU-US cooperation on cyber security and cyberspace, No. 14326/01, 26 March 2014, available at: http://www.eeas.europa.eu/statements/docs/2014/140326_01_en.pdf, last accessed 29 December 2014 (henceforth cited as: *EU External Action*, 2014).

568 *EU External Action*, 2014, ibd, p. 2.

569 *EU External Action*, 2014, ibd, p. 2.

570 *EU External Action*, 2014, ibd, p. 1.

571 *NIS Directive*, loc. cit. Fn. 8.

572 See the European Parliament press release: http://www.europarl.europa.eu/news/en/news-room/20160701IPR34481/Cybersecurity-MEPs-back-rules-to-help-vital-services-resist-online-threats, last accessed 10 July 2016. Published in O.J. L 194 dated 19 July 2016, available here: http://eur-lex.europa.eu/legal-content/EN/TXT/PDF/?uri=OJ:L:2016:194:FULL&from=EN, last accessed 4 August 2016.

the infrastructure. Security incidents have to be reported to national authorities. However, micro and small digital companies are exempt.

EU member states will then have 21 months to transpose the NIS Directive into their national laws and six additional months to identify operators of essential services.

Pursuant to Art. 1 NIS Directive, the provisions aim to ensure a high common level of network and information security within the EU internal market. It establishes security requirements for market operators and public administrations. Pursuant to Art. 2 para. 1 NIS Directive, the rules governing the processing of personal data apply.

It is technically not feasible to operate with network and information systems that store, process, retrieve or transmit computer stored data without affecting the transmission security requirements stipulated by the Directive 95/46/EC and now the GDPR.

The security of information is defined in Art. 4 para. 2 NIS Directive as "*the ability of network and information systems to resist, at a given level of confidence, any action that compromises the availability, authenticity, integrity or confidentiality of stored or transmitted or processed data or the related services offered by, or accessible via, those network and information systems.*"

If the integrity and confidentiality of personal data is compromised by a privacy breach, it is a consequence of a security breach because the network and information system did not resist the attack. Consequently, the NIS Directive cannot factually be without prejudice and interconnection to provisions concerning the protection of personal data. The interrelation of the NIS Directive with data protection provisions will continue to increase with the new GDPR. Pursuant to Art. 15 para. 4 NIS Directive, the national authorities in charge of enforcing NIS shall work closely with the national authorities in charge of personal data protection when addressing incidents resulting in personal data breach.

There are three main mechanisms to ensure NIS. Firstly, EU Member States shall establish a national framework for NIS, Art. 7 NIS Directive. Secondly, the competent authorities to ensure NIS shall form a cooperation network to exchange information, circulate early warnings and risks and discuss strategies, Art. 11 NIS Directive. ENISA is mandated to assist through expertise and advice, Art. 11 para. 2 NIS Directive. Thirdly, there are security and notification requirements for market operators stipulated in Art. 14 NIS Directive. These provisions directly address the private sector with compliance requirements. Pursuant to Annex III, reference to Art. 5 para. 4 NIS Directive, the sectors concerned are online marketplaces, online search engines and cloud computing service providers.

The security requirements stipulated in Art. 16 NIS Directive apply to all market operators providing services within the EU internal market, Art. 16 para. 1. This means that the requirements will target any private entity – with disregard to the registered seat of the company - that is not a microenterprise as defined by Commission Recommendation 2003/361/EC dated 6 May 2003, Art. 14 para. 11 NIS Directive. Security requirements include that companies adopt state of the art technical measures to ensure the level of security to prevent and minimize the impact of incidents that could affect the NIS and the core services the company provides, Art. 16 para. 1.

Both national authorities and the EU Commission will determine the specifics of the technical requirements. Pursuant to Art. 16 para. 9, the Commission may issue implementing acts to define the technical formats and procedures for the notification requirements.

12.5 Enforcement and sanctions

Art. 15 para. 2 lit. a and lit. b NIS Directive mandates EU Member State authorities to request information from private companies in order to check for their compliance with security policies. Furthermore, they can be obligated to undergo a security audit performed by a third party or the competent public authority. Art. 17 para. 1 NIS Directive authorizes Member States to stipulate effective, proportionate and dissuasive rules for sanctioning information and network security breaches. Pursuant to Art. 17 para. 2, the sanctions concerning personal data breaches must be consistent with the GDPR.

12.6 Conclusion

The NIS Directive shows that privacy and data protection becomes more interwoven into civil and criminal law security regulation. The compliance demands will increase on both hardware and software components as the basis of data management platforms that handle personal data. The Commission has an increasingly heavy hand in not just the legal requirements but also the technical standard settings to ensure network and information security. From a practitioner's point of view, this means that a data security breach of a data center processing EU citizens' personal data triggers incident notification requirements under the NIS Directive and the GDPR.

Recent political and international affairs led the EU policy and lawmakers to move more quickly towards a coherent cyber security and data privacy regime. For private actors, this means that the density of compliance regulations and potential audits will increase.

13 Conclusions and Outlook

The two largest obstacles cloud service providers face on the EU market is the lack of a predictable legal environment and gaining the market's trust to adopt cloud-based solutions for business and private utilization model. The customers demand a higher level of accountability from cloud service providers in the EU in comparison to the U.S.

Cloud computing is a new technology. As a new technology, it faces an abundance of regulations that are undergoing large changes. Investing in this new technology as a customer also means that there is a risk of legal uncertainty under current and future provisions. The scope of the liability is not fully foreseeable at this stage. But the first waves of the new EU data privacy regime can already be seen in *Google Spain SL, Google Inc. v Agencia Española de Protección de Datos (AEPD), Mario Costeja González*[573] and the right to be forgotten. Designing contracts with tight and detailed rules around data collection, retention, transmission and deletion have become the primary tool of cloud service providers to navigate EU laws. The relationship between the service provider and the customer is largely governed by their contractual relationship on the level of private ordering. Now, companies need to go back and revise these contracts to meet the stricter requirements of the GDPR and the Privacy Shield, especially with regard to onward transfers to sub-processors.

This thesis described the basic technical parameters of cloud computing and the legal framework it operates in. The main two reasons to make legal provisions more technology-driven are the technical feasibility of remedies and the mirroring of business needs in the IT sector. Firstly, legal provisions require technical implementation. The right to be forgotten clearly illustrates that implementation is furthermore not just a binary decision. There are multiple options, depths and ways of compliance. What is legally desirable is not always technically feasible. And technical possibilities must be mirrored in the law to make sure the legally required protection levels are feasible. Secondly, the law must reflect the market's business realities. The cloud services sector is aiming at making geographical boundaries obsolete. The infrastructure, platform and services are accessible from anywhere around the globe with an internet connection. This level of availability is catering to consumers on an unprecedented scale and people rely on these services increasingly. The law must ensure that

573 *Google/Costeja,* C-131/12, loc. cit. Fn. 4.

the business need for data transfer, retention and utilization are sufficiently accounted for in order to keep providing these services. The different understandings of data privacy in the EU and the U.S. leave regulatory gaps behind that are still not accounted for in the GDPR.

At this stage, the best strategy for the near future is to have a clear direction in the law. The uncertainty is what makes compliance with the law so expensive, burdensome and in the end a discouragement to engage with the EU internal market. Mirroring this, legal uncertainty contributes to lacking trust on the consumers' side in adopting cloud solutions despite their economic benefits. This has negative effects for all parties involved. Consumers in the EU should be able to profit from innovative products and services and service providers should not have to forego participating in this market due to conflicting or prohibitively expensive compliance requirements. In the following, I will summarize the key findings of the research. Lastly, I will provide recommendations for possible technical, organizational and legal remedies to shed light on the key issues of the legal environment cloud service providers operate in today.

13.1 Benefits and risks of the cloud

Cloud computing is an innovation accelerator. Its characteristics such as elasticity and utility payment schemes have reduced the barriers to market entry because of scalable IT resources. Market entrants now need a substantially less upfront IT infrastructure because cloud services can be provisioned on demand. The vast amount of idle resources through overprovisioning can be reduced because the hardware is no longer taken care of by each user individually. Customers can rely on an optimal use of resources and pay only for the computing power needed. Movements towards cloud standardization and higher uniform cloud security standards also contribute to making the cloud more attractive to customers who are on the very risk adverse side. Lastly, taking part in cloud computing ensures that the customers do not miss out on technological progress because of lacking funds to continuously upgrade the IT in-house infrastructure.

Currently, cloud services are also associated with several downsides. Cloud service customers face lacking standardization. This in connection with losing control over the data leads to significant switching costs and lock-in effects. Furthermore, privacy and data protection standards remain a concern for the vast majority of cloud service customers. In connection with intransparent billing schemes, this still has as a deterring effect.

13.2 In-house IT transformation

Once the customer has decided to implement a cloud solution, the internal IT processes need to be prepared. In this regard, there are two types of cloud users. On the one hand, there is the customer that is starting the business from scratch and decides to rely on cloud solutions from the get-go. For this customer bracket the IT transformation process does not pose an implementation challenge beyond the cost and time needed to set up the IT infrastructure on the front end. On the other hand, there is the cloud customer with pre-existing IT infrastructure. There, the IT transformation process can pose an additional challenge with the in-house IT department. Information and data streams must be identified in-house and then made ready for transformation into the new cloud structure. For that, the in-house IT team must identify the specific applications that can be migrated to the cloud and those that cannot. For that, the companies must answer numerous preparatory questions. Certain types of data may not be suitable for hybrid cloud migration because of data privacy requirements. Also, companies must figure out how to process governmental requests for information. For example, when the district attorney's office inquires for court-ordered access to telecommunication interception of a suspect pursuant to § 100a of the German Criminal Procedure Code, this must be processed by the system within the required time frame.

Cloud service providers offer localized "compliant clouds" in specific jurisdictions to mitigate some of the customers' privacy and security concerns. This approach takes away a few benefits of the cloud. A key technological step of cloud computing is that physical geographic location does not play a role in accessing, transmitting and processing data. Fragmenting the service into jurisdictional and geographic parameters takes away from this achievement but meets local accountability demands of the customer.

13.3 Cloud market exposure to EU and Member State data protection law

The cloud market has exposure to data privacy laws on EU and Member State level. Firstly, this is very important to stay current on the applicable data privacy laws. Currently, Directive 95/46/EC is the valid data privacy law regime, in combination with the implementing national laws. In Germany this is the Federal Data Protection Act – *Bundesdatenschutzgesetz.* With the current legislative process, the new GDPR has introduced an elevated and modernized standard of privacy and data protection that will come into effect on 25 May 2018. In contrast to Directive 95/46/EC, the GDPR will be directly applicable in Member States as its legal nature is a Regulation.

Firstly, the right to be forgotten will not only have data privacy law implications and technical challenges but also affects the dimension of freedom of speech and the press. In this regard, American and German constitutional law and society's view on freedom of speech and the press are different. Being compliant with the right to be forgotten will not only be a question of implementing IT processes in line with the law. It is also a politically charged provision. Its implementation by U.S. technology companies will be an issue that draws in the spotlight. Secondly, the requirements for data collection, consent structures, retention, transmission, notification and deleting time frames will become more complex and densely regulated under the GDPR. Compliance mechanisms should be implemented as early as possible, keeping the future stricter standard in mind. With that, contract adjustment and IT transformation will require fewer resources once the changes are implemented. Particular attention must be paid to consent structures. Mirroring the business reality of "click and consent", this is not a sufficient level of customer protection. Consent requirements will increase, as it will need to be explicit for the processing of sensitive data, and linked to more formal requirements. Thirdly, current political developments have made the data transfer standards more burdensome. Several thousand companies were self-certified through the EU-U.S. Safe Harbor framework and over half of them used the certification to transfer human resources data.[574] As of 1 August 2016, the successor of the EU-U.S. Safe Harbor, the EU-U.S. Privacy Shield, is open for self-certification. Certifying companies now need to make sure that their data processing activities are compliant with the Privacy Shield Privacy Principles and complete the certification requirements on www.privacyshield.gov.

13.4 General Data Protection Regulation

The GDPR is the result of a need to a uniform privacy and data protection laws. The GDPR should be seen in the larger context as well. It is not only a reform of the privacy and data protection standards. It also stands for a political response to the transatlantic developments in data security. In light of this, there are two main issues the GRPR should have placed an emphasis on: Meta data protection and the clear distinction between causality and correlation.

574 *EU Commission*, Communication on the Functioning of the Safe Harbour, loc. cit. Fn. 9.

Firstly, the information value derived from meta data is oftentimes higher than the actual data. The GDPR does not consider the protection from pseudonomyzed meta data separately from personal data protection. This distinction would be important because meta data is able to show a complete systematic movement pattern of the data subject even without knowing its human identity. It has lower storage capacity requirements and can therefore be retained for a longer period of time than the actual communication contents. Taking technical abilities more into consideration when drafting legal provisions would cover loopholes like these. If customer protection is a high priority of the GDPR, a specific regulation with regard to meta data gathering, use, retention, resale and data mining is necessary.

Secondly, correlation of two events does not mean that they are causally linked. This distinction becomes particularly important with regard to criminal law. Big data is able to uncover correlation between events that have been hidden knowledge before. For example at Walmart, the sale of strawberry frosting cupcakes increases exponentially when there is a hurricane alert. Without the shopping data evaluation, very likely neither an outsider nor a Walmart store manager would have uncovered this opportunity to increase sales. Using the same mechanism with regard to human profiling is able to fundamentally challenge the principle of "innocent until proven guilty". If previous behaviors in combination correlate with a criminal rate, it can also serve as an indicator to future criminal conduct of the data subject. This however, preempts the assumption of innocence and is in breach of the constitutional pillar of the assumption of innocence. The GDPR does not incorporate this distinction explicitly. Mistaking correlation for causation in law enforcement is the most detrimental harm data analysis can cause to any individual. It lacks consent, remedy and transparency and leads to adverse effects that are beyond the individual defendant's control. The GDPR should have included safeguards to prevent these data use cases.

13.5 Cloud market exposure to EU competition law

The innovations of cloud computing pose a large challenge to the current competition law framework. The market definition structured by geographic, product and timely considerations do not fit seamlessly for this business model. This is owed to the nature of the cloud service. It is designed to innovate away considerations of geographic boundary and national limits of access. In my view, the geographic parameters will be rendered less significant whereas the timely component of the market – given the rate of innovation – will gain importance and weight in the assessment process. From a market integration perspective, the assessments will likely focus on neighboring or up-and downstream markets. With cloud computing being an outsourcing model, the number of actors involved has increased. With that, the number of contractual relationships has increased as well. The number of exposed customers to cloud risks and benefits increases. This must play a role in assessing the correct demand and supply side product market.

Even if the cloud computing service provider is headquartered outside the EU, as soon as market activity is touching on the EU internal market, competition law is applicable. Hence, the physical location of the data centers, the taxing jurisdiction or other factors are not able to prevent applicability of competition law. Also, the SLA may stipulate the governing law of the contract to be outside the EU. That is a valid legal provision under conflict of laws regulation for rules that are at the disposition of the contracting parties. But mandatory regulations such as competition law and its enforcement cannot be circumvented on a private ordering level. The major gate for competition law exposure of a cloud computing service provider is data privacy. In recent competition and antitrust law development, qualitative data protection concerns have been made an argument within the pro-and anticompetitive case analysis, most notably in *TomTom/Teleatlas* and *Google/DoubleClick*.[575] Under EU law, the self-regulatory behavior of the market participant is an expected form of conduct, i.e. under Art. 101 para. 3 TFEU. For the correct market conduct, the market player needs to understand what is expected of him and how self-regulatory behavior works. Strategic alliances are very useful to make cooperators out of competitors. However, their competition law boundaries under Art. 101 TFEU are very narrowly defined.

13.6 What can U.S. cloud service operators do to stay compliant with EU laws?

Cloud service providers are exposed to EU and Member State laws and policies. Compliance with the law on its face is oftentimes not possible without an IT transformation. Because of this, we should distinguish between technical, business organizational and legal measures to achieve compliance.

575 See in detail Chapters 7.2.1 and 7.2.3 on *Google/DoubleClick* – FTC File No. 071–0170 (Federal Trade Commission) and Case COMP/M.4731 – *Google/DoubleClick* (European Commission) and *TomTom/Tele Atlas* – Case COMP/M.4854 dated 14 May 2008.

Cloud service operators face technical exposure on multiple levels. With regard to this thesis, ensuring interoperability is a crucial factor. Interoperability ensures data portability, and with that mitigates lock-in effects on customers. But interoperability also increases the companies' exposure to cyber attacks. It is disproportionately more difficult to protect an interoperable IT system in comparison to a proprietary platform. A second point of exposure is compliance with privacy and data protection laws on a technical level. The easiest but most resource intensive and expensive solution is to duplicate all IT facilities and keep the EU and U.S. markets separate from each other. This however, may not be feasible for every company. For startups, this is a prohibitively expensive solution to compliance issues. For large corporations, it may not be feasible to separate its business activities along geographic borders. Certifications pursuant to ISO 19600, ISO/IEC 27001 or IDW PS 980 did not provide a clear and holistic solution either. This is a process in transformation since ISO/IEC 27018 was released in August 2014. ISO/IEC 27018 is an important tool to close the gap between the legal requirements and technical integrity of information management platforms.

Cloud service providers must also show a sophisticated internal organization layout to deal with compliance requirements and notification reporting lines in case of privacy breaches. For that, the new GDPR will impose a dense set of rules on corporate offices, compliance officers and notification specialists. Under the GDPR, data controllers and data processors are obligated to appoint a data protection officer if the company fits the criteria of Art. 37 GDPR.

Cloud service operators can limit their liability for tying and exclusionary practices if they are clear up front about their terms of service. For that, the cloud service provider should explicitly show his billing scheme and list what cloud service components are charged for. If the services are offered in aggregate, the customer should be informed whether or not he has the option of segmenting the service package and what that would do to the pricing of the service. The way the consumer is informed must not be taking advantage of the imbalance of information between the contractual parties. The terms of service are subject to the member state national law equivalent of Sec. 305 et. seqq. German Civil Code for a validity check.

In terms of strategic alliances, cloud service operators must be aware of both the benefits and the risks that sharing knowledge comes with. When entering into a standardization agreement, the boundaries of Art. 101 TFEU are tightly set. Data protection standards are on track to becoming a legitimate exemption argument pursuant to Art. 101 para. 3 TFEU, but the general rule of a prohibited hard core cartel under Art. 101 para. 1 TFEU still applies. Also, no de minimis safe harbor can be stipulated to in case of a hard-core cartel.

There is a connection between innovation and interoperability. The higher the interoperability, the better the market enables the players to participate in the process of incremental innovation. A lower rate of interoperability leads to less common ground between market players. This in turn means that the rate of incremental innovation on the market will be lower. However, at the same time this enables forces and incentives for radical innovation. Because it is not possible to "rest on" a high level of interoperability, competitors are forced to innovate around the barrier.

Cloud service operators face substantial privacy and data protection law exposure. Working with these laws is a challenge on several levels. In transatlantic relationships, data transfer compliance requirements play a major role in lowering transaction costs for companies relying on data transfer possibilities for their business operations. The EU-U.S. Privacy Shield entails stricter requirements than its predecessor, the EU-U.S. Safe Harbor, and gives individuals several remedies to complain about the companies' data processing activities. Another compliance alternative is the implementation of BCRs or SCCs that many companies have already opted for.

With regard to consent structures, cloud service providers must ensure that the customer's contract or consent covers the full scope of the company's personal data use, retention and transmission. It would make sense to combine the data subject's consent with a provision on the right to be forgotten. If the data subject waives or keeps its rights to an ex post claim on deleting search queries on the grounds of the right to be forgotten, the legal situation would be clearer in the future. Abiding by stricter standards from the start is easier than a roll-out, data migration and IT transformation once it becomes mandatory. Also, this would have a signaling effect for higher consumer protection standards.

Vertical integration of the company may generate the benefit of data availability. If data is available in-house through subsidiaries of the same conglomerate, data transfer provisions only apply in limited scope. This way, accessing more data becomes easier. Secondly, the SLA's contractual provisions may be tailored to the client location depending on the governing role. Flanking dispute resolution clauses may be added to avoid conflicting data privacy regulations. Cloud service providers could use a system of "check boxes" whereby the customer can select the jurisdictions it touches upon. This way, the cloud service provider knows its exposure first hand from its customer. Hand in hand goes the idea that the cloud service provider should implement an internal checklist for the parameters that are relevant for the overall cost of data privacy levels depending on the jurisdiction. Lastly, engaging in a strategic alliance with other actors on the relevant market helps with jointly upholding the standard.

The data protection officer in a company will carry a steadily increasing responsibility to stay in line with self-certification and self-assessment procedures as they become standard under the GDPR. It can be expected that competition law, privacy and data protection law and big data will go hand in hand in the future with ever tighter cooperation between the government agencies. It can be expected that competition authorities will increasingly coordinate with data privacy agencies to fulfill their legal mandate.

14 Annex: Interview questions for market assessment

In the course of research, I have conducted interviews with startups, large corporations and consultancies in the technology sector. The below is a list of questions along which the interviews were conducted. The questions below are provided in German and English.

14.1 Questionnaire in English

I. Questions on interoperability

- In which legal regime (and why there) consider cloud service providers their IPRs and business secrets – in particular the APIs – protected to the highest degree?
- How is interoperability between the cloud components, i.e. infrastructure and software components, ensured?
- Between which components is interoperability indispensable and which component manufacturer offers more than one component to avoid interoperability problems?
- The information allowing receiving and sending of information at the platform may be seen as interoperability information in terms of an essential facility under competition law (Art. 102 TFEU) to which TPA rights may have to be granted. Do the cloud service providers have a strategy developed to defend themselves against TPA-claims?
- How high is the probability considered that elements of the cloud will be considered essential?
- Which possibilities does a user have to switch between cloud service providers and "take their data with them"? How often do these switches occur?

II. Questions on data privacy

- How are the contractual clauses in the service level agreement drafted with regard to data privacy?
- Which parameters are relevant for the calculation of costs of data privacy?
- On the basis of which incentive mechanisms are cloud operators willing to burden costs for data privacy?
- How are cloud service providers preparing themselves to buffer the effects of the reputation mechanism regarding data privacy questions?

- Are there initiated plans to expand as a vertically integrated company i.e. through a merger to mitigate data privacy concerns and to enlarge the available data within the company?
- Is there empirical value of cloud service providers active in the United States regarding the Stored Communications Act 1986 that had to take position to data privacy law questions?

III. Questions on standardization agreements

- Is there an exchange of thoughts (or even an agreement) between cloud service providers to enter a standardization agreement in pursuit of lowering the costs of data privacy provision?
- Are there cases of cloud service providers that have approached the European Commission or any other (competition/antitrust) agency with the purpose of arguing for the admissibility of such a standardization agreement?
- If such standardization agreement does not exist, which parameters form the competitive pressure for higher data privacy?

14.2 Questionnaire in German

I. Fragen zur Interoperabilität

- In welcher Rechtsordnung (und wieso dort) halten die Cloud-Anbieter ihre Rechte aus geistigem Eigentum und ihre Geschäftsgeheimnisse, insbesondere die APIs (Application Programming Interfaces), am stärksten geschützt?
- Wie wird die Interoperabilität der Cloud-Komponenten, z. B. die Infrastrukturkomponenten, Softwarekomponenten, etc., sichergestellt?
- Zwischen welchen Komponenten ist die Interoperabilität unerlässlich und welcher Komponentenhersteller bietet mehr als nur eine Komponente an, sodass die Interoperabilität keine Schwierigkeit darstellt? (Als Parallele für diese Frage vergleichbar mit Microsoft Word und dem Windows-Betriebssystem, nur für Cloud-Komponenten)
- Die Informationen, wie die Plattform Informationen empfängt und sendet, könnte als Interoperabilität als eine wesentliche Einrichtung/essential facility im Sinne des Wettbewerbsrechts angesehen werden (Art. 102 AEUV), zu der Drittzugangsrechte eingeräumt werden müssten.
- Haben die Unternehmen bereits eine Strategie, sich gegen mögliche Nutzungs- und Zugangsrechte Dritter zu wehren?
- Wie hoch wird die Wahrscheinlichkeit eingeschätzt, dass Teile der Cloud als wesentliche Einrichtung eingestuft werden?

- Welche Möglichkeiten hat ein Nutzer, zwischen Cloud-Anbietern zu wechseln und seine Daten "mitzunehmen"? Wie häufig sind solche Wechsel?

II. Fragen zum Datenschutz

- Wie sind die Vertragsklauseln um den Datenschutz in einem Service Level Agreement ausgestaltet?
- Welche Parameter spielen für die Bemessung der Höhe der Kosten für den Datenschutz eine Rolle?
- Aufgrund welcher Anreizmechanismen sehen sich Cloud-Anbieter in der Lage, Kosten für den Datenschutz aufzubringen?
- Wie wird bei datenschutzrechtlichen Fragen der Reputationsmechanismus der Cloud-Anbieter geschützt?
- Gibt es aufgrund von datenschutzrechtlichen Hürden die Bestrebung, als vertikal integriertes Unternehmen z. B. im Wege der Fusion zu expandieren, damit die verfügbaren Daten innerhalb eines Unternehmens genutzt werden können?
- Gibt es Erfahrungswerte von Cloud-Anbietern, die in den Vereinigten Staaten aktiv sind und mit dem Stored Communications Act 1986 zu datenschutzrechtlichen Fragen bereits Stellung nehmen mussten?

III. Fragen zu Standardisierungsvereinbarungen

- Gibt es unter den Cloud-Anbietern einen Austausch (oder schon eine Vereinbarung) zur Senkung der Kosten des Datenschutzes eine Standardisierungsvereinbarung einzugehen?
- Gibt es Fälle von Cloud-Anbietern, die an die Europäische Kommission oder an eine andere (Kartell-)Behörde herangetreten sind, um für eine Zulässigkeit von solchen Standardisierungsvereinbarungen zu argumentieren?
- Wenn eine solche Standardisierungsvereinbarung nicht existiert, welche Parameter bilden den Wettbewerbsdruck um höhere Datensicherheit und Datenschutz?

15 Bibliography

Abdallah/Wadhwa, Collaborating with your rivals: Identifying sources of coopetitive performance, Paper to be presented at the Summer Conferences 2009, Copenhagen Business School, 17–19 June 2009.

Adam/Maier-Rigaud, The Law and Economics of Article 82 EC and the Commission Guidance Paper on Exclusionary Conduct, Journal of Competition Law/ Zeitschrift für Wettbewerbsrecht (ZWeR) Vol. 1 2009, pp. 131–146.

AEA, Study on Risk Governance of European Critical Infrastructures in the ICT and Energy Sector, Final Report to European Commission Directorate-General Justice, Freedom and Security, 4 September 2009, also available at: http://ec.europa.eu/energy/infrastructure/studies/doc/2009_10_risk_governance_report.pdf, last accessed 9 May 2012.

Ahlborn/Evans, The Microsoft Judgment and its Implications for Competition Policy Towards Dominant Firms in Europe, Antitrust Law Journal Vol. 75 No. 3 2009, also available at http://papers.ssrn.com/sol3/papers.cfm?abstract_id=1115867##, last accessed 23 October 2012.

Ahmed, Google search finds seafaring solution, The Sunday Times, 15 September 2008 available at: http://technology.timesonline.co.uk/tol/news/tech_and_web/the_web/article4753389.ece, last accessed 20 February 2011.

Andreşan-Grigorio, European Union/United States Data Protection Relations, University of Oxford under the supervision of Prof. Derrick A Wyatt, September 2002.

Antitrust Modernization Commission, Chair *Deborah A. Garza*, Report and Recommendations, April 2007, available at http://govinfo.library.unt.edu/amc/, last accessed 24 August 2012.

Antonelli, Technological Knowledge as an Essential Facility, Working paper No. 04/2005 of the Dipartimento di Economia, S. Cognetti de Martiis, Laboratorio di Economia dell'Innovazione, Franco Monigliano 2005.

Areeda, Essential Facilities: An Epithet in Need of Limiting Principles, Antitrust Law Journal Vol. 58, 1990 at p. 841.

Areeda/Hovenkamp, Fundamentals of Antitrust Law, 4th Ed. 2011, Loseleave Wolters Kluwer Law & Business.

Armbrust/Fox/Griffith/Joseph/Katz/Konwinski/Lee/Patterson/Rabkin/Stoica/Zaharia, Above the Clouds: A Berkeley View of Cloud Computing, Electrical Engineering and Computer Sciences University of California at Berkeley, Technical Report No. UCB/EECS-2009–28, 10 February 2009.

Armbrust/Fox/Griffith/Joseph/Katz/Konwinski/Lee/Patterson/Rabkin/Stoica/Zaharia, Clearing the clouds away from the true potential and obstacles posed by this computing capability, Communications of the ACM, Vol. 53 No. 4, April 2010.

Asendorpf, Die Zeit, Ab in die Wolken. Keine Festplatte, nirgends: Wenn Programme und Daten vom lokalen Rechner auf ferne Server wandern, spricht man von Cloud Computing. Wie zuverlässig funktioniert die ‚Rechenwolke'?, dated 17 February 2011.

Asendorpf, Die Zeit Online, Spionage inklusive – Für kostenlose Cloud-Angebote zahlen die Nutzer mit ihren Daten, dated 17 February 2011, available at: http://www.zeit.de/2011/08/Cloud-privat, last accessed 14 Mach 2011.

Averitt/Lande, Consumer Sovereignity: A Unified Theory of Anitrust and Consumer Protection Law, 65 Antitrust Law Journal 713, 1997.

Barrett, The European Commission's Antitrust Analysis of High-Technology Joint Ventures and Strategic Alliances: A Diverging Analysis?, The Transnational Lawyer Vol. 12, 1999.

BBC News, Microsoft to give access to code, dated 26 January 2006 available under: http://news.bbc.co.uk/2/hi/business/4649348.stm , last accessed 29 December 2014.

Benkard, Patentgesetz, Commentary 10th Edition 2006, Verlag C. H. Beck München.

Benkler, Yokai, Sharing Nicely: On Shareable Goods and the Emergence of Sharing as a Modality of Economic Production, The Yale Law Journal Vol. 114, 2004, pp. 273–358.

Bessey, Terrance L, Comity and Computers in the Common Market: The IBM Case, Northwestern Journal of International Law & Business, Vol. 4 No. 2, 1982, p. 626 et seqq.

Bester, Theorie der Industrieökonomik, 4th Edition 2007, Springer.

Bodoni/Newman, at *Bloomberg*, Microsoft Settled EU Case Not Knowing Vote Was 7 to 6, Bloomberg dated 5 September 2008, also available at http://www.bloomberg.com/apps/news?pid=newsarchive&sid=avY9xtzrv2Zs&refer=e, last accessed 19 October 2012 2008.

Boyd/Crawford, Critical Questions for Big Data, Provocations for a cultural, technological, and scholarly phenomenon, Information, Communication & Society, Vol. 15, Issue 5, 2012, Special Issue: A decade in Internet time: the dynamics of the Internet and society, also available at: http://www.tandfonline.com/doi/abs/10.1080/1369118X.2012.678878#.VJ2C9UAsFA, last accessed 27 December 2014.

Broy, Report on Case COMP/C-3/37.792, Lehrstuhl für Software & Systems Engineering, Institut für Informatik, Technische Universität München, dated15 February 2006, available at: http://www.microsoft.com/presspass/download/legal/EuropeanCommission/ECSO_6_Annex%204 %20-%20Broy%20 Report%20(NC%20Version).pdf, last accessed 14 March 2011.

Bundesverband Informationswirtschaft, Telekommunikation und neue Medien e. V. (BITKOM), Cloud Computing – Evolution in der Technik, Revolution im Business; BITKOM-Leitfaden, October 2009, also available at: http://www.bitkom.org/de/themen/36129_61111.aspx, last accessed 30 August 2011.

Buyya/Yeo/Venugopal/Broberg/Brandic, Cloud Computing and Emerging IT Platforms: Vision, Hype and Reality for Delivering Computing as the 5th Utility, Grid Computing and Distributed Systems Laboratory, Department of Computer Science and Software Engineering, University of Melbourne, Australia; Manjrasoft Pty Ltd, Melbourne, Australia; Institute of Information Systems, Vienna University of Technology, Vienna, Austria, 2009.

Carrier, Innovation for the 21st Century: Harnessing the Power of Intellectual Property and Antitrust Law, Oxford University Press, 2009.

Candeub, Trinko and Re-grounding the Refusal to Deal Doctrine, University of Pittsburg Law Review, Vol. 66, 2005, pp. 821–869.

Carlton/Perloff, Modern Industrial Organisation, 4th Edition 2005, Pearson.

Chang/Tsai, How Do Strategic Alliances Affect Suppliers, Customers and Rivals?, National Cheng Kung University, 1 February 2008.

Codd, Edgar Frank, A Relational Model of Data for Large Shared Data Banks, Communication of the ACM, Vol. 13 No. 6, 1970, pp. 377–387.

Czajkowski, Grzegorz, Sorting 1 PB with MapReduce, The Official Google Blog, 21 November 2008, available at: http://googleblog.blogspot.com/2008/11/sorting-1pb-with-mapreduce.html, accessed 20 February 2011.

Czapracka, Intellectual Property and the Limits of Antitrust: A Comparative Study of U.S. and EU Approaches, Cheltenham, U.K., Edward Elgar, 2009.

Der Spiegel Online, Snowdens Deutschland-Akte: Die Dokumente im PDF-Format, available at: http://www.spiegel.de/netzwelt/web/snowdens-deutschland-akte-alle-dokumente-als-pdf-a-975885.html, last accessed 15 August 2014.

Easterbrook, The Limits of Antitrust, Texas Law Review Vol. 63 No. 1, 1984, also reprinted as University of Chicago Law School Occasional Paper No. 21.

Easterbrook, Ignorance on Antitrust, in: *Jorde/Teece* (eds.), Antitrust, Innovation, and Competitiveness, Oxford University Press 1992.

Elmuti/Kathawala, An overview of strategic alliances, Management Decision 2001, p. 205–217.

Ezrachi, EC Competition Law – An Analytical Guide to the Leading Cases, Hart Publishing 2008.

Ezrachi, Article 82 EC: Reflections on its Recent Evolution, Oxford 2009.

Ezrachi/Maggiolino, European Competition Law, Compulsory Licensing, and Innovation, Journal of Competition Law & Economics, Vol. 8 Issue 3, September 2012, pp. 595–614.

Feinstein, Jeremy, Transcending the Cloud, A Legal Guide to the Risks and Rewards of Cloud Computing, Chapter 7: Tying Up the cloud: A Study in Antitrust Issues in Cloud Computing, ReedSmith 2011.

Federal Trade Commission, Protecting Consumer Privacy in an Era of Rapid Change: Recommendations for Businesses and Policymakers, March 2012, also available at: http://www.ftc.gov/reports/protecting-consumer-privacy-era-rapid-change-recommendations-businesses-policymakers, last accessed 31 August 2014.

Financial Times news report by Nikki Tait, IBM faces EU antitrust complaint over 'tying' claims, also available at: http://www.ft.com/cms/s/0/085a371e-36e5-11df-bc0f-00144feabdc0.html, last accessed 29 December 2014.

Flohr/Pohl, in: *Martinek/Semler/Habermeier/Flohr*, Vertriebsrecht, 3rd Edition C. H. Beck 2010.

Foley, Why Google And Microsoft Are Building Data Centers In Iowa, Information Week dated 4 August 2008, available at: http://www.informationweek.com/blog/229210089, accessed 10 May 2011.

Forbes Magazine report by Kashmir Hill, How Target Figured Out A Teen Girl Was Pregnant Before Her Father Did, available at: http://www.forbes.com/sites/kashmirhill/2012/02/16/how-target-figured-out-a-teen-girl-was-pregnant-before-her-father-did/, last accessed 27 December 2014.

Fu/Chase/Chun/Schwab/Vahdat, SHARP: An Architecture for Secure Resource Peering, Department of Computer Science, Duke University, Intel Research Berkeley and Network Associates Laboratories, 2003, available under: http://issg.cs.duke.edu/publications/sharp-sosp03.pdf, last accessed 31 May 2011.

Gasser/Palfrey at: *The Berkman Center for Internet & Society at Harvard Law School and Research Center for Information Law University of St. Gallen*, Breaking Down Digital Barriers – When and How ICT Interoperability Drives Innovation, 14 November 2007, also available at: available at: http://cyber.law.harvard.edu/interactive/events/2007/11/Palfrey_Gasser, last accessed 19 January 2014.

Giffordal/Kudrle, Antitrust Approaches to Dynamically Competitive Industries in the United States and the European Union, Journal of Competition Law & Economics, September 2011, p. 5.

Ginsberg/Mohebbi/Patel/Brammer/Smolinski/Brilliant, Detecting influenza epidemics using search engine query data, Nature 457 (7232) 2009, pp. 1012–1014, also available at: http://www.nature.com/nature/journal/v457/n7232/full/nature07634.html, last accessed 25 December 2014 and at the free of charge source provided by the authors at http://static.googleusercontent.com/external_content/untrusted_dlcp/research.google.com/en/us/archive/papers/detecting-influenza-epidemics.pdf, last accessed 25 December 2014.

Gilder, The Information Factories. Wired, Vol. 14 No. 10, 2007.

Gleeson, Computing industry set for a shocking change, Moneyweek dated 24 April 2009, available at: http://www.moneyweek.com/investment-advice/computing-industry-set-for-a-shocking-change-43226, last accessed 10 May 2011.

Google Inc., Summary description of US Patent No. US8612136 B2, published 17 December 2013, date of priority 27 August 2008, available at: http://www.google.com/patents/US8612136, last accessed 25 December 2014.

Götting, Gewerblicher Rechtsschutz, 9th Edition 2010, Verlag C. H. Beck.

Greenwald, Glen: No Place to Hide: Edward Snowden, the NSA, and the U.S. Surveillance State, Metropolitan Books, 13 May 2014.

Hamel/Doz/Prahalad, Collaborate with Your Competitors – and Win, Harvard Business Review, January-February 1989.

Harbour/Koslov, Section 2 in a Web 2.0 World: An Expanded Vision of Relevant Product Markets, Antitrust Law Journal, Vol. 76, 2010 p. 769 et seqq.

Hardy, The Death of Hardware, Forbes Magazine, 11 February 2008, available at: http://www.forbes.com/forbes/2008/0211/036.html, accessed 20 February 2011.

Hay/McMahon, The Diverging Approach to Price Squeezes in the United States and Europe, Journal of Competition Law & Economics, Vol. 8 No. 2, April 2012, pp. 259–296.

Hovenkamp/Janis/Lemley, IP and Antitrust: An Analysis of Antitrust Principles Applied to Intellectual Property Law, ring-bound loose leaf edition, Aspen Law & Business, 1 December 2002 onwards.

IBM, Seeding the Clouds: Key Infrastructure Elements for Cloud Computing, February 2009, available at www.ibm.com with document reference No. OIW03022-USEN-00.

IBM, Cloud computing insights from 110 implementation projects, IBM Academy of Technology Survey, Thought Leadership Whitepaper, dated October 2010.

Information Systems Audit and Control Association (ISACA), Essential Characteristics of Cloud Computing, also available at: http://www.isaca.org/Groups/

Professional-English/cloud-computing/GroupDocuments/Essential%20 characteristics%20of%20Cloud%20Computing.pdf, last accessed 29 December 2014.

Institute for Public Auditors in Germany, Principles for the Proper Performance of Reasonable Assurance Engagements Relating to Compliance Management Systems, 2011, also available at: http://www.idw.de/idw/portal/n589244/n589350/n611308/index.jsp, last accessed 29 December 2014 .

International Competition Network (ICN), International Competition Network, Report on the Objectives of Unilateral Conduct Laws, Assessment of Dominance/Substantial Market Power, and State-Created Monopolies, prepared by The Unilateral Conduct Working Group (UCWG), presented at the 6th Annual Conference of the ICN Moscow, May 2007.

International Competition Network (ICN), Unilateral Conduct Workbook Chapter 3: Assessment of Dominance, prepared by The Unilateral Conduct Working Group, Presented at the 10th Annual ICN Conference, The Hague, May 2011, also available at: http://www.internationalcompetitionnetwork.org/working-groups/current/unilateral.aspx, last accessed 9 February 2012.

International Organization for Standardisation (ISO), Risk management – Principles and Guidelines, ISO 31000:2009 dated 13 November 2009.

International Organization for Standardisation (ISO), Information technology -- Security techniques -- Code of practice for protection of personally identifiable information (PII) in public clouds acting as PII processors, ISO 27018:2914 dated 1 August 2014.

Ivaldi/Jullien/Rey/Seabright/Tirole, The Economics of Tacit Collusion, Final Report for DG Competition, European Commission, IDEI, Toulouse, March 2003, also available at http://ec.europa.eu/competition/mergers/studies_reports/the_economics_of_tacit_collusion_en.pdf, last accessed 24 October 2012.

Jacobs, Adam, The Pathologies of Big Data, Communications of the ACM, Vol. 52, Issue 8, August 2009, pp. 36–44, also available at: http://dl.acm.org/citation.cfm?id=J79&picked=prox, last accessed 27 December 2014.

Jaeger/Jin/Grimes/Simmons, Where is the cloud? Geography, economics, environment, and jurisdiction in cloud computing, First Monday, Vol. 14 No. 5, May 2009.

Jorde/Teece (eds.), Antitrust, Innovation, and Competitiveness, Oxford University Press 1992.

Kaplow, On the Meaning of Horizontal Agreements in Competition Law, California Law Review Vol. 99 No. 3, June 2011, pp. 683–818.

Katz, Making Sense of Nonsense: Intellectual Property, Antitrust and Market Power, Arizona Law Review Vol. 49, 2007, pp. 837–909.

Katz, Intellectual Property Rights and Antitrust Policy: Four Principles for a Complex World, Telecommunications & high Technology Law, Vol. 1, 2002, pp. 325–353.

Käseberg, Intellectual Property, Antitrust and Cumulative Innovation in the EU and the US, Hart Studies in Competition Law No. 1, June 2012.

Kerr, Orin S., A User's Guide to the Stored Communications Act – and a Legislator's Guide to amending it, George Washington Law Review, Vol. 72, p. 1700 et seqq., also available at: http://courses.ischool.berkeley.edu/i205/s10/readings/week10/kerr-storedcomm.pdf, last accessed 29 December 2014.

Kerr/Teng, Cloud Computing: Legal and Privacy Issues, Prepared for the Academy of Business Disciplines' Conference, taking place 10 to 13 November 2010 in Ft. Myers, Florida, dated 15 September 2010, also available at: http://www.g-casa.com/conferences/vietnam/paper/JDK_CLOUDING_9_21_10_Paper-1[11].pdf, last accessed 29 December 2014.

Khajeh-Hosseini/Sommerville/Sriram, Research Challenges for Enterprise Cloud Computing, available through the Cornell University Library under http://arxiv.org/abs/1001.3257, last accessed 29 December 2014.

Kimball, Ralph, The Data Warehouse Toolkit: Practical Techniques for Building Dimensional Data Warehouses, John Wiley & Sons 1996, New York.

Kirchner/Käseberg, Cloud Computing im Lichte des europäischen Wettbewerbsrechts, in: *Bechtold/Jickeli/Rohe* (eds.), Recht, Ordnung und Wettbewerb: Festschrift zum 70. Geburtstag von Wernhard Möschel, Nomos, 5 July 2011.

Kling/Thomas, Kartellrecht, Verlag Franz Vahlen München 2007.

Kolasky, Antitrust Enforcement Guidelines For Strategic Alliances, presented at the Federal Trade Commission's Hearings on Joint Ventures, 1 July 1997.

Korah, Intellectual Property Rights and the EC Competition Rules, Hart Publishing, 2006.

Lemley, Mark, A New Balance Between IP and Antitrust, Southwestern Journal of Law and Trade in the Americas, Vol. 13, April 2007, pp. 1–20; see as well John M. Olin Program in Law and Economics, Stanford Law School, Working Paper No. 340, April 2007, also available at: http://ssrn.com/abstract=980045, last accessed 24 September 2012.

MacCormick, John, Nine algorithms that changed the future – The ingenious ideas that drive today's computers, Princeton University Press 2011.

Mayer-Schönberger/Cukier, Big Data: A Revolution That Will Transform How We Live, Work, and Think, Eamon Dolan/Houghton Mifflin Harcourt; 1st Ed. 2013.

McKinsey Global Institute, Manyika/Chui/Brown/Bughin/Dobbs/Roxburgh/Byers, Big data: The next frontier for innovation, competition and productivity, 2011, available at: http://www.mckinsey.com/insights/business_technology/big_data_the_next_frontier_for_innovation, last accessed 26 December 2014.

Mell/Grance with the *National Institute of Standards and Technology (NIST)*, The NIST Definition of Cloud Computing, 2009, also available at: http://csrc.nist.gov/publications/drafts/800-145/Draft-SP-800-145_cloud-definition.pdf, last accessed 9 November 2010.

Microsoft, United States District Court for the District of Columbia, Memorandum Opinion on *State of New York, et al., v. Microsoft Corporation*, Civil Action No. 98–1233 (CKK), available at http://www.microsoft.com/en-us/news/download/legal/RemediesTrial/Lit11-1.pdf, last accessed 3 October 2012.

Microsoft, Best Practices for the Design of Large-Scale Services on Azure Cloud Services dated 14 October 2014, available at: http://msdn.microsoft.com/en-us/library/azure/jj717232.aspx, last accessed 29 December 2014.

Monti, Mario quoted in *Reynolds/Best,* Article 102 and innovation: the journey since Microsoft, 39th annual Fordham Conference on International Antitrust Law and Policy, 20–21 September 2012.

Monti, Mario, The Concept of Dominance in Article 82, European Competition Journal Vol. 2, 2006, pp. 31–52.

Nägele/Jacobs, Rechtsfragen des Cloud Computing, Zeitschrift für Urheber- und Medienrecht (ZUM) 2010, p. 281.

North, Douglass C, Ideology and Political/Economic Institutions, Cato Journal, Vol. 8 No. 1, Spring/Summer 1988.

O'Donoghue/Padilla, The Law and Economics of Article 82 EC, Oxford and Portland 2006.

OECD, Competition Law & Policy, Organisation for Economic Cooperation and Development, Policy Roundtables, The Essential Facilities Concept, General Distribution, OCDE/GD(96)113, 1996.

OECD, Report on Fighting Hard Core Cartels: Harm, Effective Sanctions and Leniency Programmes, 2002, available at: http://www.oecd.org/dataoecd/49/16/2474442.pdf, last accessed 14 May 2011.

OECD, Working Party No. 3 on Co-operation and Enforcement, Unilateral Disclosure of Information with Anticompetitive Effects (e.g. Through Press Announcements), OECD Directorate for Financial and Enterprise Affairs, Competition Committee, European Union, DAF/COMP/WP3/WD(2012)21, dated 14 February 2012.

Patel/Ranabahu/Sheth, Service Level Agreement in Cloud Computing, Knoesis Center, Wright State University, USA and DA-IICT, Gandhinagar, India, 2010.

Pavel/Mattes, Cloud Computing: Großes Wachstumspotential, Wochenbericht des DIW Berlin Nr. 48/2010, available at: http://www.diw.de/documents/publikationen/73/diw_01.c.364145.de/10-48-3.pdf, accessed 14 March 2011.

Pereira Teles/Souto Maior de Barros, Towards Standardization and Interoperability of Database Backups, International Journal of Computer Science and Network Security (IJCSNS), Vol. 12 No. 8, August 2012, available at: http://paper.ijcsns.org/07_book/201208/20120803.pdf, last accessed 29 December 2014.

Picker, Competition and Privacy in Web 2.0 and the Cloud, Chicago John M. Olin Law & Economics Working Paper No. 414 (2D Series), June 2008.

Popofsky, Section 2 Litigation: Is Aspen Still Viable? – Unilateral Refusals to Deal: The History and Future of Aspen Skiing, ABA Section of Antitrust Law Spring Meeting, 28 to 30 March 2012, 60th Annual Antitrust Conference. The conference materials are available through www.americanbar.org.

Posner, Antitrust in the New Economy, Chicago John M. Olin Law & Economics Working Paper No. 106, 2nd Series, 2000, available at: http://papers.ssrn.com/paper.taf?abstract_id=249316, last accessed 29 December 2014.

Posner, Antitrust Law, 2nd Ed., University of Chicago Press, 2001.

Prahalad/Hamel, The Core Competence of the Corporation, Harvard Business Review, May-June 1990.

PriceWaterhouseCoopers, Invest in Iceland Agency, Benchmarking Study on Iceland as a Location for Data Centre Activity, 2007, available at: http://www.invest.is/resources/files/invest.is/BDC%20Report.pdf, accessed 15 May 2010.

William Jeremy Robinson, Free at What Cost? Cloud Computing Privacy Under the Stored Communications Act, The Georgetown Law Journal, Vol. 98 No. 4, 2010, pp. 1195 et seqq.

Rohwetter, Intel – Gefräßige Chips, Die Zeit, 26 May 2011, available at: http://www.zeit.de/2011/22/Chip-War-Intel-vs-ARM, last accessed 30 May 2011.

Roth, Zur Berücksichtigung nichtwettbewerblicher Ziele im europäischen Kartellrecht – eine Skizze, in: *Engel/Möschel* (eds.), Recht und spontane Ordnung; Festschrift für Ernst-Joachim Mestmäcker zum achtzigtsen Geburtstag, Nomos 2006.

Salesforce, A Complete History of Cloud Computing, available at: http://www.salesforce.com/uk/socialsuccess/cloud-computing/the-complete-history-of-cloud-computing.jsp, last accessed 29 December 2014.

Sakr, Majd F, Introduction to cloud computing, lecture at Carnegie Mellon Qatar dated 14 January 2010, also available at: http://www.qatar.cmu.edu/~msakr/15319-s10/lectures/lecture02.pdf, last accessed 29 December 2014.

Schmidt/Rosenberg, How Google Works, John Murray Publishers 2014.

Schrems, Maximilian, Facebook v. Europe, Rapid Press Update: Facebook & NSA-Surveillance: Following "Safe Harbor" decision, Irish Data Protection Commissioner to bring EU-U.S. data flows before CJEU again, 26 May 2016, available at: http://www.europe-v-facebook.org/PA_MCs.pdf, last accessed 10 July 2016.

Sidak/Teece, Dynamic Competition in Antitrust Law, Journal of Competition Law & Economics, 2009 p. 581–631.

Sluijs/Larouche/Sauter, Cloud Computing in the EU Policy Sphere, Journal of Intellectual Property, Information Technology and e-Commerce Law 3(1) 2012 and also available through TILEC Discussion Paper 2011–036.

Sunosky, Privacy online: A primer on the European Union's directive and the United States' Safe Harbour privacy principles, International Trade Law Journal Vol. 9 pp. 80–88.

Surgient, Dave Malcom, The Five Defining Characteristics of Cloud Computing, ZDNet, Virtualization, dated 9 September 2009, also available at: http://www.zdnet.com/article/the-five-defining-characteristics-of-cloud-computing/, last accessed 29 December 2014.

The Boyd Company, Location Factors for Data Centers, Area Development, Site and Facility Planning, August 2009, available at: http://www.theboydcompany.com/pdf/Area_Development_Data_Centers.pdf, last accessed 15 May 2011.

The New York Times: Charles Duhigg, How companies learn your secrets, available at: http://www.nytimes.com/2012/02/19/magazine/shopping-habits.html?pagewanted=9&_r=1&hp, last accessed 27 December 2014

van Schewick, Barbara, Network Neutrality and Quality of Service, What a Non-Discrimination Rule Should Look Like, Center for Internet and Society Whitepaper, 11 July 2012.

Välimäki/Oksanen, DRM Interoperability and Intellectual Property Policy in Europe, European Intellectual Property Review 11/2006, Vol. 26 No. 11, pp. 562–568.

Vigen, Tyler, Spurious Correlations, available at: http://www.tylervigen.com/, last accessed 27 December 2014.

Waller, In Search of Economic Justice: Considering Competition and Consumer Protection Law, Chicago Law Review 631, 2005.

Williamson, Oliver E, The Economic Institutions of Capitalism – Firms, Markets, Relational Contracting, The Free Press 1985.

World Health Organization, Influenza factsheet 2003, available at: http://www.who.int/mediacentre/factsheets/2003/fs211/en/, last accessed 25 December 2014.

Woyke, Identifying The Tech Leaders In LTE Wireless Patents, Forbes Magazine, 21 September 2011, available at: http://www.forbes.com/sites/elizabethwoyke/2011/09/21/identifying-the-tech-leaders-in-lte-wireless-patents/, last accessed 28 June 2012.

Wyld, David C, The Utility of Cloud Computing as a New Pricing and Consumption Model for Information Technology, International Journal of Database Management Systems (IJDMS), Vol. 1 No. 1, November 2009.

Zins, Chaim, Journal of the American Society for Information Science and Technology, 58(4) 2007, pp. 479–493, also available at: http://www.success.co.il/is/zins_definitions_dik.pdf, last accessed 19 January 2014.

EU Documents

Article 29 Working Party, Opinion 01/2016 on the EU – U.S. Privacy Shield draft adequacy decision, dated 13 April 2016, available here: http://ec.europa.eu/justice/data-protection/article-29/documentation/opinion-recommendation/files/2016/wp238_en.pdf, last accessed 10 July 2016.

Charter of Fundamental Rights of the European Union, 7 December 2000, O.J. L C 364/01, available at: http://www.europarl.europa.eu/charter/pdf/text_en.pdf, last accessed 31 August 2014.

Consolidated Version of The Treaty of The Functioning of the European Union, Official Journal of the European Union C 115/47, 9 May 2008.

Council of the European Union, press release No. 10578/14 on the 3319th Council meeting of Justice and Home Affairs, Luxembourg, 5 and 6 June 2014, available at: http://www.consilium.europa.eu/uedocs/cms_data/docs/pressdata/en/jha/143119.pdf, last accessed 30 August 2014.

Council Directive 2008/114/EC of 8 December 2008 on the identification and designation of European critical infrastructures and the assessment of the need to improve their protection, O.J. L 345/75 dated 23 December 2008.

Council Directive 91/250/EEC on the legal protection of computer programs, O.J. L 122 dated 14 May 1991.

Council Directive 95/46/EC of the European Parliament and of the Council of 24 October 1995 on the protection of individuals with regard to the processing of personal data and on the free movement of such data, O.J. L 281, 23 November 1995, p. 31–50.

Council Directive 2002/58/EC of the European Parliament and of the Council of 12 July 2002 concerning the processing of personal data and the protection of privacy in the electronic communications sector (Directive on privacy and electronic communications), O.J. L 201 dated 31 July 2002, p. 37–47.

Council Directive of the European Parliament and of the Council concerning measures to ensure a high common level of network and information security across the Union, COM(2013) 48 final, 2013/0027 (COD), 7 February 2013, (NIS Directive), as made available in O.J. L 194, dated 19 July 2016, available here: http://eur-lex.europa.eu/legal-content/EN/TXT/PDF/?uri=OJ:L:2016:194:FULL&from=EN, last accessed 4 August 2016.

Council Regulation (EC) No 1/2003 of 16 December 2002 on the implementation of the rules on competition laid down in Articles 81 and 82 of the Treaty, O.J. L 1 dated 4 January 2003, p. 1–25.

Council Regulation (EU) No 182/2011 of the European Parliament and of the Council of 16 February 2011 laying down the rules and general principles concerning mechanisms for control by Member States of the Commission's exercise of implementing powers.

Court of Justice of the European Union, An internet search engine operator is responsible for the processing that it carries out of persona ldata which appear on web pages published by third parties, Press Release No. 70/14 on Judgment in Case c-131/12 dated 13 May 2014.

EU Commission, Cloud Service Level Agreement Standardization Guidelines dated 24 June 2014, available at: http://ec.europa.eu/digital-agenda/en/news/cloud-service-level-agreement-standardisation-guidelines, last accessed 29 December 2014.

EU Commission, Commission Decision of 5 February 2010 on standard contractual clauses for the transfer of personal data to processors established in third countries under Directive 95/46/EC of the European Parliament and of the Council (notified under document C(2010) 593), O.J. L 39/5, 12 February 2010.

EU Commission, Guidelines on Vertical Restraints, SEC(2010) 411, p. 9, also available at: http://ec.europa.eu/competition/antitrust/legislation/guidelines_vertical_en.pdf, last accessed 29 December 2014.

EU Commission, Communication Notice from the Commission, Guidelines on the application of Article 81 (3) of the Treaty, O.J. C 101/97 dated 27 April 2004.

EU Commission, Communication from the Commission, Guidance on the Commission's enforcement priorities in applying Article 82 of the EC Treaty to abusive exclusionary conduct by dominant undertakings, 2009/C 45/02, O.J. C 45/7 dated 24 February 2009.

EU Commission, Commission Notice on agreements of minor importance which do not appreciably restrict competition under Article 81(1) of the Treaty establishing the European Community (De Minimis), O.J. C 368 dated 2 December 2001.

EU Commission, Commission Notice on the definition of the relevant market for the purposes of Community competition law, O. J. C 372 dated 9 December 1997.

EU Commission, Commission Staff Working Paper, Impact Assessment Accompanying the document Regulation of the European Parliament and of the Council on the protection of individuals with regard to the processing of personal data and on the free movement of such data *(General Data Protection Regulation)* and Directive of the European Parliament and of the Council on the protection of individuals with regard to the processing of personal data by competent authorities for the purposes of prevention, investigation, detection or prosecution of criminal offences or the execution of criminal penalties, and the free movement of such data, SEC(2012) 72 final, 25 January 2012, also available at: http://ec.europa.eu/justice/data-protection/document/review2012/sec_2012_72_en.pdf, last accessed 29 December 2014.

EU Commission, Commission Staff Working Paper, Interpretative Note on Directive 2998/73/EC concerning Common Rules for the Internal Market in Natural Gas – Third-Party Access to Storage Facilities, dated 22 January 2010.

EU Commission, Commission Staff Working Document on "Towards a general policy on the Fight against Cyber Crime" – SEC 2007/ 641, 642, Brussels dated 22 May setting out the future approach of the EU-wide combat against cyber crime.

EU Commission, Communication from the Commission to the European Parliament and the Council on the Functioning of the Safe Harbour from the Perspective of EU Citizens and Companies Established in the EU, COM(2013) 847 final dated 27 November 2013, available at: http://ec.europa.eu/justice/data-protection/files/com_2013_847_en.pdf, last accessed 31 August 2014.

EU Commission, Communication from the Commission to the European Parliament, the Council, The European Economic and Social Committee and the Committee of the Regions, Safeguarding Privacy in a Connected World, A European Data Protection Framework for the 21st Century, COM (2012) 9 final, Brussels, 25 January 2012, available at: http://eur-lex.europa.eu/legal-content/EN/TXT/PDF/?uri=CELEX:52012DC0009&from=en, last accessed 16 July 2014.

EU Commission, Communication of Unit 5.2 of the EU Commission, DG Communications Networks, Content and Technology, available at: http://ec.europa.eu/dgs/connect/en/content/software-services-cloud-european-cloud-computing-strategy, last accessed 29 December 2014.

EU Commission, Factsheet on the "Right to be Forgotten" ruling (C-131/12) dated 13 May 2014, available at: http://ec.europa.eu/justice/data-protection/files/factsheets/factsheet_data_protection_en.pdf, last accessed 30 August 2014.

EU Commission, Guidelines on the assessment of horizontal mergers under the Council Regulation on the control of concentrations between undertakings, 2004/C 31/03, O.J. C 031 dated 5 February 2004, pp. 5–18.

EU Commission, Joint Communication to the European Parliament, the Council, the European Economic and Social Committee and the Committee of the Regions, Cybersecurity Strategy of the European Union: An Open, Safe and Secure Cyberspace, JOIN(2013) 1 final, Brussels dated 7 February 2013.

EU Commission, Memo titled: Progress on EU data protection reform now irreversible following European Parliament vote, Strasbourg, 12 March 2014 available at: http://europa.eu/rapid/press-release_MEMO-14-186_en.htm, last accessed 16 July 2014.

EU Commission, Press release: European Commission welcomes European Parliament's vote to extend mandate of ENISA and strengthen EU Cybersecurity, dated 16 April 2013, available at: http://europa.eu/rapid/press-release_MEMO-13-341_en.htm, last accessed 29 December 2014.

EU Commission, Press release: Commission proposes a comprehensive reform of data protection rules to increase users' control of their data and to cut costs for businesses, dated 25 January 2012, also available at: http://europa.eu/rapid/press-release_IP-12-46_en.htm?locale=en, last accessed 29 December 2014.

EU Commission, Proposal for a Directive of the European Parliament and of the Council concerning measures to ensure a high common level of network and information security across the Union, COM(2013) 48 final, 2013/0027 (COD), 7 February 2013.

EU Commission, Proposal for a Directive of the European Parliament and of the Council on the protection of individuals with regard to the processing of personal data by competent authorities for the purposes of prevention, investigation, detection or prosecution of criminal offences or the execution of criminal penalties, and the free movement of such data, COM (2012) 10 final, 2012/0010 (COD), {SEC(2012) 72 final} {SEC(2012) 73 final}, Brussels, 25 January 2012, available at: http://eur-lex.europa.eu/legal-content/EN/TXT/PDF/?uri=CELEX:52012PC0010&from=en, last accessed 16 July 2014.

EU Commission, Proposal for a Regulation of the European Parliament and of the Council on the protection of individuals with regard to the processing of personal data and on the free movement of such data (General Data Protection Regulation), dated 25 January 2012, available at: http://ec.europa.eu/justice/data-protection/document/review2012/com_2012_11_en.pdf, last accessed 19 January 2015.

EU Commission, Unleashing the Potential of Cloud Computing in Europe, Communication from the Commission to the European Parliament, the Council, the European Economic and Social Committee and the Committee of the Regions, COM(2012) 529 final, dated 27 September 2012.

EU Commission, XXVth REPORT on Competition Policy, Published in conjunction with the "General Report on the Activities of the European Union 1995, available at http://ec.europa.eu/competition/publications/annual_report/1995/en.pdf, last accessed 19 October 2012.

EU Commission, Committee on Civil Liberties, Justice and Home Affairs, Draft Report on the proposal for a regulation of the European Parliament and of the Council on the protection of individual with regard to the processing of personal data and on the free movement of such data, COM(2012)0011 – C7-0025/2012–2012/0011(COD)); available at: http://www.europarl.europa.eu/meetdocs/2009_2014/documents/libe/pr/922/922387/922387en.pdf, last accessed 19 January 2015.

EU Commission, DG COMP, Best Practices for the submission of economic evidence and data collection in cases concerning the application of Articles 101 and 102 TFEU and in Merger Cases, also available at: http://ec.europa.eu/competition/consultations/2010_best_practices/best_practice_submissions.pdf, last accessed 12 April 2011.

EU Commission, DG COMP, Best Practices on the conduct of proceedings concerning Articles 101 and 102 TFEU, also available under: http://ec.europa.eu/competition/consultations/2010_best_practices/best_practice_articles.pdf, last accessed 12 April 2011.

EU Commission, DG COMP, Discussion paper on the application of Article 82 of the Treaty to exclusionary abuses, Brussels, December 2005, also available at: http://ec.europa.eu/competition/antitrust/art82/discpaper2005.pdf, last accessed 20 October 2009.

EU Commission, DG Justice, Model Contracts for the transfer of personal data to third countries, available at: http://ec.europa.eu/justice/data-protection/international-transfers/transfer/index_en.htm, last accessed 10 July 2016.

Eurobarometer, Attitudes on Data Protection and Electronic Identity in the European Union, 2010, available at: http://ec.europa.eu/public_opinion/archives/ebs/ebs_359_en.pdf, last accessed 29 December 2014.

Eurobarometer, Attitudes on Data Protection and Electronic Identity in the European Union, 2010 Fact Sheet for Germany, available at: http://ec.europa.eu/public_opinion/archives/ebs/ebs_359_fact_de_en.pdf, last accessed 16 July 2014.

European Committee for Interoperable Systems, A Chronology of the EU's Microsoft Proceedings: 1998–2007, available at: www.ecis.eu, last accessed 29 December 2014.

European Committee for Interoperable Systems, A History of Antitrust Problems: Microsoft Settlements to Resolve Antitrust Disputes 2003 to 2007, available at: www.ecis.eu, last accessed 29 December 2014.

European Network and Information Security Agency (ENISA), Cloud Computing – Benefits, risks and recommendations for information security, 20 November 2009, available under: www.enisa.europa.eu, last accessed 12 May 2011.

European Parliament, Draft Report of European Parliament Committee on Civil Liberties, Justice and Home Affairs on the U.S. NSA surveillance Program, 21 February 2014, (2013/2188(INI)), available at: http://www.europarl.europa.eu/sides/getDoc.do?type=REPORT&reference=A7-2014-0139&language=EN#title1, last accessed 31 August 2014. ("*LIBE Report*").

European Parliament, Draft Report on the proposal for a regulation of the European Parliament and of the Council on the protection of individual with regard to the processing of personal data and on the free movement of such data (General Data Protection Regulation); (COM(2012)0011–C7-0025/2012–2012/0011(COD); dated 17 December 2012.

European Union External Action, Factsheet EU-US cooperation on cyber security and cyberspace, No. 14326/01, 26 March 2014, available at: http://www.eeas.europa.eu/statements/docs/2014/140326_01_en.pdf, last accessed 29 December 2014.

The European Advisory Group on Competition Policy (EAGCP), An economic approach to Art. 82, July 2005, available at: http://ec.europa.eu/dgs/competition/economist/eagcp_july_21_05.pdf, last accessed 2 February 2012).

List of Cases

Airtours/First Choice – Case No. IV/M.1524 dated 22 September 1999.

Aspen Highlands Skiing Co., 738 F.2d 1509 (10th Cir. 1984), aff'd, 472 U.S. 585 (1985)

Associated Press v. United States, 326 U.S. 1 (1945).

British Airways plc. v. Commission; Case C-95/04 P, 2007, E.C.R. I-2331, 4 C.M.L.R. 22, dated 15 March 2007.

British Airways plc. v. Commission; Case C-95/04 P, 2007, E.C.R. I-2331, 4 C.M.L.R. 22, dated 15 March 2007, Opinion of *Advocate General Kokott* in Case C-95/04 P, E.C.R. I-2336, delivered on 23 February 2006, also available at http://eur-lex.europa.eu/LexUriServ/LexUriServ.do?uri=CELEX:62004CC0095:EN:PDF, last accessed 20 October 2012.

Broadcom Corp. v. Qualcomm Inc., 501 F.3d 297, U.S. Court of Appeals 3rd Cir., No. 06–4292, 4 September 2007.

BVerfG, Urt. des Ersten Senats vom 15. Dezember 1983, 1 BvR 209/83 u. a. – *Volkszählung*; BVerfGE 65, 1.

Comcast Corp. v. FCC, [1] 600 F.3d 642.

Flughafen Frankfurt/Main AG - IV/34.801 FAG, O.J. No. L 072, pp. 30–50 dated 14 January 1998.

Data General Corporation, et. Al., v. Grumman Systems Support Corporation, 36 F.3d 1147, United States Court of Appeals, First Circuit, 1994; No. 93–1637. Decided 14 September 1994.

Delaware & Hudson Ry. Co. v. Consolidated Rail Corp., 902 F. 2d 174 (2d Cir. 1990).

Deutsche Telekom AG – Case COMP/C-1/37.451, 37.578, 37.579 dated 21 May 2003, O.J. [2003] L 263/9.

Griswold v. Connecticut, 381 U.S. 479, 483 (1965).

GlaxoSmithKline Services Unlimited v. Commission of the European Communities, Case T-168/01 [2006] ECR II-2969, Judgment of the CFI, 4th Chamber, 27 September 2006.

Glaxo Welcome – Case COMP IV/36.957/F3, Commission Decision dated 8 May 2011, C 2001/791/EC).

Google/DoubleClick – Case COMP/M.4731 Commission Decision dated 11 March 2008.

Google/DoubleClick – FTC File No. 071–0170 dated 20 December 2007.

Google/DoubleClick – Statement of the Federal Trade Commission concerning Google/DoubleClick, FTC File No. 071–0179, available at: www.ftc.gov/os/caselist/0710170/071220statement.pdf, last accessed 14 March 2011.

Google Spain SL, Google Inc. v Agencia Española de Protección de Datos (AEPD), Mario Costeja González, Case C-131/12, OJ C 165, 9 June 2012, Court of Justice, Judgment of the Court (Grand Chamber) of 13 May 2014.

Hoffmann-La Roche & Co. v. Commission, Case 85/76, 13 February 1979, ECJ [1979] ECR 461, [1979] 3 C.M.L.R. 211.

IBM Corp. v. E.C.Commission, Case 60/81 dated 11 November 1981, 32 C.M.L.R. 93, 1981.

IBM Italia v UBIS, Case COMP/M.6921, O.J. C 163 dated 8 June 2013.

IBM Maintenance Services – Case COMP/C-3/39.692, Commission Decision dated 13 December 2011.

IMS Health GmbH & Co. OHG v. NDC Health GmbH & Co. KG, Case C-418/01, CFI [2000] ECR I-5039, [2004] 4 C.M.L.R. 28.

In re International Busines Machines Corp., 687 F.2d 591 (2d Cir 1982), Ref. 594.

Interface Group, Inc. v. Massachusetts Port Auth., 816 F.2d 9 (1st Cir. 1987).

Internationale Handelsgesellschaft v. Einfuhr- und Vorratsstelle für Getreide und Futtermittel, 1970, ECR 1125, Case 11/70.

Kodak I (1927) – Eastman Kodak Co. of New York v. Southern Photo Materials Co., 47 S.Ct. 400 Supreme Court of the United States, 273 U.S. 359 (1927), 21 February 1927.

Kodak II (1992) – Eastman Kodak Co. v. Image Technical Services, Inc., 112 S.Ct. 2072 Supreme Court of the United States, 504 U.S. 451 (1992), 8 June 1992.

Maximillian Schrems v Data Protection Commissioner, Court of Justice of the European Union, judgment C-362/14 dated 6 October 2015, O.J. C398/5 dated 30 November 2015. The case is available here: http://eur-lex.europa.eu/legal-content/EN/TXT/?uri=CELEX%3A62014CJ0362, last accessed 10 July 2016.

MCI Communications Corp. v. American Tel. & Tel. Co., 708 F.2d 1081 (7th Cir. 1983), 464 U.S. 891 (1983).

Micro Leader Business v Commission, Judgment of the CFI (3rd Chamber) dated 16 December 1999, Case T-198/98, E.C.R. 1999 p. II-03989.

Microsoft – Case COMP/C-3/37.792, Commission Decision dated 24 March 2004.

Microsoft – Case COMP/C-3/37.792, final report of the hearing officer, O.J. C 26/5 dated 6 February 2007.

Microsoft – Case COMP/C-3/37.792, Supplemental Response of Microsoft Corporation to the Statement of Objections by The European Commission dated 21 December 2005, available under: http://www.microsoft.com/presspass/download/legal/EuropeanCommission/03-02-06SupplementaryResponseSOfinalNC.pdf, last accessed 29 December 2014.

Microsoft Corp. v. Commission, Case T-201/04 CFI [2007] 5 C.M.L.R. 11 .

Microsoft Corp. v. Commission, Case T-167/08, Judgment of the General Court (Second Chamber) dated 27 June 2012.

NDC Health GmbH & Co. KG and NDC Health Corporation v. Commission, Case C-481/01 P(R) [2002] E.C.R. I-3401 [2002], 5 C.M.L.R. 1.

Nederlandsche Banden Industrie Michelin v. Commission, Case 322/81, ECJ [1983] ECR 3461, [1985] 1 C.M.L.R. 282 dated 9 November 1983.

Oscar Bronner GmbH & Co. KG v. Mediaprint Zeitungs- und Zeitschriftenverlag GmbH & Co. KG; Case C-7/97 [1998] E.C.R. I-7791, [1999] C.M.L.R. 112.

Oscar Bronner GmbH & Co. KG v. Mediaprint Zeitungs- und Zeitschriftenverlag GmbH & Co. KG, Case C-7/97 [1998] E.C.R. I-7791, [1999] C.M.L.R. 112, Opinion of Advocate General Jacobs delivered on 28 May 1998, available at http://eur-lex.europa.eu/LexUriServ/LexUriServ.do?uri=CELEX:61997C0007:EN:HTML, last accessed 19 October 2012.

Otter Tail Power Co. v. United States, 410 U.S. 366 (1973).

Pacific Bell Telephone Co., dba AT&T California, et al. v linkLine Communications Inc., et al., 129 S. Ct. 1109, 555 U.S. 438 U.S. Supreme Court dated 25 February 2009.

Radio Telefis Eireann (RTE) and Independent Television Publications Ltd. (ITP) v. Commission; Joined Cases C-241/91 P and C-242/91 P, [1995] E.C.R. I-743 [1995] 4 C.M.L.R. 718.

Sea Containers v. Stena Sealink; Commission Decision - IV/34.689 – O.J. No. L 15 dated 21 December 1993.

Sony/BMG – Case COMP/M.3333 dated 3 October 2007.

Telemarketing – Centre Belge d'Études de Marché-Telemarketing (CBEM) v. SA Compagnie Luxembourgeoise de Télédiffusion (CLT) and Information Publicité Benelux (IPB); Case 311/84, 1985 E.C.R. 3261, 1986, 2 C.M.L.R. 558.

Tetra Pak International SA v. Commission, Case C-333/94, E.C.R. I-5951, 4 C.M.L.R. 662, 1996.

Tierce Ladbroke SA v. Commission; Case T-504/93, CFI [1995] E.C.R. II-923, [1997] 5 C.M.L.R. 309.

TomTom/Tele Atlas – Case COMP/M.4854 dated 14 May 2008.

United Brands Company and United Brands Continental BV v. Commission, Case 27/76 [1978] E.C.R. 207, [1978] 1 C.M.L.R. 429.

United States v. Colgate & Co., U.S. 300, 307 (1919).

United States v. E. K. du Pont de Nemours & Co., 351 U.S. 377 (1956).

United States v. IBM, Action No. 69–200 (S.D.N.Y.) (D.N.E.) dated 17 January 1969.

United States v. Jones, 132 S. Ct. 949 (2012).

United States v. Microsoft Corp, 253 F.3d 34 U.S. Court of Appeals, District of Columbia Cir., No. 00–5212 and 00–5213, 28 June 2001.

United States v. Terminal Railroad Association, 224 U.S. 383 (1912).

Van den Bergh Foods – Case T-65/98, Judgment of the CFI (5th Chamber) dated 23 October 2003.

Verizon v. FCC, 740 F.3d 623 (D.C. Cir. 2014).

Verizon Communications Inc. v. Law Office of Curtis v. Trinko, 540 U.S. 398 (2004).

Volvo v. Erik Veng (UK) Ltd.; Case 238/87, 1988 E.C.R. 6211, 1989, 4 C.M.L.R. 122.

Veröffentlichungen des Instituts für deutsches und europäisches Wirtschafts-, Wettbewerbs- und Regulierungsrecht der Freien Universität Berlin

Herausgegeben von Franz Jürgen Säcker

Band 1 Franz Jürgen Säcker (Hrsg.): Deutsch-russisches Energie- und Bergrecht im Vergleich. Ergebnisse einer Arbeitstagung vom 31. März / 1. April 2006. 2007.

Band 2 Franz Jürgen Säcker / Walther Busse von Colbe (Hrsg.): Wettbewerbsfördernde Anreizregulierung. Zum Anreizregulierungsbericht der Bundesnetzagentur vom 30. Juni 2006. 2007.

Band 3 Dirk Zschenderlein: Die Gleichbehandlung der Aktionäre bei der Auskunftserteilung in der Aktiengesellschaft. Zum Problem der Zulässigkeit der Weitergabe von Informationen an einzelne Aktionäre und Dritte. 2007.

Band 4 Simone Kirchhain: Die Anwendung der Vertikal-GVO auf innerstaatliche Wettbewerbsbeschränkungen nach der 7. GWB-Novelle. 2007.

Band 5 Franz Jürgen Säcker: Der Independent System Operator. Ein neues institutionelles Design für Netzbetreiber? 2007.

Band 6 Stefanie Otto: Allgemeininteressen im neuen UWG. § 1 S. 2 UWG und die wettbewerbsfunktionale Auslegung. 2007.

Band 7 Jochen Eichler: Vertragliche Dritthaftung. Eine Auseinandersetzung mit der Frage der Dritthaftung von sogenannten Experten und anderen Auskunftspersonen im Rahmen des § 311 Abs. 3 BGB. 2007.

Band 8 Markela Stamati: Die Anforderungen der operationellen Entflechtung nach den Beschleunigungsrichtlinien der Europäischen Kommission. Umsetzung in Deutschland und Griechenland. 2008.

Band 9 Franz Jürgen Säcker: The Concept of the Relevant Product Market. Between Demand-Side Substitutability and Supply-Side -Substitutability in Competition Law. 2008.

Band 10 Renate Rabensdorf: Die Durchgriffshaftung im deutschen und russischen Recht der Kapitalgesellschaften. Eine rechtsvergleichende Untersuchung. 2009.

Band 11 Franz Jürgen Säcker: Der beschleunigte Ausbau der Höchstspannungsnetze als Rechtsproblem. Erläutert am Beispiel der 380-kV-Höchstspannungsleitung Lauchstädt – Redwitz – Grafenrheinfeld mit Querung des Rennsteigs im Naturpark Thüringer Wald. 2009.

Band 12 Helen Mahne: Eigentum an Versorgungsleitungen. 2009.

Band 13 Franz Jürgen Säcker (Hrsg.): Russisches Energierecht - Gesetzessammlung. 2009.

Band 14 Franz Jürgen Säcker / Maik Wolf: Integrierte Energieversorgung in geschlossenen Verteilernetzen. Zum Gestaltungsspielraum des Gesetzgebers zur Neuregelung des § 110 EnWG im Lichte des Dritten EG-Energiepakets. 2009.

Band 15 Franz Jürgen Säcker (Hrsg.): Das Dritte Energiepaket für den Gasbereich. Deutsch-Englische Textausgabe mit einer Einführung. 2009.

Band 16 Franz Jürgen Säcker (Hrsg.): Das Dritte Energiepaket für den Elektrizitätsbereich. Deutsch-Englische Textausgabe mit einer Einführung. 2009.

Band 17 Thomas Dörmer: Die Unternehmenspacht. Rechtsstellung der Vertragsparteien unter besonderer Berücksichtigung der Pflicht des Unternehmenspächters zur ordnungsgemäßen Unternehmensführung sowie der Rechtslage bei Vertragsbeendigung. 2010.

Band 18 Klaas Bosch: Die Kontrolldichte der gerichtlichen Überprüfung von Marktregulierungsentscheidungen der Bundesnetzagentur nach dem Telekommunikationsgesetz. 2010.

Band 19 Geng-Sook Leem: Einheitliche Corporate Governance-Grundsätze für die Europäische Aktiengesellschaft (SE). Eine rechtsvergleichende Untersuchung anhand der Ausgestaltung der SE im deutschen und britischen Recht. 2010.

Band 20 Wiebke Gebhardt: Gentechnik und Koexistenz nach der Gesetzesnovelle von 2008: Zivilrechtliche Haftung im Vergleich Deutschland und USA. 2010.

Band 21 Cathrin Isenberg: Die Geruchsmarke als Gemeinschaftsmarke. Schutzfähigkeit und Einsatzmöglichkeiten. 2010.

Band 22 Franz Jürgen Säcker / Jochen Mohr / Maik Wolf: Konzessionsverträge im System des europäischen und deutschen Wettbewerbsrechts. 2011.

Band 23 Judith Antonia Loeck: Die unzumutbare Belästigung nach der UWG Novelle 2008 und dem Gesetz zur Bekämpfung unerlaubter Telefonwerbung und zur Verbesserung des Verbraucherschutzes bei besonderen Betriebsformen. 2011.

Band 24 Jörg Jaecks: Konzernverrechnungsklauseln und verwandte einseitige Verrechnungsbefugnisse im Mehrpersonenverhältnis. 2011.

Band 25 Franz Jürgen Säcker: Marktabgrenzung, Marktbeherrschung, Markttransparenz und Machtmissbrauch auf den Großhandelsmärkten für Elektrizität. 2011.

Band 26 Susanne Wende: Die einheitliche Auslegung von Beihilfen- und Vergaberecht als Teilgebiete des europäischen Wettbewerbsrechts. 2011.

Band 27 Leonie Kempel: Die Anwendung von Art. 102 AEUV auf geistiges Eigentum und Sacheigentum. Die Voraussetzungen des Kontrahierungszwangs nach Art. 102 AEUV und der Essential-Facility-Doktrin unter besonderer Berücksichtigung der Unterschiede zwischen geistigem Eigentum und Sacheigentum. 2011.

Band 28 Christoph Schuldt: Werbejingles – schützenswerte Kompositionen!? Die urheberrechtliche und markenrechtliche Schutzfähigkeit von Werbejingles vor unbefugter Nachahmung. 2012.

Band 29 Lydia Scholz: Die Rechtfertigung von diskriminierenden umweltpolitischen Steuerungsinstrumenten. Eine Untersuchung der Reichweite der Warenverkehrsfreiheit und ihrer Begrenzung durch den Umweltschutz als Vertragsziel am Beispiel der deutschen Energiefördergesetze EEG und KWKModG. 2012.

Band 30 Franz Jürgen Säcker: Investitionen in Kraftwerke zur Sicherung einer zuverlässigen Elektrizitätsversorgung nach der Energiewende. Rechtliche und ökonomische Rahmenbedingungen. 2012.

Band 31 Florian Leib: Kartellrechtliche Durchsetzungsstrategien in der Europäischen Union, den USA und Deutschland. Eine rechtsvergleichende Darstellung. 2012.

Band 32 Holger Hoch: Marktverschlusseffekte und Effizienzen vertikaler Zusammenschlüsse. Kartellrechtliche Beurteilung nach europäischem und deutschem Recht. 2012.

Band 33 Sebastian Kemper: Gasnetzzugang in Deutschland und in Spanien. 2012.

Band 34 Elena Timofeeva: Unbundling in der russischen Elektrizitätswirtschaft im Vergleich zum deutschen und europäischen Energierecht. 2012.

Band 35 Gisela Drozella / Harald Krebs: Marktbeherrschung im Bereich Stromerzeugung / Stromgroßhandel. Eine kritische Analyse der neueren Sicht des Bundeskartellamts. 2013.

Band 36 Christian Rehm: Die Einzel- und Gesamtverantwortung der Vorstandsmitglieder der Aktiengesellschaft. Die Verantwortung für die Leitung und Geschäftsführung im mehrköpfigen Vorstand in der unabhängigen und der herrschenden AG. 2013.

Band 37 Ann-Christin Richter: Mengen- und umsatzbezogene Rabatte marktbeherrschender Unternehmen in den Grenzen des Art. 102 AEUV. 2013.

Band 38 Nikolaos Pitsos: Die erhebliche Behinderung des wirksamen Wettbewerbs (SIEC-Test) im Fusionskontrollrecht. Zugleich ein Beitrag zur Problematik der oligopolistischen Marktbeherrschung unter Vergleich mit dem amerikanischen SLC-Test. 2013.

Band 39 Mirko Heinemann: Das Markenzeichen als Anknüpfungspunkt des Markenimages. 2013.

Band 40 Sylvia Lorenz: Der Immaterialgüterschutz virtueller Ladengeschäfte. Ein Vorschlag für die rechtliche Erfassung virtueller Güter. 2014.

Band 41 Anke Reimers: Wettbewerbsrechtliche und regulatorische Analyse der Kapazitätenvergabe an Grenzkuppelstellen im Elektrizitätsbinnenmarkt. 2014.

Band 42 Franz Jürgen Säcker / Carsten König / Lydia Scholz: Der regulierungsrechtliche Rahmen für ein Offshore-Stromnetz in der Nordsee. 2014.

Band 43 David Preisendanz: Der Humor in der vergleichenden Werbung. 2014.

Band 44 Martin Gerig: Vollendung des EU-Energiebinnenmarktes vs. nationale Marktabschottungen. Europarechtskonformität mitgliedstaatlicher Fördermaßnahmen und Kapazitätsmärkte am Beispiel Deutschlands. 2014.

Band 45 Jan Patrick Ehinger: Dritthaftung für Kunstexpertisen und Aufnahmebestätigungen in den Catalogue raisonné. Ein Beitrag zur Expertenhaftung. 2014.

Band 46 Julia Gerzen: Das Recht der Gesellschafter-Fremdkapitalfinanzierung. Rechtsvergleichende Analyse der Behandlung von Gesellschafterdarlehen vor und in der Insolvenz der GmbH nach deutschem und russischem Recht. 2014.

Band 47 Laura Börger: Die gerichtliche Kontrolldichte bei der Überprüfung von Entscheidungen der Europäischen Kommission auf dem Gebiet der Fusionskontrolle. 2014.

Veröffentlichungen des Instituts für Energie- und Regulierungsrecht Berlin

Band 48 Daniel Simon Travers: Kopplungsangebote. Eine Studie zum Vertrags- und Lauterkeitsrecht. 2015.

Band 49 Anna Olbryś-Sobieszuk: EU-rechtliche Schranken der Glücksspielwerbung in Deutschland, Großbritannien und Polen. 2015.

Band 50 Franz Jürgen Säcker/Lydia Scholz/Thea Sveen: Renewable Energy Law in Europe. Challenges and Perspectives. 2015.

Band 51 Lina Berezgova: Festlegung von Stromnetzentgelten in Deutschland und Russland. Eine rechtsvergleichende Untersuchung der anreizbasierten Regulierungsvorgaben. 2015.

Band 52 Fengliang Jin: Aufgreifkriterien in der Fusionskontrolle. Eine rechtsvergleichende Untersuchung des europäischen (Art. 3 FKVO), deutschen (§ 37 GWB), taiwanesischen (§ 6 FHG) und festlandchinesischen (§ 20 AMG) Rechts. 2015.

Band 53 Vasileios Triantafyllidis: Die Einordnung der Passing-On-Defense in das allgemeine Schadensersatzrecht. Eine rechtsvergleichende, dogmatische Studie. 2015.

Band 54 Peipei Liu: Die Inhaltskontrolle von Allgemeinen Geschäftsbedingungen und formularmäßigen Vertragsklauseln im deutsch-chinesischen Vergleich. 2016.

Band 55 Evelyn Kozak: Zur Notwendigkeit eines arbeitsrechtlichen und haftungsrechtlichen Whistleblowerschutzes. 2016.

Band 56 Genevieve Baker: Der bereicherungsrechtliche Nutzungsanspruch. 2017.

Band 57 Maria Zaykova: Der rechtliche Rahmen für den bergbaulichen Zugang zu den Erdöl- und Erdgaslagerstätten in der Russischen Föderation im Vergleich zum deutschen Bergrecht: Der bereicherungsrechtliche Nutzungsanspruch. 2017.

Band 58 Qian Luan: Geldschöpfungsprozess und Geld als abstraktes Schuldversprechen. Die europäisch-verwaltungsrechtliche Betrachtung des Geldschöpfungsprozesses der EZB und die Rechtsnatur von Zentralbankgeld und Geschäftsbankengiralgeld. 2017.

Band 59 Sára Gabriella Hoffman: Regulation of Cloud Services under US and EU Antitrust, Competition and Privacy Laws. 2017.

www.peterlang.com

Lightning Source UK Ltd.
Milton Keynes UK
UKHW042012170621
385614UK00002BA/97

9 783631 677391